Women Succeeding in the Sciences

Women Succeeding in the Sciences

Theories and Practices across Disciplines

edited by
Jody Bart

PURDUE UNIVERSITY PRESS

West Lafayette, Indiana

04   03   02   01   00   5   4   3   2   1

⊗ The paper used in this book meets the minimum requirements of American
National Standard for Information Sciences—Permanence of Paper for Printed
Library Materials, ANSI Z39.48–1992.
Printed in the United States of America

Library of Congress Cataloging-in-Publication Data
Women succeeding in the sciences : theories and practices across disciplines
    / edited by Jody Bart.
        p.   cm.
    Includes bibliographical references and index.
    ISBN 1–55753–121–8 (cloth : alk. paper).—
    ISBN 1–55753–122–6 (pbk. : alk paper)
    1. Women in science. 2. Science—study and teaching. 3. Women—
Education. I. Bart, Jody, 1960– .
    Q130.W676 1999
    507.1—dc21   99–26055
                                                                CIP

Contents

Acknowledgments

Any work of this magnitude is a function of the efforts of many people, and this project is no different. First, many thanks to Sweet Briar College Administration for supplying the Ewald endowment funding and the Sue Reid Slaughter funding for producing the conference "Women Succeeding in the Sciences: Theories and Practices across the Disciplines." Special thanks to the staff of Sweet Briar College for their contributions to making a successful conference and to the members of the Women and Gender Studies Advisory Committee for their ideas and energies. I owe a tremendous debt of gratitude to my many students who worked hard on the conference, produced the undergraduate conference as part of the main conference, and—by their wit and energy—keep me young and inspire me to strive to provide them with interesting scholastic activities. Many thanks to my editor, Margaret Hunt, whose tireless work on this anthology is primarily responsible for its release. Finally, as always, thanks to my parents, Jana and Teddy Bart, for always encouraging me to reach beyond myself and for having instilled in me early an insatiable curiosity for all intellectual and creative activities.

Preface

This book, and the conference that gave rise to it, are a reflection of the recent—by which I mean in the last twenty years—growing scholastic interest in the topic of women in science. This interest extends across a wide variety of disciplines, from philosophy, sociology, and education to areas of the so-called hard sciences. The issues raised by this topic are the questions surrounding the fact that women as a social category have entered into study, practice, and research in science in ever higher numbers. These questions also surround the use of women as subjects of scientific research. Some of these questions are theoretical, some practical, but all of them involve some interest in whether the gendered social experience of women, and the differences between this experience and the lived social experience of men, have any bearing on women's contributions to scientific inquiry theory formation. They relate to the validity of women's experiences to the way women ought to be trained as scientists; that is, to the way women learn. Thus, the interdisciplinary field of Women and Gender Studies properly becomes the academic backdrop against which discussions of these issues can take place across the disciplines.

The essays in this anthology resulted from a conference called Women Succeeding in the Sciences: Theories and Practices across the Disciplines, given at Sweet Briar College in Sweet Briar, Virginia. As the director of the Women and Gender Studies Program at the college, I wanted to do something to bridge the conceptual gap between the sciences and the humanities that seems to be endemic at all universities and colleges throughout the country. In short, even at this small liberal arts college for women, the two main branches of a liberal arts education were seen as severely separate, both pedagogically and politically. This state of affairs seemed ineffectual to many of us at the college because it left students without a clear understanding of why these two branches of their liberal arts education were required of them, or what relationships the branches had to each other. Quite frankly, at that time even the faculty at this institution (then only 61 members) held no clear idea of the conceptual connections between these disciplines, and competition between the departments struck many of us as counterproductive to our mission of shaping a coherent liberal arts education.

It became apparent that the program of Women and Gender Studies, through this conference, could provide the perfect response to this state of affairs, begin to educate both students and faculty on the relationships between the humanities and the sciences, and exhibit why students need an understanding of both scientific methodologies and practices, as well as of the history, philosophy, and sociology of science. The field of Women and Gender Studies is inherently interdisciplinary, incorporating information on nearly every aspect of human endeavor, from history to literature to the social sciences to the physical sciences as well. Women have been entering the sciences in every aspect, as academics and in the private sector, in ever greater numbers over the last twenty years, but women have always been in science and have always made significant contributions that the historical record—until recently—has only treated peripherally. This conference was designed to bring people together not only to talk about the historical contributions of women in the sciences but also to share various pedagogical methodologies for teaching science to women and teaching about women in science; to share practices for "doing" science in ways that take gender into consideration as a research subject or use gender sensitive models of including women in research projects; and to share ideas about philosophies regarding women and science, from women's participation in theory formation to women as objects of scientific investigation.

The essays in this anthology reflect both the spirit and content of this highly successful conference and serve as excellent tools for teaching both students and educators across many disciplines about the topic of women in science.

Helen Brooke Taussig (1898–1986)

A Biography of Success

Laura Malloy

Helen Brooke Taussig was the designer of the first surgical treatment for so-called blue babies and the founder of the medical specialty of pediatric cardiology. A devoted scholar and teacher, she wrote the first standard reference text for pediatric cardiology (*Congenital Malformations of the Heart*, 1947) and established the clinical criteria for diagnosing heart malformations. She was the first woman to achieve the rank of full professor at Johns Hopkins University College of Medicine and the first woman to be president of the American Heart Association. Her professional experience with birth defects and her personal concern for the welfare of children and families also led her to play an instrumental role in publicizing the devastating effects of the sleeping tablet thalidomide. Her testimony before Congress helped to prevent its release in the United States.

Taussig's accomplishments are all the more significant because she had to overcome learning disabilities, deafness, and a medical culture that was not ready for women. Her insight and perseverance were nurtured by her early experiences of hardship, the passion and pleasure she found in her intellectual life, and the understanding that being an outsider can present opportunities as well as limitations. With the support of family, friends, teachers, and students, she was able to sustain her vision and determination in the face of resistance to her ideas and her very presence in medicine. With skillful documentation and a flexible approach to problem solving, as well as a smattering of good luck, she integrated her understanding of physiology with the clinical needs of children who were desperately ill.

1

Blue Babies

There are many different ways in which the heart or the blood vessels around it can be malformed. Different malformations can all cause a lack of oxygen in the red blood cells, which gives a child the characteristic blue color of a so-called blue baby. There are also wide variations in the severity of this condition: Certain malformations can resolve themselves with time, allowing children a perfectly normal life. Others are so severe as to be acutely life-threatening at birth. Still others, the ones most debilitating to children and difficult for families and physicians alike, allow enough oxygen to enter the blood for minimal survival but are accompanied by episodic attacks of extreme cyanosis (dangerously low oxygen levels).

Before Taussig's pioneering work, children with serious cardiac defects rarely lived to adulthood because normal growth could place impossible demands on their respiratory and circulatory systems. Further, the quality of life that these children experienced, even with the assistance of oxygen tanks, was severely compromised. Growing blue babies endured continuous fatigue, frequent dizzy spells, shortness of breath, and extreme difficulty with physical exertion. Taussig remarked that she often saw children squatting in the waiting room of the cardiac clinic, trying to relieve the discomfort by developing external pressure on their chests. She advised parents to hold small children over their shoulders, in a similar bent position, so that the increased pressure might help to increase blood flow to the lungs.

Hopeless Cases

The heart-lung bypass machine, which takes over the work of the heart and lungs during heart surgery, did not yet exist in the 1930s when Taussig started her work at the Pediatric Cardiac Clinic of Johns Hopkins University Hospital. It was not used successfully in humans until 1953, after twenty years of research and development conducted by Dr. John Gibbon and an engineering team from IBM Corporation. Thus open-heart surgery as we know it today was unheard-of in Taussig's clinic. To the extent that surgical corrections of heart defects existed at all, they were a risky business. Because surgeons lacked technologically sophisticated life-support and anatomical-imaging systems, they had to rely on the ability of the patient's body to withstand oxygen deprivation. Their surgical speed was essential in both diagnosis and correction of even the simplest problems. It is little wonder that children with extensive cardiac birth defects were considered hopeless cases.

Further, little was known about the relationship between specific anatomical defects and their functional characteristics. Dr. Maude Abbott had written the first article on congenital heart disease (1915) and later published an atlas (1936) that documented the anatomy of one thousand cases of congenital malformations, dividing them into some functional classifications. However, classifications made from autopsy data were difficult to use or verify, and it was nearly impossible to recognize the specific malformations from only the symptoms presented by a living patient. To provide a meaningful set of diagnostic criteria for the many different kinds of malformations in existence would have required extensive patient testing, evaluation, and follow-up, a tedious task at best. Most cardiologists were not interested in addressing this technically difficult problem, because the prevailing viewpoint was that even if congenital malformations could be accurately diagnosed, nothing could be done about them.

During this period, rheumatic fever, a life-threatening infection that could cause permanent cardiac damage, reached nearly epidemic proportions. Far more children were at risk from this infectious disease than from cardiac birth defects. Thus far more research interest focused on rheumatic fever. When clinicians recognized that rheumatic heart disease followed streptococcal infections of the throat, steps could be taken toward preventing its contagion. With the advent of first sulfa drugs and later penicillin, physicians were able to have a dramatic impact on its treatment. Thus, there was little incentive to pursue the largely arcane problem of congenital malformations when more pressing and exciting work remained to be done.

Dead-end Specialty

Despite her excellent record in medical school and the publications that resulted from her cardiovascular research projects as a medical student in the laboratory of Dr. Edward P. Carter, Taussig was denied a medical internship after she completed medical school in 1927. It seemed unlikely that she would be able to pursue a career specialty in cardiology. She was, however, encouraged to pursue a research fellowship for the year after graduation and then a fifteen-month internship in pediatrics. When the new chief of pediatrics, Dr. Edwards A. Park, established a pediatric cardiac clinic with the explicit intention of improving the quality of care for chronically ill children, Taussig recognized the opportunity to combine her interests in cardiology with pediatrics.

Though friends warned her that pediatric cardiology could be a very narrow, dead-end specialty, her primary mentors in medical school, Carter and Park, encouraged her. Taussig returned home to Boston upon completion of her internship in pediatrics. In the fall of 1930, two years after Park established the Pediatric Cardiac Clinic at Johns Hopkins, he invited her to return to become its director.

However, according to Taussig, this clinic was unpopular with other physicians in the hospital. Because she treated children with rheumatic fever in addition to those with cardiac malformations, the perception at first was that her clinic was "robbing" the medical residents in other departments of the opportunity to learn from these cases. Further, her internship training was in pediatrics, not cardiology, and she had no more years of training than other residents in the hospital. Thus, though Carter and Park recognized her superior expertise, some colleagues who knew her less well were reluctant to trust her judgment. As a result, only the ambiguous cases of rheumatic fever or the hopeless cases of cardiac malformations were referred to her clinic.

Crossword Puzzles

Park, as head of pediatrics, provided Taussig with equipment and the assistance of a social worker and a technician, who doubled as her secretary. With their help and the recently developed technology of a fluoroscope, Taussig began her long-term study: she spent the remaining fifty-six years of her life working toward documenting, understanding, correcting, and preventing congenital malformations of the heart. She and her team began by working methodically through a list of two hundred young patients for whom there were no diagnoses. They accumulated a comprehensive set of clinical characteristics for each child. The fluoroscope permitted Taussig to take X-ray images of the heart with greater clarity than a standard X-ray machine. She used fluoroscopy and chest X rays to look at the anatomy of the heart and great vessels from four different angles. She used electrocardiograms and blood pressure measurements to assess both electrical and mechanical aspects of cardiovascular function. She also relied heavily on detailed histories and hands-on physical examinations.

Taussig pursued this work with dedication in the face of a greater challenge: she began to lose her hearing at age thirty-one. She used a hearing aid and a specially amplified stethoscope. She also became expert at using her sense of touch to detect the characteristics of a heartbeat. Her physical exams included palpation of the heart, a difficult technique that uses the pressure of hands against the chest wall to detect the frequency and strength of pressure changes in and around the heart. This approach provided her with a form of direct information that many physicians omitted from examinations.

By correlating her fluoroscopic observations of anatomy with results from her functional examinations using stethoscope, blood pressure cuff, electrocardiogram, and heart palpation, Taussig began to deduce which heart structures were enlarged or malformed. She called these deductions the "crossword puzzles" of the cardiac clinic. She would predict the anatomical variations and track the patients through their lifetime. When the child died—which was most often the case—she would correlate her predictions with autopsy findings. With these data she was able to recognize distinct patterns of symptoms shared by patients born with the same malformations. Further, she made inferences about the functional significance of those malformations, predicting how blood flow, blood pressure, or blood oxygenation might change as a result of a malformed or misplaced blood vessel.

It took her years to assemble and present her findings about congenital heart defects. Her textbook, *Congenital Malformations of the Heart,* was published in 1947. With comprehensive illustrations and lucid explanations, it established the clinical criteria for the diagnosis of heart malformations and became the standard reference text for pediatric cardiology. When asked why she would devote so much effort to what was viewed as an impractical and obscure intellectual curiosity, Taussig wrote, "If you stay in academic medicine and learn anything, you are morally obligated to make that knowledge available to others."[1]

Ductus Arteriosus

Taussig's most influential and celebrated contribution to pediatrics was the insight that the negative effects of complex cardiac malformations might still be treated with simple surgical steps. Though it might not be possible to rebuild the circulation to exactly duplicate that of a normal child, she reasoned that ways could be found to compensate for the physiological problems caused by the malformations. Because she had paid attention to the functional implications of many different types of congenital malformations, she thought in terms of functional compensation rather than structural repair. Taussig suspected that the root cause of death in most blue babies was not heart failure, as was thought at the time, but insufficient blood flow through the lungs. She asserted that if differences in blood flow could explain the clinical symptoms of some blue babies, then it was possible to correct some problems by redirecting the blood flow.

One cardiac birth defect that Taussig saw frequently was a condition known as patent, or open, ductus arteriosus. In a normal fetus, whose lungs are not yet in use, the blood vessel known as the ductus arteriosus shunts some blood around and away from the lungs. After birth, when the lungs inflate, this blood vessel normally closes off to permit increased blood flow to the functional lungs. If this vessel remains open after birth, it prevents adequate blood flow to the lungs, making some babies look blue from lack of oxygen. In 1939 Dr. Robert Gross at Harvard University successfully developed a surgical procedure to close off patent ductus arteriosus.

The critical inference that Taussig made about other blue babies was an apparent paradox: in children with more than one defect, a ductus arteriosus that remained open after birth could help, rather than harm, the child. She realized this after observing two children who died shortly after the ductus spontaneously closed off, as it sometimes does. She reasoned that when multiple defects prevent adequate blood flow to the lungs through normal pathways, blood flow through the ductus might reverse and redirect blood toward the lungs. This would improve the oxygenation of the blood and help the children survive. Her goal then became to find some other way to redirect blood to the lungs, one that would not require direct surgery on the heart and one that would not close off with time.

In 1939, when Gross's procedure to close the ductus was published, Taussig traveled to Harvard to seek his collaboration in trying to build a ductus for patients in whom this would be a corrective procedure. Gross was riding on his recent success and quite skeptical. Though he said he had the expertise to redirect additional blood flow to the lungs, he rebuffed what he considered an irrelevant proposal. He is reported to have said, "Madame, I close ductuses, I do not create them."[2] After this meeting, while Taussig visited with family in Boston, she explained her dilemma to her father. He advised her to go where she was wanted rather than where she was just tolerated. Subsequently, Taussig abandoned the idea of working with Gross and returned to Johns Hopkins.

The Blalock-Taussig Surgery

Taussig waited two years to find a surgeon willing to collaborate on this project. Some colleagues found Taussig's persistence merely egotistical or territorial. Some suggested that her deafness was responsible for her directness and tenacity. The profession remained skeptical of her insights. Years after her surgical approach proved successful, Dr. Richard Bing asserted that Taussig came up with the right surgery for the wrong reasons. His position was that Taussig's ideas about restricted lung circulation were physiologically naive, because they emphasized the defect that narrows the size of the artery carrying blood to the lungs rather than an accompanying defect, a hole in the heart that can redirect functional blood flow away from the lungs. Yet Taussig's proposal for compensatory surgery addressed the single fundamental physiological problem created by both these defects: she sought to create a mechanism to get more functional blood flow through the lungs. In 1941, Dr. Alfred Blalock was appointed chairman of surgery at Johns Hopkins. Taussig was impressed with his skill as a vascular surgeon and explained her thoughts on the surgical palliation of complex congenital cardiovascular defects. Blalock, known for his openness and flexibility, was intrigued by her ideas.

Blalock took the project into the research laboratory to work out the surgical steps in animals, relying heavily on the support and insight of Vivien Thomas, the team's research technician for animal surgery. Blalock and Thomas developed the technique over a period of three years, performing nearly two hundred surgical experiments with dogs before it could be attempted in humans. Thomas, an African American man who had begun work as a research technician after financial difficulties made it impossible for him to complete undergraduate studies, wrote a book entitled *Pioneering Research in Surgical Shock and Cardiovascular Surgery* and was awarded an honorary doctoral degree from Johns Hopkins in recognition of his essential role in these research studies. When the surgical interventions were carried over into the clinical setting, both Blalock and Taussig relied on Thomas in the operating room for technical advice during the human surgery.

On November 29, 1944, a critically ill fifteen-month-old girl was the first patient to undergo surgery to redirect blood flow from an artery in the arm to the lungs. Though the child began to improve significantly two weeks after the surgery, her recovery period was difficult and the results were not as dramatic as Taussig had hoped. In the second surgery, on a declining eleven-year-old girl, the child's unique anatomy required a last-minute change in the procedure. The team redirected a different artery, and the surgery yielded such improved results that they decided to try this approach for subsequent surgeries. It was the third operation, on a six-year-old boy whose anatomical defects were slightly less complex, where the results were most immediate and exciting. Writing about it years later, Taussig said, "I suppose nothing would ever give me as much delight as seeing the first patient change from blue to pink in the operating room.... There the little patient was with bright pink cheeks and bright lips. Oh, what a lovely color.... The child woke up, looked at Dr. Blalock, blinked his eyes a little and said, 'Is the operation over, may I get up now?'.... And from that day on he was raring to go and we realized we had won."[3]

In 1945, Blalock and Taussig reported the results of the first three operations in a landmark paper. Together they assembled a diverse and cooperative group of physicians, nurses, and technicians that performed hundreds of successful operations on blue babies. Furthermore, the striking success of this treatment inspired others to develop new surgical techniques to treat the functional problems created by other cardiac defects. Taussig later reflected on the role these efforts played in the development of treatments for congenital heart malformations. She was well aware that medical research is a cooperative enterprise and was happy to recognize the contributions of her colleagues and collaborators, even those less generous to her. She wrote: "Dr. Gross unlocked the gate to surgical treatments of congenital malformations of the heart. I opened it; Dr. Blalock and I galloped in, quickly followed by a stream of patients, surgeons, cardiologists, and pediatricians."[4] These events led to the growth of pediatric heart clinics all over the United States.

Pediatric Cardiology

In the twenty years following the first Blalock-Taussig surgery, Taussig treated hundreds of patients and trained more than one hundred pediatric cardiologists. She remained deeply concerned for both the physical and psychological well-being of her patients and their families. She was adamant that surgery not be performed on a child who was not emotionally ready for the procedure. She listened carefully to her young patients and parents, by lipreading and with the help of her hearing aid. She insisted that her residents take the time to listen and answer questions as well and reminded them that families were pressed to extremes when children have chronic congenital problems.

Taussig applied for funding from the National Institutes of Health and the Children's Bureau to start a formal academic training program in pediatric cardiology with both clinical and research components. Subsequently, the American Academy of Pediatrics established a cardiology section, and Taussig helped define the national standards for certification in pediatric cardiology as a founding member of its Board of Pediatric Cardiology. Her text, techniques, and training methods became the model for education in this discipline. Her evaluation and reassessment of patients treated with the Blalock-Taussig surgery, which spanned more than thirty years, provided her students with exposure to an analytical approach that was a model for a systematic and meticulous scientific method. Annually Taussig hosted a two-day continuing-education scientific symposium to bring former fellows in contact with current students and to encourage further development of the field.

Thalidomide

Late in 1961, when Taussig was nearing retirement age, she was visited by a former fellow from Germany, Dr. Alois Beuren, who told her about some striking birth defects he had seen: children born with missing limbs or flipperlike hands without arms. Taussig was struck by the urgency of understanding this problem. In February 1962 she went to Germany on a personal fact-finding tour. She learned that the sedative thalidomide was suspected as the cause of these impairments. Taussig saw evidence that she considered conclusive. Thalidomide had been taken by the mothers of all the children showing the birth defects, and these impairments were absent within the United States Army population in Germany, to which thalidomide was not available. It appeared that even a small quantity of the drug taken once in early pregnancy could have devastating results.

Taussig returned to the United States with pictures and clinical statistics to report her observations throughout the medical community. Her information was used by the Food and Drug Administration to prevent the release of thalidomide in the United States. Taussig's efforts not only helped to prevent an outbreak of birth defects in the United States but also highlighted the need for greater control over the evaluation and marketing of new drugs. Taussig testified before the Senate's Kefauver Committee, created to draft legislation to address this issue, and she called for specific language in the law to address birth defects. Although the thalidomide affair was her last widely publicized contribution to medicine, she spent the remaining twenty-four years of her life conducting research and working toward a better understanding of pediatric heart disease.

Evolution

During her tenure at Johns Hopkins, Taussig held academic appointments in the medical school as instructor in pediatrics (1930–46), associate professor of pediatrics (1946–59), professor of pediatrics (1959–63), and professor emeritus (1963–86). After her retirement, she continued her research work as the Thomas M. Rivers Research Fellow and also wrote about the history of medicine and about her adaptation to hearing loss. She continued to collect data for the follow-up research project on patients who had been treated surgically for malformations of the heart. She followed them through adulthood, parenthood, and successful, productive lives. Even in retirement she served as a mentor for former fellows, and her active intellectual life (she published approximately forty papers after she retired) served as a model for them as well.

With a view toward addressing prevention rather than correction of congenital defects, Taussig also began a new project on the evolutionary implications of cardiac malformations. She investigated the incidence of cardiac malformations within families and examined parallels between malformations in bird hearts and human hearts in order to understand the extent to which both hereditary and evolutionary factors contribute to the incidence of congenital heart defects. She completed her manuscript "Evolutionary Origins of Cardiac Malformations" just a few days before she died.

Privilege, Hardship, and Perseverance

The path Helen Taussig took through this distinguished career as a healer, scientist, writer, teacher, and public figure began with appreciation for service and intellectual curiosity, characteristics she learned from a supportive and privileged academic family. Taussig took pleasure in assembling information, experiences, and ideas into meaningful patterns. She had a superb memory for people and their histories. Throughout her career she demonstrated intellectual focus and flexibility of thought in looking for opportunities and in solving problems. These qualities grew of necessity from her struggles to overcome personal loss and learning difficulties that began in childhood.

Taussig was born in Cambridge, Massachusetts, on May 24, 1898, the youngest of four children in an academically and professionally accomplished family. Her paternal grandparents were Adele (Wuerpel) and William Taussig, of St. Louis, Missouri. William Taussig was a physician who had emigrated from Bohemia in 1846 and established a medical practice to treat children with impaired eyesight. He helped establish the William Taussig School for Handicapped Children in St. Louis. He also held positions as judge of the St. Louis County Court, president of the St. Louis Board of Education, and head of the St. Louis Terminal Railroad Association.

Helen Taussig's mother, Edith (Guild) Taussig, was one of the earliest students enrolled in Radcliffe College. Her primary academic interests were education and the natural sciences, particularly botany and zoology. She shared those interests with her children and in particular tried to interest her daughter Helen in botany. The family owned a summer home on Cape Cod, which no doubt provided a wonderful resource for collections and studies of natural history. It is likely that Helen Taussig developed her appreciation for patterns in the natural world as well as her lifelong fondness for gardening at this summer retreat. Later in life Taussig recalled with affection the freedom and exuberance she and her brother and sisters shared there. Edith Taussig died in 1909, when Helen was eleven years old, after a two-year illness that was first diagnosed as Hodgkin's disease and later recognized as tuberculosis. While her prolonged illness and premature death limited her time with her daughter, she demonstrated a confidence in Helen's strength and an optimism about her future that left her daughter with warm and vivid memories of her mother.

Frank Taussig was the Henry Lee Professor of Economics at Harvard University and the cofounder of the Harvard School of Business Administration. He held A.B. (1879), A.M. (1883), and Ph.D. (1883) degrees from Harvard University, and an LL.B. (1886) from Harvard Law. Highly respected as a teacher and scholar, he wrote a pivotal textbook, *The Principles of Economics* (1911), published widely on international economics and tariffs, pursued scholarship at both Harvard and the University of California at Berkeley, and was a member of the National Tariff Commission in Washington, D.C.

Her father's devotion to scholarship and service for the public good served as a model for professional values that Helen Taussig emulated throughout her life. Frank Taussig's custom of reserving summer mornings at their home on Cape Cod exclusively for writing also provided her with an example of routine and discipline that she successfully imitated as an adult. Throughout her career, Taussig's father urged the family to respect her writing time without interruption, as they had respected his. Further, like her father, Taussig considered it a social responsibility to share her research findings in print. Frank Taussig often advised his daughter on her academic and career decisions and supported her choices. She remained deeply appreciative of his help and encouragement throughout her life and was very conscious of the great privilege she experienced growing up in an academic atmosphere.

Both illness and a learning disability complicated Helen Taussig's early education. She was a frail baby and, like her mother, contracted tuberculosis. This restricted her to attending school only half-time for two or three years. She graduated from the Cambridge School for Girls in 1917, but her efforts in school were made arduous by difficulties in reading, spelling, number recognition, and languages. Though her father privately wondered if she would even finish grammar school, he tutored her for many hours with extreme patience and encouragement. According to Taussig, he did not express his concerns about her to his ailing wife, nor did he chide her for her shortcomings. As an adult, Taussig concluded that her early academic problems were symptomatic of dyslexia. She compensated for these difficulties by taking more time to read and review her work. Though her academic performance was exemplary by the time she reached college, she always harbored some self-doubt about her capabilities. Even as an adult, reading and number recognition did not come easily to her, and she never considered reading a pleasure. But the methodical approaches to study that her father helped her to develop as survival strategies in childhood served her well.

Independence

Taussig followed her mother's example and enrolled in Radcliffe College in 1917, where she continued to improve as a student and also became a tennis champion. However, at the end of her first year at Radcliffe, she was somewhat disappointed in her experience and considered transferring to the University of California at Berkeley. She had visited Berkeley with her father and was impressed by what she saw. She also had a friend who was a student at Berkeley. Many of her local friends in Cambridge had moved on. Further, her father had moved to Washington, D.C., to serve as chairman of the U.S. Tariff Commission, and he remarried in August 1918. At the same time, Taussig felt a need to become more self-reliant, and at Radcliffe she was always known as her father's daughter. At her father's recommendation she remained at Radcliffe for a second year to improve her grades. She transferred to Berkeley in the fall of 1919.

Taussig's attempts to grow independently from family reputation had a shaky start. Though no relation, the regent at Berkeley was also named Taussig, and she was repeatedly mistaken for his daughter. The regent was unpopular with faculty, and there was some cynicism about any academic potential that could be demonstrated by his daughter. One of her professors was so impressed with one of Taussig's papers, yet so suspicious of her intellectual potential, that he complained to a colleague. He could not imagine how the regent's daughter could have honestly and independently written such an outstanding piece of work, though there was no evidence to the contrary. Ironically, she had traveled across the continent to escape a helpful family reputation only to be confronted with unfounded and unhelpful connections. Taussig recalled this incident with humor, though clearly it meant that in her new environment she had new and unexpected challenges to overcome. She did overcome them, flourished academically at Berkeley, and graduated in 1921, B.A., Phi Beta Kappa, having made it on her own.

Contaminating Medical Education

When Taussig then began to consider a career in medicine, she met with obstacles that presented the first serious social resistance to her presence in the academic world. At first, her father recommended that she pursue a degree in public health, because it might be a more suitable and hospitable career for a woman. Harvard University, whose medical school did not admit women, had just opened its School of Public Health. Taussig met the dean of the new school, Dr. Milton J. Rosenau, to inquire about the program. In a 1978 interview in the *Medical Times,* she recalled that meeting. She was told that women were permitted to take courses in the public health program and that the first two years of the program were the study of medicine. However, women could not be admitted as degree candidates. When Taussig inquired, "Who is going to be such a fool as to spend four years studying and not get a degree?" the dean replied, "No one, I hope." Taussig answered, "I'll not be the first to disappoint you."[5] She dismissed the idea of the public health program and decided to study medicine however she could.

By special permission Taussig was able to enroll at Harvard in the fall of 1921. There she was permitted to take only two courses: bacteriology and histology. She was seated in an isolated corner of the lecture hall for classes and placed in a room alone to look at slides. Reflecting upon this toward the end of her career, she conjectured that this was to prevent her from "contaminating" the male students. She may have benefited indirectly from this imposed isolation, however, because she received individual attention from her histology professor, Dr. John Lewis Bremmer. He supported her efforts, met with her daily, and came to respect her work. Ultimately he recommended that she switch to Boston University. There she would be permitted to take anatomy (a course generally deemed as an unsuitable pursuit for women at Harvard). Further, she could carry a full course load over the entire year, instead of slipping into courses here and there. She took his advice and after traveling in Europe with her family for eight months, returned to her studies in the fall of 1922 as a research student with Dr. Alexander Begg, dean of Boston University Medical School and professor of anatomy.

Begg encouraged Taussig to pursue research studies outside the classroom and to get interested in some important physiological system. He sparked her interest in cardiology when he asked her to work on the anatomy of the muscle bundles of the heart. She spent some time dissecting a beef heart he had given her but was reluctant to show the preparation to Begg because she had so completely pulled it apart. Finally, when she had no choice, she showed him the dissection. To her surprise, he was impressed with her work and asked her to continue. Through these efforts Taussig developed a strong appreciation for the interdependence of structure and function within the cardiovascular system, an appreciation that contributed to insights she had in the most productive stages of her career. As she became more interested in the functional characteristics of the heart, she began physiological studies of spontaneous cardiac muscle contraction, which resulted in her very first publication in 1925.

A Place for a Woman

After she completed courses in anatomy, physiology, and pharmacology, there was little more that Boston University could offer Taussig. Like Harvard, Boston University did not admit women for a medical degree. Begg advised her to apply to medical school at Johns Hopkins University, where women were admitted to the medical program. A wealthy benefactress had left Johns Hopkins a considerable sum with the provision that the university admit women to the school of medicine. In the 1920s the university met the letter of the bequest by making a place for just one or two women per year. Taussig obtained strong support for her application from Dr. Walter Cannon, an eminent professor of physiology at Harvard and a family friend. Cannon appreciated her work and wrote that if women were admitted to Harvard, he would support her admission. She was admitted to the Johns Hopkins program, and in 1924 she began her lifetime affiliation with this institution.

Taussig pursued research throughout her medical school training. She was disappointed that the physiology department did not support her interests or permit her to work late in the lab. She then established a working relationship with Dr. Edward P. Carter, at the Johns Hopkins Heart Station. There she immersed herself in cardiovascular medicine, spending evenings, weekends, and all of her elective course time on clinical and research work. She completed her M.D. degree in 1927, having published three scholarly articles as a medical student. However, she was denied a medical internship at Johns Hopkins because there was only one place for a woman. The grades of the other woman candidate were two-tenths of a point higher than Taussig's.

Subsequently, Carter invited her to continue her research and take the Archibald Fellowship at the Johns Hopkins Heart Station for one year. She accepted this position and followed it with an internship in pediatrics under Dr. Edwards A. Park. Park recognized both her clinical expertise and the advanced understanding of cardiovascular function she had gained from her student and postdoctoral research. Further, because her options as a woman physician were somewhat limited, he surmised that she would be a permanent member of the staff. Park encouraged her to focus her interests on the comprehensive study of congenital malformations. The general lack of interest in this subspecialty meant that it was wide open when Taussig began her medical career. Park's judgment was correct on both counts: Taussig's position at Johns Hopkins's Pediatric Cardiac Clinic became a lifetime career. Together, Parks and Carter have been credited for guiding her toward the study of cardiac birth defects, which led to her most renowned contributions to medicine. Certainly, their support and overlapping interests in cardiology and pediatrics paved the way for Taussig's efforts in establishing this area as a full-fledged medical specialty. Good fortune, family connections, and her insight into the characters of her colleagues no doubt permitted Taussig to find these strongly supportive teachers, who were essential to her many successes.

Opening Gates

The convoluted route that Taussig followed to complete her medical education illustrates how her uniquely personal characteristics shaped her achievements as well. The metaphor she used to describe the significance of the blue baby operations could easily describe her approach to her entire career: if her mentors and supporters unlocked the gate to opportunity, it was she who opened it and rushed in. Throughout her education Taussig vigorously followed those opportunities that presented themselves and recognized where her efforts were not welcome. Her interaction with the dean of Harvard's School of Public Health and her decision not to waste her time there demonstrates that she was both astute and blunt. She did not suffer fools gladly. Nor did she hesitate to take the indirect route when a more obvious one failed to present itself. She was willing to go from Harvard to Boston University to Johns Hopkins in the pursuit of not just a medical education but also its accompanying empowerment: a medical degree and certification. She sought out a place to do research in a clinical setting when her efforts to continue basic research in the physiology department at Johns Hopkins were discouraged. Further, she was persistent and patient, working and waiting for a medical internship in pediatrics when she was denied one in cardiology.

In addition to her flexibility of thought and realistic vision of life's possibilities, Taussig had a reputation for dogged determination and stubborn adherence to her convictions. This disposition enabled her to overcome institutionalized resistance to her work, but it also fueled the resentment and envy of some colleagues. One of her fellows, Dr. Charlotte Ferencz, acknowledged in her eulogy that while Taussig enjoyed a warm, generous spirit and the admiration of students and patients, she suffered from the intense conflicts that accompanied her successes. Although she presented a determined face to the world, close colleagues knew that at times she struggled with self-doubt, on occasion unsure of her intellect and her abilities. This seemed to offset much of the pleasure she might have taken in the public recognition of her efforts.

Though Taussig achieved both recognition and social change during her career, her primary motivation was the personal need to find an arena where she could work and learn. This pragmatic strategy allowed her to overcome insecurities, to reshape disappointments into opportunities, and to persist when options seemed discouragingly limited. It is precisely this creative and tenacious approach that she used when she and Blalock opened the gate and "galloped" in to develop the earliest surgical treatments for cardiac birth defects.

The Round Table

Taussig remained the physician in charge of the Harriet Lane Home Cardiac Clinic at Johns Hopkins from 1930 until her retirement in 1963.

Though her academic appointment remained at the level of instructor for sixteen years, she was promoted to associate professor after the celebrated success of the Blalock-Taussig surgery. After twenty years of leadership in pediatric cardiology, in 1959—just four years before her retirement—she was promoted to the rank of full professor, becoming the first woman in the history of Johns Hopkins University College of Medicine to achieve such recognition.

Throughout her career Taussig remained passionate about her roles there as healer and teacher. She demonstrated regard for her patients and their families as individuals and repeatedly advised that her patients should be treated like any other child. She affirmed that their medical conditions did not warrant isolation from others, which could only impede their normal emotional development. She said, "We don't want to forget that after we've got all the laboratory data together we are taking care of patients or the health of the community. We are dedicated to making life better for humanity.... Our art in medicine is quite a different thing. Our essential ingredients are kindness and compassion and human understanding."[6] Her first instructions to pediatric cardiology residents were to use patience and tact with children and their families.

Taussig served as a role model of personal concern and professional rigor in her discipline, and she viewed it as her responsibility to foster the next generation of pediatric cardiologists. Taussig trained many accomplished visiting physicians. Of the approximately 130 fellows she trained, 34 became heads of cardiology or pediatric cardiology divisions themselves. Among her students were Drs. Mary Allen Engle, Catherine Neill, Ruth Whittemore, Charlotte Ferencz, Dan McNamara, James Manning, Alois Beuren, and Caroline Bruins.

Taussig had high expectations of these students. "Teachers are very odd creatures," she wrote in 1979. "We want to share everything we can with our students. We want them to excel us and expect them to surpass us."[7] In fact, her training program was an intense experience. In addition to their clinical work, she called upon her students to make public presentations and to discuss cases and research with visiting physicians. Taussig also held that it was essential to balance work with relaxation, and she insisted that there be days off to make the most of the pleasures of life. Yet even during vacation time she worked with students, teaching them how to write a scientific abstract and organize papers for presentation and publication. She understood that a student's self-confidence grows not just from succeeding but also from the challenge of fearing that she might not succeed and persevering in spite of it. She included both students and assistants as coauthors on publications and made a point to acknowledge the contributions of support staff in her efforts. The annual symposium that she hosted served not only to reunite the scores of pediatric cardiologists and surgeons she had influenced but also to establish a culture of cooperation in this new medical subdiscipline.

Taussig's students were personally important to her, and she to them. She followed up on them to see how they were doing, made sure that those who had traveled from abroad to study with her were adjusting to their new environment, and showed regard even for the progress of her students' students. Responding with warmth and enthusiasm, her students called themselves "the knights of Taussig" or her "round table." They quoted her favorite poems and her philosophy of medicine, remarked on her romantic ideals, and were moved by the beauty she saw in a healthy heart and the joy she experienced from a child's recovery. Those initially drawn to her clinic by its fame and perhaps intimidated by its rigor left it to practice a compassionate and ethical medical specialty.

Public Life and Personal Values

Undoubtedly, Dr. Helen Taussig was widely recognized for her contributions in pediatric cardiology. She was awarded twenty honorary degrees, including D.Sc. degrees from Boston University School of Medicine (1948), Columbia University (1951), the University of Athens, Greece (1956), Harvard University (1959), Göttingen University, Germany (1960), the University of Vienna, Austria (1965), and Duke University (1968). She particularly appreciated her honorary degree from Boston University, where she had begun her research career, and relished the recognition from Harvard University, where she had been turned away as a degree candidate. Between 1947 and 1987 she was honored with forty-eight awards, citations, prizes, medals, fellowships, symposia, and leadership positions. She was the first woman to receive many of these acknowledgments. Two cardiac clinics were named in her honor, at the University of Göttingen and at her career home, Johns Hopkins University. She received the Presidential Medal from the Republic of Peru and the single highest honor awarded to a civilian in the United States, the Medal of Freedom, which was awarded by President Lyndon B. Johnson on September 14, 1964.

Taussig was very conscious of this personal good fortune and subscribed to the public ethic of intellectuals of her time, believing that privilege must carry with it social responsibility. Her sense of civic duty was guided by the conviction that though some ethical situations may be by nature ambiguous, those actions that are in the best interest of both the individual and the public good are inherently just. Her conduct heeded the warning: "The hottest places in hell are reserved for those who, in times of great moral crisis, maintain their neutrality."

Taussig was an active participant in the political process. In 1967 she was a member of the United States deputation to the World Health Assembly in Geneva, Switzerland. In the same year she helped express concerns for war-injured Vietnamese children as the honorary chair of the Physician's Committee for Social Responsibility. In the 1970s she was an early and outspoken proponent of the need for a nationalized health insurance and for revisions in malpractice laws to discourage the practice of litigation-defensive medicine. Anticipating what would become a national dialogue in the 1990s, she expressed concerns about rising costs of medical care and about the quality of life of patients born with severe congenital malformations.

As an outgrowth of her professional experience with birth defects and her personal concern for the welfare of patients and families, Taussig was also a strong supporter of the extensive testing of drugs for their developmental side effects and of a patient's right to reproductive choice. The concerns she raised with Congress about thalidomide underscored the need for the Food and Drug Administration to take a more proactive role in drug evaluation. Taussig argued for greater understanding of the viral and chemical causes of birth defects, for better prenatal care, and for abortion as a last resort. In her characteristically direct style, in 1978 she stated: "Ninety percent of parents would prefer a child with a normal heart born a year later than to have the anxiety and sorrow of a child with a congenital malformation of the heart."[8] "When they are able to diagnose cardiac malformations prenatally, I don't think the answer is prenatal surgery. . . . I think the answer is abortion and trying again. Bringing a healthy child into the world is the important thing."[9]

While Taussig recognized the value of her work in the palliation of one kind of congenital abnormality, she realized that "children passionately long to be normal."[10] She was convinced that prevention of birth defects was the only thing that could truly relieve the suffering of children and their families. Her efforts to improve drug testing and her final work on the evolutionary and genetic history of cardiac malformation together represent a call for a broad shift in medical perspective: from treatment to prevention.

Like many of the upper-class professionals of her generation, Taussig also believed that hard work and exceptional performance were the only real determinants of success. Her liberal vision, though ahead of its time, did not extend far beyond her own experience. She expected herself to be adaptable even in the face of unjust circumstances and encouraged her patients and students to do the same. This strategy is one she used often through her life: even at the age of eighty-three, she urged her readers to "make a determined effort to adjust to society and not expect society to adjust to you."[11] Thus, though Taussig experienced disability and discrimination, her character and background shielded her from being victimized herself and yet limited her, sometimes leading her to judge harshly those less resilient than she. She survived gender bias largely by ignoring it. While she was deeply concerned about the well-being of women and children, believed in social change, and served as a role model and mentor for many women and men physicians, she rejected, perhaps inappropriately, the notion of herself as a feminist pioneer.

Helen Taussig never married or had children, although she encouraged her women students to do both. She maintained close ties with her immediate family and maintained a home on Cape Cod as a refuge and a link with her childhood. She treasured her relationships with her family and her academic mentors, Bremmer, Begg, Carter, and especially Park. When she had middle ear surgery at the age of sixty-five, Park accompanied her to the operating room as her friend and colleague. Though her hearing improved, she continued to use palpation of the heart as a fundamental diagnostic strategy and encouraged her students and colleagues to do the same. Throughout her life Taussig remained open to new and close personal relationships, fully integrating her personal and professional lives. She often spoke of her patients and research fellows as her extended family and their children and students as her grandchildren. She visited them, participated in family celebrations, and kept holidays with them. In later life Taussig mourned the losses of several research fellows whom she survived.

On May 20, 1986, just four days before her eighty-eighth birthday, Helen Taussig was involved in a car accident close to her retirement home in Crosslands, Kennett Square, Pennsylvania. She may have failed to see an oncoming car as she drove out of a parking area while taking a friend to a polling place. She died an hour later in Chester County Hospital. In May 1987 she was posthumously awarded the Association of American Physicians' George M. Kober Medal, and her final scholarly paper was published in 1988.

A Role Model for Today

The history of Dr. Helen Taussig's career underscores the interdependence among experience, character, and viewpoint in shaping a life. Her family's resources and emotional support and her many supportive mentors and collaborators certainly laid foundations for her accomplishments. The pleasure she took in finding patterns and her persistence and flexibility at problem solving allowed her to demonstrate the importance of observations that others ignored. Most importantly, her early experience in overcoming hardship and frustration, her perspective as an outsider, and her generous spirit allowed her to translate those observations into the far-reaching contributions she made to the lives of thousands of children. The effects of her scholarship, mentoring, and approach to medicine continue to have an impact on medical practice. Her work endures.

Notes

1. Taussig, "Little Choice and a Stimulating Environment," 44.
2. Ross, "Presentation of the George M. Kober Medal (posthumously) to Helen B. Taussig," cxii–cxiii.
3. Taussig, "Difficulties, Disappointments, and Delights in Medicine," 8.
4. Taussig, "Little Choice and a Stimulating Environment," 44.
5. Harvey, "A Conversation with Helen Taussig," 30.
6. Taussig, "Difficulties, Disappointments, and Delights in Medicine," 7.
7. Ibid.
8. Taussig, "Pediatric Cardiology: Past, Present, and Future," 115.
9. Harvey, "A Conversation with Helen Taussig," 42.
10. Taussig, "Pediatric Cardiology: Past, Present, and Future," 115.
11. Taussig, "How to Adjust to Deafness," 39s.

Bibliography

Abbott, M. E. "Congenital Cardiac Disease." In vol. 4 of *Osler and McCrae's Modern Medicine,* 2nd ed., ed. W. Osler and T. McCrae. Philadelphia: Lea and Febiger, 1915.

————. *Atlas of Congenital Cardiac Disease.* New York: American Heart Association, 1936.

Baldwin, J. *To Heal the Heart of a Child: Helen Taussig, M.D.* New York: Walker, 1992.

————. "A Troubling Tribute: Jamie Wyeth's Painting of Dr. Helen Taussig." *American Medical News* 32, no. 44 (1989): 27.

Bing, R. J. "The Johns Hopkins: The Blalock-Taussig Era." *Perspectives in Biology and Medicine* 32, no. 1 (1988): 85–90.

Blalock, A., and H. B. Taussig. "Landmark Article May 19, 1945: The Surgical Treatment of Malformations of the Heart in Which There Is Pulmonary Stenosis or Pulmonary Atresia." Republication. *Journal of the American Medical Association* 251, no. 16 (1984): 2123–38.

————. "The Surgical Treatment of Malformations of the Heart in Which There Is Pulmonary Stenosis or Pulmonary Atresia." *Journal of the American Medical Association* 128 (1945): 189–202.

Bruins, Caroline L. D. C. "A Remembrance from Europe." *International Journal of Cardiology* 14, no. 2 (1987): 260–61.

Dietrich, H. J., Jr. "Helen Brooke Taussig, 1898–1986." *Transactions and Studies of the College of Physicians of Philadelphia* 8, no. 4 (1986): 265–71.

Engle, M. A. "Dr. Helen Brooke Taussig, Living Legend in Cardiology." *Clinical Cardiology* 8, no. 6 (1985): 372–74.

Gross, R. E., and J. P. Hubbard. "Surgical Ligation of a Patent Ductus Arteriosus: Report of First Successful Case." *Journal of the American Medical Association* 112 (1939): 729–31.

Harvey, A. M. "Helen Brooke Taussig, May 24, 1898–May 20, 1986." *1986 Yearbook of the American Philosophical Society of Philadelphia,* 1987, 180–85.

Harvey, W. P. "A Conversation with Helen Taussig." *Medical Times* 106, no. 11 (1978): 28–44.

————. "A Warm Thank You to Helen Taussig." *Medical Times* 106, no. 11 (1978): 17–18.

Malloy, L. G. "Helen Brooke Taussig." In *Women in the Biological Sciences,* ed. L. Grinstein, C. Bierman, and R. Rose, 524–33. Westport, Conn.: Greenwood Press, 1997.

————. "John Gibbon Develops the Heart-Lung Machine." In *Great Events in History II: Science and Technology,* ed. F. N. Magill, 1024–29. Pasadena, Calif.: Salem Press, 1991.

McNamara, D. G. "Helen B. Taussig, the Original Pediatric Cardiologist." *Medical Times* 106, no. 11 (1978): 23–27.

————. "Helen Brooke Taussig: 1898–1986." *Pediatric Cardiology* 7, no. 1 (1986): 1–2.

McNamara, D. G., et al. "Helen Brooke Taussig: 1898 to 1986." *Journal of the American College of Cardiology* 10, no. 3 (1987): 662–71.

Neill, C. A. "Dr. Helen Brooke Taussig, May 24, 1898–May 21, 1986: International Cardiologist." *International Journal of Cardiology* 14, no. 2 (1987): 255–61.

———. "A Tribute to Helen Brooke Taussig, 1898–1986." *Circulation* 74 (1986): 1180.

Ross, R. S. "Presentation of the George M. Kober Medal (posthumously) to Helen B. Taussig." *Transactions of the Association of American Physicians* 100 (1987): cxii–cxxv.

Taussig, H. B. *Congenital Malformations of the Heart*. New York: The Commonwealth Fund, 1947.

———. *Congenital Malformations of the Heart*. Rev. ed. Vol. 1, *General Considerations*; vol. 2, *Specific Malformations*. Cambridge, Mass.: Published for The Commonwealth Fund by Harvard University Press, 1960.

———. "Congenital Malformations of the Heart." *Medical Times* 94, no. 4 (1966): 455–73.

———. "Difficulties, Disappointments, and Delights in Medicine." *The Pharos* 42 (1979): 6–8.

———. "Evolutionary Origin of Cardiac Malformations." [Review.] *Journal of the American College of Cardiology* 12, no. 4 (1988): 1079–86.

———. "How to Adjust to Deafness." *Medical Times* 109, no. 2 (1981) 39s–43s.

———. "Little Choice and a Stimulating Environment." *Journal of the American Medical Women's Association* 36, no. 2 (1981): 43–44.

———. "Pediatric Cardiology: Past Present and Future." *Medical Times* 106, no. 11 (1978): 107–15.

Taussig, H. B., et al. "Long-Time Observations on the Blalock-Taussig Operation. VII, Transpositions of the Great Vessels and Pulmonary Stenosis." *Johns Hopkins Medical Journal* 135 (1974): 161–70.

Taussig, H. B., and F. L. Meserve. "Rhythmic Contractions in Isolated Strips of Mammalian Ventricle." *American Journal of Physiology* 72 (1925): 89–98.

"Taussig, Helen B." *Current Biography* (1966), 401–3.

"Taussig, Helen B." *New York Times,* May 22, 1986, B16.

"Taussig, Helen Brooke." *The National Cyclopaedia of American Biography,* vol. K, 501–3. New York: James T. White and Co., 1967.

"Taussig, William." *The National Cyclopaedia of American Biography,* vol. A, 457–58. New York: James T. White and Co., 1926.

Thomas, T. V. *Pioneering Research in Surgical Shock and Cardiovascular Surgery: Vivien Thomas and His Work with Alfred Blalock*. Philadelphia: University of Pennsylvania Press, 1985.

Frankenstein's Native

Elizabeth Stassinos

There is something cruel, Ruth, in your mad love of psychic irregularities.
Do you not feel that you extract your loveliness from a mutely resisting
Nature who will have her terrible revenge?

—Edward Sapir to Ruth Fulton Benedict, August 18, 1925

An intimate and understanding study of a genuinely disoriented culture
would be of extraordinary interest.

—Ruth Fulton Benedict, *Patterns of Culture*

The deviant ceased to be either a tragic or merely pathetic figure, and became more and more a measuring device against which the pattern itself
could be understood. The sharper the appreciation of the deviance, the
keener the recognition of the strength of the pattern.

—Margaret Mead, from her contribution to
"Ruth Fulton Benedict, A Memorial"

Between 1923 and 1938 Ruth Fulton Benedict rewrote a study of a Shasta
shaman's initiation five times: once in her dissertation on the diffusion of
the "guardian spirit complex" in North America (1974 [1923]), once in "Anthropology and the Abnormal" (1959 [1934]), twice in *Patterns of Culture*
(1934), and one final time in "Religion," a chapter she wrote for Franz
Boas's *General Anthropology* (1938). In this essay I trace her successive uses
of this biographical fragment. I argue that tracing the development of this
piece as an analytical tool helps us see Benedict's work as a particular kind
of Boasian science, cosmography, the subjective science of history and literature, and not, in the way some in the secondary literature have interpreted her work since Judith Schachter Modell's first full-length biography

in 1983, as literary criticism, satire, or precocious feminist postmodernism (Geertz 1988; Babcock 1995 [1993]). In fact, Benedict's repeated use of this biographical fragment of a woman who, she says, would be stigmatized as abnormal in the West helps us trace her development of the notion of cultural patterns for both personal narrative and cultural ethnography, two genres that today fit under the cultural studies term "biography." I will use George W. Stocking's reading of Boas to clarify Benedict's subjective science and will return to what Stocking's method has in common with Benedict's at the end of this piece. But first, and before we meet either of their monsters, I should briefly clarify how my approach differs from that of others writing in the secondary literature.

The secondary literature on Benedict since Modell's effort (1983) has emphasized Benedict's biography over her theory, the "real" Ruth, so to speak. Modell and those who write after her read Benedict as a poet turned scientist and as an accidental anthropologist. Although this approach is helpful in giving attention to Benedict's earlier favorite genre and self (she wrote poetry under pseudonyms), it also has distracted us from the use to which we can put Benedict's work today as a counter to hermeneutical trends and the overly autobiographical ethnography that they have led to. It is true that biographies about Benedict do as they were intended—fill in the gaps of Mead's enigmatic (and ironically autobiographical) "at work" portrait of Benedict. In the process, they wonderfully complicate the story of the grand theory being employed at the time. But a biographical approach to Benedict (especially the early Benedict as a poet only) does not fully take into account Benedict's also early experimentation in biography or her movement from poetry through biography to ethnography. Benedict wrote one biographical paper in 1919, "Mary Wollstonecraft," and switched to ethnography, as Mead says, when she "widened the range of 'vicarious living' " that she could do from biographical portraits of the "highly enslaved" individual to writing cultures already colonized as analogies to personalities (1959, 116). But Benedict's more private experiments with authority and genre are the best evidence that biography is not the appropriate genre for the job. Not only in poetry but throughout her life, Benedict used a series of pseudonyms crafted to a variety of genres. She even thought of her married name, Ruth Benedict, as a pseudonym (in Mead 1959, xix).

My view is that, even without considering the other features of her case, Benedict's use of different pseudonyms for different genres complicates the biographical picture beyond the limits of that genre, beyond the bounded homogenous individuals (as a kind of synonym to bounded individual nations) that biography needs to assume. Any Benedict that we must write of in the 1990s deserves a more complex treatment, one that privileges her theory of culture as subjective science and as potentially useful for us today, and remembers that culture theory was the genre that she felt eclipsed all her other efforts at writing. It is in this sense that Stocking's project of distinguishing between Boas's objective or physicist's methods of deducing laws and the cosmographical model of intuiting a model or pattern from an individual's ("native" as well as Western) experience that Mead and Benedict used matters (Stocking 1974). If biography is my idea of a monstrous model for Benedict's life, let us quickly meet Benedict's monster and get down to the business of Benedict's science, a science that contains and encourages its own critique without destroying itself in the process.

Early in *Patterns of Culture,* Benedict attacks James Frazer's model of culture, his habit of using ethnocentric categories to group observed "bits of behavior":

> Studies of culture like *The Golden Bough* and the usual comparative ethnological volumes are analytical discussions of traits and ignore all the aspects of cultural integration. Mating or death practices are illustrated by bits of behavior selected indiscriminately from the most different cultures, and the discussion builds up a kind of mechanical Frankenstein's monster with a right eye from Fiji, and a left from Europe, one leg from Tierra del Fuego, and one from Tahiti, and all the fingers and toes from still different regions. Such a figure corresponds to no reality in the past or present, and the fundamental difficulty is the same as if, let us say, psychiatry ended with a catalogue of the symbols of which psychopathic individuals make use, and ignored the study of patterns of symptomatic behavior—schizophrenia, hysteria, and manic-depressive disorders—into which they are built.... There is as great an unreality in similar studies of culture. (1934, 49)[1]

In this passage, Benedict uses Mary Shelley's monster's body to make the Boasian shift from Frazer's categories to meaningful wholes.[2] She does this by juxtaposing Frazer's model to that monster. Her claim is that Frazer's science embodies a moral error. Benedict's cultures, described as analogies not to origins or organisms but to psychiatric wholeness, make a myth out of this personality writ large without reifying any particular psychiatric mechanism or vocabulary, while at the same time they embody a moral use of anthropological science. In her translation of the Boasian tack, traits are to be treated like symptoms, and random ethnocentric observations, like "the symbols" of the psychopath, are to be helpful in the diagnosis and treatment of the patient's or culture's psychic integration.

But there is more than just a shift to meaning or psychiatric wholeness in Benedict's critique: Just as important is the shift in time frames that Benedict makes. She takes Shelley's monster literally as a statement about the moral vision of a future science. In her reading, the Frankenstein monster represents both the past, Frazer's bad old evolutionary model, and the future, the potentially horrible consequence of treating other cultures like creatures that Western science cannot yet even make. For Benedict, models and other creations of human culture have a life of their own. There is no guarantee against an idea or model, like the monster in the novel, running amok, seeking to kill off the kith, kin, and culture of the very scientist that spawned it. But these creations and their independence from their creators are what anthropologists, as Boasian cosmographers and novelists/biographers, have in common. For the physicist, like Dr. Frankenstein (or Benedict's literary colleague Alfred Kroeber), who never included himself as a "mind of the observer" in his monster/model, loses control of that monster/model, lets it become disconnected from the causality that rules human emotions. On the other hand, in Benedict's model, the cosmographer is the subjective scientist, the opposite of the physicist who uses facts only to derive abstract rules. Benedict's model cosmographer in the case of her critique of functionalism is Mary Wollstonecraft (Mary Shelley's mother), a creator always connected to her creation, her model for a better world.

Benedict's vision of the Frankenstein monster as an analogy for anthropological mistakes also graphically embodies her analogy of culture and the personality. Here the body of the Frankenstein monster is a symbol of a world-personality, a body as globe, "with a right eye from Fiji, a left from Europe." Later in Benedict's writings culture is merely "personality writ large." But how does this transition from a disjointed geography to personal history or biography written large come about? Benedict gives us a clue as to what she wanted from "personality," monster, science, self:

"to master an attitude toward life which will somehow bind together these episodes of experience into something that may conceivably be called life" (in Mead 1974, 10).[3] That is, Benedict's Frankenstein monster not only represents a passionate monster and bad scientific model but also is first and foremost a projection of Benedict's notion of a Western attitude. In two articles, Richard Handler tells us that Benedict's notion of Western cultural achievement was publishing her "self," owning her own "answer" to life through academic writing (1986, 1991). Earlier in *Patterns of Culture*, and with precise indirection, Benedict both reiterates what writing and distance have in common and relocates her Frankenstein monster when she tells us she cannot study Western culture the same way that she can study other cultures in her "primitive laboratory":

> This laboratory has another advantage. The problems are set in simpler terms than in the great Western civilizations. With the inventions that make for ease of transportation, international cables and telephones and radio transmission, those that ensure permanence and widespread distribution to the printed page, the development of competing professional groups and cults and classes and their standardization over the world, modern civilization has grown too complex for adequate analysis except as it is broken up for the purpose into small artificial sections. And these partial analyses are inadequate because so many outside factors cannot be controlled.... In primitive society, the cultural tradition is simple enough to be contained within the knowledge of individual adults, and the manners and morals of the groups are moulded to one well-defined general pattern. (1934, 18)

Western culture, when analyzed, is her original monster of "small artificial sections," a body with as many autonomous patterns or contexts or geographical and experiential limits or "episodes" as it has parts (today, read: ethnicities, identities, races). So for Benedict, the West cannot be studied for the same reason that these "primitive cultures" can, that is, by reason of its own, very different diversity. In her reading, the monstrousness of the West is in fact spawned by its figurative "longings," or as Benedict R. Anderson would say, its own means of production of communications, its unreal unity or "imagined community" (1991). Here is Benedict as Frankenstein's native, an anthropologist who uses "the printed page" as her form of permanence and to locate her own "longings" and moral vision. Her use of writing counters the tendencies of her own culture's use of writing to fragment itself into yet more artificial sections or constituencies. It is the West and its literature that informs her laboratory, not the other way around. The laboratory of "primitive forms" is privileged in Benedict's work, but not as in Claude Lévi-Strauss's, in which it is primarily a means of theoretical illustration. It is the struggle of the individual to fit in a culture that drives Benedict's own and her projected "personalities," however ill equipped they are to conform.

We also see in this passage one reason that Benedict went from writing "Mary Wollstonecraft" and biography to writing *Patterns of Culture.* Benedict's "Mary Wollstonecraft" is the mother of the monster-maker and a woman who died after giving birth to her daughter. It is Mary Wollstonecraft whose vision for women was, like Frazer's model, the vision of just one artificial section of the population. For Benedict, Wollstonecraft could have learned from her daughter to temper her politics with science. Benedict rejects Wollstonecraft's moral vision for culture, in which Wollstonecraft reified and separated her notion of women from her idea of culture. Benedict's move away from overtly feminist constructs of culture seems to be a way of saying that Wollstonecraft, Elsie Clews Parsons, and even Mead were making Frankenstein monster's parts out of women's sphere, trying to liberate women from the context of which they were an integral and inseparable part. Ultimately Benedict follows Wollstonecraft's daughter's path of science fiction, using her "science of culture" in tandem with Shelley's critique of a Western "culture of science." Benedict, like Shelley, sees that a culture of technology will ultimately need to create a culture with values that deal with its inherently dehumanizing bent, if not for the lonely Frankenstein monster then for later similar monsters, perhaps the Internet hackers of the next millennium.

Despite her critique, Benedict seems to prepare us for a kind of Frankenstein monster and concept of culture that are paradoxically "abnormal" but nevertheless not monstrous. Her Frankenstein monster is artificial in the sense of being an individual for her to "think with," to use analogically to develop a model. But he is not monstrous in that he is more than an inventory of parts, "bits of behaviour," experience, even lonely shards of patriarchy. Benedict never overtly delivers a better Frankenstein monster in *Patterns of Culture,* nor does she call for an integrated West, but instead leaves the reader stewing in satiric juices and asks merely for more tolerance of America's cultural Others (Geertz 1988). But I think I have found the hidden monster of Benedict's plan for a better America in Benedict's five descriptions of the Shasta shaman. This woman is described over and over in Benedict's work, even twice in *Patterns of Culture*. She is a Shasta woman who, as Benedict says, would be seen as abnormal from the point of view of a West that stigmatizes her catalepsy, but who, among the Shasta, is seen as a leader for just that same "talent" for trance.

Shamans and Seizures

We first meet the shaman in Benedict's corpus as a case that illustrates trait diffusion over North America. In her dissertation, shamanism is the Shasta way of achieving relations with "guardian spirits." Benedict emphasizes all that is conventional in the initiate's procurement of a guardian spirit; she notes that shamans all have "stereotyped dreams" that forewarn them of their calling, and she describes the Axeki (pain) or very tiny man with a bow who is the guardian spirit and who threatens and empowers the bodies of all shamans. She also describes in detail the goods that all initiates need to accumulate in order to validate their power (1974 [1923], 14).[4]

In the next text, "Anthropology and the Abnormal," Benedict's emphasis on the shaman's role is entirely different (in Mead 1959, 262–83). Instead of dwelling on how the traits of guardian spirit and shamanism have merged, she uses the case of the Shasta shaman to make the argument that the Western notion of abnormality is culturally relative. Here Benedict notes that the vignette indicts her own culture's intolerance, for "Even a very mild mystic is aberrant." She uses this case to argue that although ecstatics are stigmatized in her Manhattan, they were once the chosen ones "when Catholicism made the ecstatic experience the mark of sainthood." I will quote the passage in full, as this version and its emphasis on the shaman, not Shasta culture, are what she depends on for the next three rewritings.

> Some of the Indian tribes of California accorded prestige principally to those who passed through certain trance experiences. Not all of these tribes believed that it was exclusively women who were so blessed, but among the Shasta this was the convention. Their shamans were women, and they were accorded the greatest prestige in the

community. They were chosen because of their constitutional liability to trance and allied manifestations. One day the woman who was so destined, while she was about her usual work, would fall suddenly to the ground. She had heard a voice speaking to her in tones of the greatest intensity. Turning, she had seen a man with drawn bow and arrow. He commanded her to sing on pain of being shot through the heart by his arrow, but under the stress of the experience she fell senseless. Her family gathered. She was lying rigid, hardly breathing. They knew that for some time she had had dreams of a special character which indicated a shamanistic calling, dreams of escaping grizzly bears, falling off cliffs or trees, or of being surrounded by swarms of yellow jackets. The community knew therefore what to expect. After a few hours the woman began to moan gently and to roll about upon the ground, trembling violently. She was supposed to be repeating the song which she had been told to sing and which during the trance had been taught her by the spirit. As she revived her moaning became more and more clearly the spirit's song until at last she called out the name of the spirit itself, and immediately blood oozed from her mouth.

When the woman had come to herself after the first encounter with her spirit she danced that night her first initiatory shamanistic dance. ... For three nights she had to receive in her body her power from her spirit. She was dancing, and as she felt the approach of the moment she called out, "He will shoot me, he will shoot me." Her friends stood close, for when she reeled in a kind of cataleptic seizure, they had to seize her before she fell or she would die. From this time on she had in her body a visible materialization of her spirit's power, an icicle-like object which in her dances thereafter she would exhibit.... From this time on she continued to validate her supernatural power by further cataleptic demonstrations, and she was called upon in great emergencies of life and death, for curing and for divination and for counsel. She became in other words by this procedure, a woman of great power and importance.

It is clear that, so far from regarding cataleptic seizures as blots upon the family escutcheon and as evidences of dreaded disease, cultural approval had seized upon them and made of them the pathway to authority over one's fellows.... It was precisely the cataleptic individuals who in this culture were singled out for authority and leadership. (in Mead 1959, 264)

Gone are conventions; now blood "oozes" from the shaman's magical lips. Benedict's concern with the details of diffusion has yielded to a description of the initiation as unique event and the shaman as a unique woman. But what is added in 1934 marks Benedict's "widening" of the shaman's "vicariousness" as much as it marks Benedict's own movement from biography to ethnography, from charity work to professional science. This secularization of the shaman's work continues, in many ways reflecting Benedict's own career move from charities to the academy. As she says in the passage just quoted, while it is the family of this shaman who "gathered" to help her, it is the "community," the larger social unit, by which the shaman is supported. "They" know what to expect. And it is her "friends," not family, that catch her when her life is most in danger. Likewise, the shaman's power is now seen as secular and is no longer analogically linked with Catholicism, although Benedict later returns to a different religious analogy for catalepsy.[5]

The shaman of the article is now the anti–Frankenstein monster of the book, an "abnormal" who fits her culture, neither a deviant driven to murder nor a "normal" dumbly "plastic to the moulding force of society." In 1938 the erasure of the "little man" and guardian spirit is complete, being replaced by a gender-neutral "spirit's power." Also in 1938, the Shasta's catalepsy is desecularized. Benedict finally finds the right analogy to a religion other than Western Catholicism (or is it Western "work" that constitutes Benedict's American ethic?). In 1938, Benedict says that the shaman's trance is like that of Polynesian priests whose talents for "possession" allow them to be "ranked with the highest chiefs," to become the "mouthpieces of the god" (in Boas 1938, 659).[6]

Thus we see the shift from Benedict's critique of functionalism's monster (a world without British values) to her positive use of the perceived psychological monsters of her time (women hysterics/cataleptics) and her subsequent creation of the theoretical concept of patterns. Patterns is again a crucial notion to us today, not only because it promises us an early bridge between anthropology and the humanities, a promise Benedict made in her farewell address as president of the American Anthropological Association in 1947, but because it allows for a kind of objective subjectivism, the idea that we can use the individual's testimony and even biography to test what we know of a culture without losing all of the other objective information we have about that culture. Like Roy Wagner (1981 [1975]), Benedict creates an ethnographic anchor upon which to build a description, as well as test it, by including the mind of the observer in the model. Of course Benedict uses the hysterical shaman and only alludes to her own difficult role in American culture. Nevertheless, this projection served the purpose of her holistic modernism and her liberal scientific biases at a time when it was needed.

Conclusion

We don't have to read Benedict as postmodern to claim her for our canon. She clearly believed in a real culture and a better model. She was no hermeneut, despite the advantages of that position in her day. But she also never presented any data or model without critiquing the Western culture and scientist that construct them, continually "widening her vicariousness" and lessening her fragmented sense of herself until she totally shared her Other deviant's, not Other normal's, points of view. When culture was personality writ large, anthropologists were abnormal, as were neurotics. Now that culture is writ in the margins with identity issues thrown large upon the screen, everyone's a shrink, an observer, a dysfunctional voyeur. It is time to relocate the strangeness (or maybe just the innocence) of the anthropological project and personality, not in postmodern fragmentation or the death of the ethnographer but in the shifting between genres and models and even experiences of self that mark Benedict's (and Stocking's) project. It is that aspect of the canon that Benedict will always represent. And she will always stand out among those anthropologists who are already in the minority, willing to not just compare but to resign their successive realities and models, to take the poison of their own vitiating analysis.

Notes

1. Benedict gets this model for a fragmented person from A. C. Bradley's masterful *Shakespearian Tragedy* (1904). She mentions his work, but not his similar passage, in her call for more interesting applications of life histories in her 1947 "Anthropology and the Humanities."

2. In fact, we can see Benedict's use of "Dionysian" as inspired not so much by Friedrich Nietzsche or Walter Pater but by Frazer, who, in *The Golden Bough*, has a chapter about the worship of the god Dionysus. In this chapter it is first Dionysus as his infant self, then those who are sacrificed to him, who are, like anti–Frankenstein monsters, dismembered, "cut into pieces," "cut ... limb from limb," only to be "pieced together, at the command of Zeus, by Apollo who buried them on Parnassus" (1963 [abridged], 388–89). In *Patterns of Culture*, Benedict, following Nietzsche, makes Dionysus over into Dionysian, an adjective or "way" of doing something, doing culture. Here is another of Benedict's "widenings of vicariousness" through juxtaposition with things Apollonian.

3. This is a bit ironic, as Benedict, perhaps of all the Boasians, recognized that, in the terms of her model, certain cultures and individuals never achieve either a recognizable coherence or, in the sense of their symptoms being unified, a meaning.

4. In her next four examples many changes occur. The Axeki, or guardian spirit, is slowly edited out, and the woman and the story of her "destiny" of being stricken and then becoming a leader in her community takes over the narrative. Beginning in "Anthropology and the Abnormal" (1959 [1934]), Benedict adds the element of the "rigidity" of the shaman in trance, something she talks about in her autobiographical fragment written for Mead. In this fragment she says that her mother's weeping "always had the same effect on [her], an excruciating misery with physical trembling of a peculiar involuntary kind which culminated periodically in rigidity like an orgasm" (1959 [1934], 98). In later versions, the graphic element of blood "oozing" from the mouth of the shaman is added.

5. This secularization of the shaman's work continues, in many ways reflecting Benedict's own career move from charities to the academy.

6. Benedict's comparison of the shaman to a Polynesian "mouthpiece of the god" is similar to the way she speaks of being possessed herself by her pseudonyms/familiars. Mead writes, "In letters to me she began to use an older name, 'Sally,' for the self who came and went and who would 'dictate' lines only when it suited her" (Mead 1959, 94).

Works Cited

Anderson, Benedict R. 1991. *Imagined Communities: Reflections on the Origin and Spread of Nationalism*. London: Verso.

Babcock, Barbara. 1995 [1993]. "Not in the First Person Singular." Reprinted in *Women Writing Culture*, ed. Ruth Behar and Deborah A. Gordon. Berkeley: University of California Press.

Benedict, Ruth Fulton. 1959 [1919]. "Mary Wollstonecraft." In *An Anthropologist at Work: The Writings of Ruth Benedict*, ed. Margaret Mead. Boston: Houghton Mifflin.

————. 1974 [1923]. *The Concept of the Guardian Spirit in North America.* Millwood, N.Y.: Kraus Reprint.

————. 1934. *Patterns of Culture.* Boston: Houghton Mifflin.

————. 1959 [1934]. "Anthropology and the Abnormal." In *An Anthropologist at Work: The Writings of Ruth Benedict,* ed. Margaret Mead. Boston: Houghton Mifflin.

————. 1947. "Anthropology and the Humanities." *American Anthropologist* 50: 585–93.

Boas, Franz. 1938. *General Anthropology.* Boston: Heath.

Frazer, James. 1963. *The Golden Bough: A Study in Magic and Religion.* Abridged ed. New York: Collier-Macmillan.

Geertz, Clifford. 1988. *Works and Lives: The Anthropologist as Author.* Stanford, Calif.: Stanford University Press.

Handler, Richard. 1986. "Vigorous Male and Aspiring Female: Poetry, Personality, and Culture in Edward Sapir and Ruth Benedict." In *Malinowski, Rivers, Benedict, and Others: Essays on Culture and Personality,* ed. George Stocking. Madison: University of Wisconsin Press.

————. 1991. "Ruth Benedict and the Modern Sensibility." In *Modernist Anthropology: From Fieldwork to Text,* ed. Marc Manganaro. Princeton, N.J.: Princeton University Press.

Mead, Margaret. 1959. *An Anthropologist at Work: The Writings of Ruth Benedict.* Boston: Houghton Mifflin.

————. 1974. *Ruth Benedict.* New York: Columbia University Press.

Modell, Judith Schachter. 1983. *Ruth Benedict: Patterns of a Life.* Philadelphia: University of Pennsylvania Press.

Stocking, George W., ed. 1974. *The Shaping of American Anthropology, 1883–1911: A Franz Boas Reader.* New York: Basic Books.

————. 1989. *Romantic Motives: Essays on Anthropological Sensibility.* Madison: University of Wisconsin Press.

Wagner, Roy. 1981 [1975]. *The Invention of Culture.* Chicago: University of Chicago Press.

Women Becoming Mathematicians

Constructing a Professional Identity
in Post–World War II America

Margaret A. M. Murray

Introduction

In recent years considerable attention has been devoted to the problem of underrepresentation of women and minorities in the traditionally male fields of science and engineering. These fields have tended to attract and retain women in inverse proportion to the degree to which their subject matter is perceived to be difficult, abstract, and inaccessible. It may also be argued that the presence of women is proportional to the friendliness and openness of the academic and professional community of the particular field. It is likely that these two factors are closely related. Typically, physics and many of the engineering disciplines attract and retain the fewest women, both numerically and proportionally, while the biological sciences seem to attract the most; mathematics has tended to fall somewhere in between, perhaps toward the lower end of the spectrum (see, for example, Harmon and Soldz 1963; Jones 1990; Kass-Simon 1990).

Mathematics occupies a unique position among scientific and technical fields. It provides a logical and quantitative framework for the empirical sciences, while at the same time having its own independent subject matter. Because the objects of mathematical study are concepts that have been abstracted from common notions of counting, measurement, geometry, and relationship, mathematics is not an empirical science in any ordinary sense of the word. So it is perhaps not surprising that even educated lay persons regard mathematics as difficult, abstract, and inaccessible. But one of the advantages of mathematics as a subject of study is precisely this: mathematical objects are portable and can be carried about in the mind, without need for any special equipment. In principle, mathematical inquiry can be carried out anywhere at all.

The sociability and conviviality of the mathematical community are somewhat more difficult to assess. Precisely because mathematics *is* abstract, however, the flowering of mathematical knowledge depends to a considerable extent on interaction with this larger community, within which the meaning and significance of the abstractions are negotiated. Women's ability to prosper as mathematicians depends, in no small part, on their access to this community.

The professional degree representing the highest level of attainment in mathematics, as in other scientific and technical fields, is the Ph.D. The activity that distinguishes the Ph.D. from other degrees is the process of creating new mathematical knowledge through research. Those who have pursued the Ph.D. have at least briefly engaged in this process of creation. With some notable exceptions, pursuit of the doctorate is necessary for membership in the mathematical community, and receipt of the degree is necessary for full acceptance there.

Engagement with the abstract subject matter of mathematics, creation of new knowledge through research, and membership in the mathematical community are key components in the process of becoming a mathematician. Once this process is under way, how do individuals construct and maintain a sense of identity as a professional in the mathematical world? Is this process different for women than it is for men? How does the "mathematical identity" develop over the life-course?

In this essay, I discuss the professional development of women who received Ph.D.'s in the mathematical sciences from American colleges and universities during the 1940s and 1950s. These decades are of particular interest for a number of reasons. World War II was a signal event in the development of American mathematics. During the war, American men were largely absent from the academic scene; in some years, women represented an extraordinarily high proportion of the Ph.D. recipients in mathematics and many other fields (Harmon and Soldz 1963).

At the end of the war, the mathematical and scientific enterprise in America underwent unprecedented expansion. The GI Bill enabled huge numbers of returning veterans, mainly men, to pursue advanced degrees, and colleges and universities expanded to meet the demand. Meanwhile, in the aftermath of the perceived success of the Manhattan Project, in which mathematicians played key roles, mathematics was as richly rewarded as the other physical sciences by the expansion of federal support for academic training and research. The National Science Foundation (NSF) was founded, and the Army, Navy, and Air Force sponsored basic scientific research of all kinds. With the baby boom population increase, all of the sciences, and mathematics in particular, looked forward to virtually limitless expansion.

In the decades prior to World War II, women received a relatively stable share of the Ph.D.'s awarded in mathematics. During the 1930s, for example, women consistently received between 10 and 20 percent of the Ph.D.'s each year. During the 1940s and 1950s, however, while the number of women receiving Ph.D.'s in mathematics remained relatively stable, their proportion of the total reached an all-time low (about 5 percent in the late 1950s). On the one hand, women did benefit from the general expansion in the sciences during the postwar years; on the other hand, they were subject to discrimination in a social milieu in which women were supposed to be at home raising families.

In the next section of this essay I will describe the situation for women seeking admission to the American mathematical research community in the years prior to World War II and the dramatic changes brought about by the war and its aftermath. The dramatic growth and prosperity of the American mathematical enterprise in the postwar years is reflected in the emergence of what I refer to as the myth of the mathematical life-course. In the third section I will describe the major features of the myth: a picture of the life-course of the ideal mathematician, well-suited to a man's life circumstances, and particularly those of a married man whose wife does no work outside the home. Then I will argue that the women who received mathematics Ph.D.'s during the 1940s and 1950s did not generally conform to this myth, and I will explore the actual avenues they took toward the development of a professional identity in the mathematical community.

This essay is significantly based upon information obtained in interviews with twenty-one of the approximately two hundred women who received Ph.D.'s during these two decades. These interviews were conducted in 1995 and 1996 as part of an oral history project that is still ongoing. Appendix 1 lists each interviewee by name, together with a brief description of her educational background and career path. Interview excerpts that appear in this essay are accompanied by a parenthetical note of the interviewee's name and the page number of the interview transcript. Appendix 2 provides some information on the women Ph.D.'s as a group, listing in particular the institutions that granted the most Ph.D.'s in mathematics to women during 1940–1959.

Women Mathematicians and the World War II Transition

The American tradition in mathematical research, and in academic research more generally, is not a particularly long one. Yale University has the distinction of awarding the first Ph.D. in the United States in any subject, as well as the first Ph.D. awarded in mathematics, during the academic year 1861–1862 (Solomon 1985, 134; Richardson 1989, 365). As Karen Parshall and others have shown (Fenster and Parshall 1994; Parshall and Rowe 1994), the mathematical research community in the United States began to emerge in the late nineteenth century, but it was during the early decades of the twentieth century that it grew substantially in size and distinction. In those early days, ongoing participation in research was not normally expected of mathematics Ph.D.'s once they had completed the work for the degree. For both men and women, the Ph.D. in mathematics was, first and foremost, a credential for postsecondary teaching (Richardson 1989).

The Great Depression of the thirties had a depressing effect upon institutions of higher education in the United States. In particular, fewer men and women were able to afford the expense of graduate education, either because they could not pay for it, or because their financial situation required them to work. World War II, on the other hand, while initially depleting the supply of talented faculty and students on campus, ultimately had an extremely salutary effect upon academic mathematics and upon the mathematical research community.

Perhaps the signal event that sealed the postwar fortunes of the mathematical community was the perceived success of the Manhattan Project in securing the Allied victory in World War II (Rees 1980). In the years immediately following the war, basic research in mathematics came to be perceived as essential to national security, and mathematics achieved a correspondingly greater status than it had had before the war. This change in status, among many other factors, changed the shape and character of the American mathematical research community and had a profound effect on the participation of women within that community.

In 1886, Winifred Edgerton (Merrill) was awarded the Ph.D. in mathematics at Columbia University, thus becoming the first woman to receive this degree from an American college or university (Green and LaDuke 1987, 13). In the years that followed, through the year 1939, 228 other women matched her achievement (Green and LaDuke 1987).[1]

Table 1 gives a breakdown by gender of Ph.D.'s in mathematics awarded during the years 1920–1994. The data is grouped in five-year aggregates, since year-to-year fluctuations are unlikely to have statistical significance. The period 1920–1934 saw an increase in the number of both men and women receiving the Ph.D. During 1935–1939, the numbers of Ph.D.'s awarded to both genders declined, most likely as a consequence of the depression. Over the entire period 1920–1939, the proportion of Ph.D.'s in mathematics awarded to women remained consistently in the 11–19 percent range.

In the period 1940–1944, comprising the first years of World War II in Europe and the first three years of American involvement in the war, the total number of Ph.D.'s awarded dropped from the late-thirties levels. As young men began to go to war, there were some individual years during this period in which women received an unusually high percentage of the degrees. For example, in 1944 women received fourteen of the forty-three Ph.D.'s awarded in mathematics—over 30 percent of the total (Harmon and Soldz 1963, 50).

The five years immediately following World War II saw the first real increase in the numbers of Ph.D.'s awarded in mathematics since the early 1930s. Men accounted for virtually the entire increase; the number of women receiving Ph.D.'s remained level. In the last half of the forties, women's percentage of the Ph.D.'s awarded in mathematics dropped back to 1925–1929 levels.

The most dramatic changes, however, occurred in the fifties. The number of Ph.D.'s awarded in the first half of the fifties represents an increase of 125 percent over the last half of the forties. This increase is almost entirely accounted for by the growing number of men earning the degree: the number of Ph.D.'s awarded to women in the first half of the fifties shows an increase of only 14 percent over the last half of the forties.

Roughly speaking, the number of women earning Ph.D.'s in mathematics during the years 1940–1959 remained flat, while the participation of men increased almost 300 percent in the same period. The net effect was to dramatically dilute the representation of women as a proportion of the total. Throughout the 1950s, women received less than 5 percent of the Ph.D.'s. awarded, and their percentage of the total did not return to the double digits until the latter half of the 1970s.[2]

TABLE **1**

Mathematics Ph.D.'s Awarded by Gender

Source: National Research Council, Survey of Earned Doctorates.

Years	# of Women	# of Men	Total	Percentage of Women
1920–24	21	93	114	18.4%
1925–29	28	210	238	11.8%
1930–34	62	334	396	15.7%
1935–39	51	333	384	13.3%
1920–39	**162**	**970**	**1,132**	**14.3%**
1940–44	43	321	364	11.8%
1945–49	44	427	471	9.3%
1950–54	51	1,008	1,059	4.8%
1955–59	58	1,208	1,266	4.6%
1940–59	**196**	**2,964**	**3,160**	**6.2%**
1960–64	115	1,967	2,082	5.5%
1965–69	248	4,077	4,325	5.7%
1970–74	503	5,684	6,187	8.1%
1975–79	583	4,107	4,690	12.4%
1960–79	**1,449**	**15,835**	**17,284**	**8.4%**
1980–84	531	3,060	3,591	14.8%
1985–89	628	3,137	3,765	16.7%
1990–94	1,062	4,191	5,253	20.2%
1980–94	**2,221**	**10,388**	**12,609**	**17.6%**

What were the social and political factors that can help to account for these dramatic changes in the number and proportion of Ph.D.'s awarded to women and to men during and after World War II?

In the early forties, as university-age men went off to war, university campuses experienced a shortage of students; as faculty men went off to war, there were faculty shortages as well. Consequently, women generally felt welcome in graduate departments of mathematics during the war years, particularly because they could serve as part-time replacement faculty. At colleges and universities, as in business and industry, women had somewhat greater opportunities to work in traditionally male-dominated fields owing to what might be called the "Rosie the Riveter effect" (see Hartmann 1982).

On university campuses, the war-induced shortages of faculty and graduate students became somewhat more acute in the years immediately following the war. After the passage of the GI Bill in 1944, a steady surge of returning armed service personnel—overwhelmingly male—flocked to the campuses, but primarily as undergraduate students (Solomon 1985, 190; Hartmann 1982, 101–20). At the same time, federal funding for basic research began to grow and develop, and this funding fueled the growth of graduate and postdoctoral fellowship programs. In these early postwar years, women continued to feel welcome in the graduate schools.

In the late forties and early fifties, however, returning servicemen who had earned bachelor's degrees in mathematics under the GI Bill were prepared to enter graduate school. As they entered in increasing numbers, the pressure to fill graduate student and faculty positions with women began to subside (Hartmann 1982; Solomon 1985, 190). Some of the women I interviewed who were enrolled in graduate school during this transitional period report that they sensed a change in the attitude toward them in midstream.

During this same period, graduate faculty in departments of mathematics experienced increased pressure to engage in research. Many departments undertook programs to upgrade the quality of their graduate faculty. Among the most dramatic transitions of this kind took place at the University of Chicago, where in 1947 Marshall Stone was hired to modernize the research faculty (MacLane 1989, 146–50). It is interesting to note that while forty-six women had earned Ph.D.'s in mathematics from the University of Chicago during the years 1892–1939, and six women earned Ph.D.'s in mathematics there during 1940–1946, there were only three Ph.D.'s awarded to women there during 1947–1959—in 1951, 1956, and 1957.[3] In general, attempts to modernize and upgrade departments of mathematics and science during this period had the effect of reducing the

representation of women among faculty and students alike, in both proportion and in absolute numbers, sometimes dramatically (Graham 1978;
Hartmann 1982; Rossiter 1995).

It is difficult to characterize the situation for women pursuing the Ph.D.
in mathematics in American institutions in the 1950s. On the one hand, it
is clear that they benefited, along with the men, from the new funding opportunities in mathematical training and research. The National Science
Foundation was founded in 1952, and women were among the recipients
of the first graduate fellowships awarded in the late fifties. Moreover, the
launching of the Soviet Sputnik satellite in 1957 led to an increasing sense
of urgency about the development and maintenance of a scientific and
mathematical elite. The sense of emergency tended to work in favor of talented young women who sought advanced training in technical fields, including mathematics. On the other hand, the 1950s brought a heightened
expectation that women would stay home, raise families, hew to traditional
gender roles, and leave the development of commerce, industry, and science to the men (see Hartmann 1982, especially chapters 9 and 10).

The perceived needs of the academy and of national security were
manifestly at odds with the societal requirement that women stay at home,
raise families, and provide private support for their husbands' public lives.
The women who embarked on mathematical careers during these years
keenly felt this conflict on a daily basis. Their lives as mathematicians required unrelenting negotiation between these competing demands.

The Myth of the Mathematical Life-Course

In the decades following World War II, it was increasingly expected that
Ph.D. mathematicians employed in colleges and universities would have
some continued involvement with research during their careers. But where
did this expectation originate? From the awarding of the first American
mathematics Ph.D.'s in the 1860s on into the 1950s, there were relatively
few institutions where it was possible to earn the doctoral degree (see
Richardson 1989). It was in the graduate school environment at these elite
institutions that most Ph.D.'s-in-training formed their first career expectations, from the information they gleaned from their teachers and mentors.

As the American mathematical research enterprise grew and developed in the early postwar years, the faculties of these elite doctoral insti-

tutions consisted of a growing number of intensely productive researchers (amply documented in Duren et al. 1989). In this environment, the myth of the mathematical life-course (hereinafter, "the myth") became a predominant model of career development for aspiring mathematicians. To a significant extent, the myth is prevalent in graduate institutions to this day.

According to the myth, mathematical talent and creative potential emerge very early in childhood. These natural gifts are focused and directed toward mathematics from this early age. It is a foregone conclusion that the college major will be mathematics, and the student proceeds from college to an elite graduate school without a break. In graduate school, the student comes under the tutelage of a powerful mentor, under whose direction he writes a doctoral dissertation that makes a deeply significant contribution to his area of study. As his graduate studies draw to a close, his mentor assists him in landing a postdoctoral research position at a similarly elite doctorate-granting department of mathematics, and afterward he goes on to one or more positions at comparably distinguished universities, where his creative achievements are rewarded with tenure.

The mathematician is extraordinarily productive in mathematical research from his late teens until his early forties; it is during this period that his best work is done. There are no interruptions during this period of scholarly productivity (except possibly for a brief tour of military duty), and to a considerable extent, the mathematician ignores or eschews other interests during this period. It is very helpful if the mathematician has a spouse who will take care of domestic and family concerns and provide him with a peaceful home environment that supports his creative work.

In the later years, research productivity continues, albeit at a somewhat lesser rate; the mathematician continues to generate creative ideas, but the working-out of these ideas falls to his younger colleagues and (especially) graduate students, who carry out the various aspects of his research program. It is perhaps possible, later in life, for the mathematician to enjoy some hobbies and diversions, but his primary concern is and continues to be mathematics.

It is reasonable to ask how many mathematicians, of either the prewar or postwar period, managed to live out the letter of the myth. But regardless of the extent to which the myth is mirrored in the reality of actual lives, there can be little doubt of its power. The myth is and has been aggressively perpetuated, in numerous popular accounts of the lives of the most productive male mathematicians of this century (see, for example, Albers et al. 1990; Halmos 1985, especially 400–401; Duren et al. 1989).

It is clear that in certain important particulars, the myth is an inappropriate one for women. Few women have supportive spouses who will shield them from distractions or exempt them from the responsibilities of home and family. To what extent did women of the wartime and postwar generations attempt to conform to the myth? To what extent did they experience conflict if they attempted to do so? To what extent were they able to ignore it, or else to adapt the myth to their own life circumstances?

And indeed, what did it mean to these women to be a mathematician? Were they able to develop, nurture, and sustain a sense of mathematical identity, particularly in cases of extreme dissonance between their own lives and the myth? In the sections that follow, we will consider the various stages of mathematical development as viewed through the eyes of twenty-one women mathematics Ph.D.'s of the 1940s and 1950s.

Early Influences

For many of these women, mathematics was an early interest that was incorporated into play activities and otherwise actively encouraged at home. For Grace Bates, mathematics is intermingled with warm memories of playing with her grandfather:

> I can't remember when I wasn't [interested in mathematics], but I think maybe the earliest recollection I have is of sitting on my grandpa's knee and having him say, "Now, tell me what one plus one is. Two plus three!" And that was fun, you know, sitting on his knee and also playing. (Bates, 1)

Violet Larney has similar early memories, of arithmetic being incorporated into play with her uncle:

> [My] interests always seemed to lie there [in mathematics] in elementary school and high school. When I played school with my uncle, when he babysat for me, I'd be teaching him the arithmetic that I learned that week. (Larney, 1)

Jean Walton appreciated the association of mathematics with play in her early school days:

I was interested in [mathematics] all the way through school. I remember doing well at arithmetic in grammar school, and loving it . . . when the teacher asked the class to have a mental arithmetic bee, like a spelling bee. . . . So [my interest] started early. (Walton, 1)

In many cases, though, mathematics was simply one among many enjoyable school subjects and did not hold a particular appeal. Tilla Weinstein recalls her school days warmly and recalls that she liked mathematics, but no more than other subjects:

I always liked *everything* that I learned in elementary school, including math. I especially enjoyed math in junior high school and high school. [But I] *never* thought of myself as particularly drawn to the subject. (Weinstein, 1)

Often mathematics became a particularly attractive school subject over time because it relied less heavily on memory than other subjects:

[In] high school, I took mathematics for four years and seemed to enjoy it. It involved less memory than history and literature and so on. It seemed logical to me. (Larney, 1)

Without identifying mathematics per se as her primary interest, Mary Ellen Rudin recalls that her performance in mathematics and science was better than in other subjects because of their lesser dependence upon memory:

I was not nearly so good in school as a friend of mine . . . who had a photographic memory. And she could answer questions about an English assignment or a history assignment or a government assignment much better than I could. And I was perhaps a little better than she was at mathematics and science and things like this. (Rudin, 3)

Contrary to the myth, what seems to set these women apart from their peers is not an early interest in mathematics per se, but rather the early formation of professional ambition. These women generally came from homes in which education, particularly education for women, was valued. With education came professional dreams, aspirations, and ambitions, which were encouraged by at least one and sometimes both parents. For Barbara Beechler, this encouragement came primarily from her father:

[My] father was thought to be a fool by all of his colleagues at the office, because he was educating his daughters. And my father was *inordinately* proud of me, and insisted that I ... was going to be a scientist. And so, ... from a very early age, I really *did* think I was going to be a professor of physics, long before I could pronounce the word "physicist"! And Daddy thought that was really very important. (Beechler, 2)

Margaret Owchar Marchand was raised in Manitoba by parents who had emigrated from Ukraine. Her father, who had little formal education himself, instilled in her the idea that education was the key to success in America. He believed in education for both of his daughters and took responsibility for it even before they went to school:

Well, my father, who learned English by taking it in night school after he came to this country [to Canada], had his little beginning reader books, and he taught us English. We started as youngsters, speaking Ukrainian. But by the time we went to school, we were bilingual. So he encouraged whatever we could do, because of the fact that it was obvious you couldn't get out of poverty without an education. (Marchand, 2)

While not actively encouraged by him, Jean Walton was significantly motivated by a desire to please her father, who held an important academic position:

I lived on the campus of a private boarding school; my father was headmaster. And I was the fourth of five girls—that was the family—and we grew up on that campus. ... [A]ll five of us went to college. It did not at the time seem at all unusual to me—it was assumed. I was very conscious of a desire, a need, that it was important to me to do things that would please my father. (Walton, 1–3)

At least two of the interviewees were strongly influenced by the unconventional professional attainments of their mothers. Maria Steinberg, who was born in Germany, has this to say about her mother:

[My mother] had a Ph.D. in history, which was unusual for her time. ... [S]he and other girls of her generation could not go to public school. I don't know the details of that. So they were tutored by a private tutor till they got to university, and they *could* go to university. And my mother spent several years at the university and then got her Ph.D. (Steinberg, 2)

Vera Pless, who grew up in Chicago, was impressed by the achievements of her mother, who studied and practiced dentistry in Russia and the United States:

[My mother] became a dentist in Russia, and they drafted her in World War I. . . . And they sent her to the front, and I think she didn't like it. . . . [S]he deserted and came here. My mother was very unusual. . . . [T]hey wouldn't accept her [dentistry] degree here, so she had to go through school again. And she went to the University of Illinois. Her English was never very great. But she did [it], and she became a dentist. (Pless, 2)

Tilla Weinstein reports that she was always much closer to her mother than to her father. She was an only child, and her mother attended very closely to her and encouraged her in almost everything she wanted to do. It is interesting that her own professional ambition originated as a reaction to her mother's dependence upon her father:

[My mother] spoke to me at great length about absolutely everything—certainly not about mathematics! And I loved listening to her and she loved listening to me. And I imagine that just being taken as seriously as I was by my mother as an individual was very important. . . . [My father] and my mother didn't get along that well together, and so it was a happy house when he wasn't there, and only sometimes happy when he was around. . . . [As a child I] had pipe dreams, almost, about the different things I might do. . . . I might be a lawyer; I might be a clothing designer; I might be a buyer for a department store. I don't think I ever thought in terms of owning a business. Entrepreneurial adventures were not for me! I thought at different times after high school of being a writer. But probably the most persistent sense was that I wanted to teach. . . . Behind all of this—which is important—was the knowledge that I was not going to put myself in the situation which I saw my mother in. I expected to work in order to not be dependent. I didn't see myself as working in order to attain some great status, or to excel particularly. (Weinstein, 1–4)

In the formation of professional ambition, a home atmosphere that was supportive of intellectual and educational pursuits seems to have been more important than an early interest in mathematics as such. Herta Freitag, who grew up in Vienna, had an intellectually lively home in which each family member followed his or her own special intellectual or artistic pursuits in the company of one another:

We had a very, very happy family life, to which I attribute ... anything that I've done with myself. What we specifically liked was to sit together—specifically, say, weekends—together, but everybody doing his thing. Father would almost invariably read the newspaper, Mother would do her embroidery, [my brother] Walter would compose, and I would do mathematics. We even coined a German name for that— it was very, very important for us—*eine wonnige Gruppierung:* a delightful *Gruppierung,* group togetherness. (Freitag-1, 2)

Joan Rosenblatt grew up in New York City, the eldest of four children born to a Columbia University faculty couple. When Rosenblatt was born in 1926, her mother "was the first woman on the faculty of Barnard College to get a maternity leave—unpaid, but with the promise of getting her job back." She describes her home environment growing up as "supportive, and stimulating," and has this to say about the breadth and depth of her family's academic commitment:

My father was a professor of philosophy of education at Teachers College of Columbia University. My mother was a professor of economics at Barnard College, Columbia University.... My father went to Wittenberg College; then he went to McCormick Theological Seminary. Then he got a Ph.D. working under John Dewey at Columbia Teachers College. My mother went to Reed College; then briefly taught at Mills College, worked for a while, for Irving Fisher, the famous economist at Yale, and then started a Ph.D. at Columbia in sociology and switched to economics.... And not only do I have parents [who both] had Ph.D.'s, I think I'm one of the relatively few people who can say I have two grandmothers [who] graduated from college. (Rosenblatt, 2)

For both Herta Freitag and Joan Rosenblatt, home was a place where intellectual excitement and creative activity were celebrated and shared. In the life of Vera Pless, the larger community played a crucial role in the support and encouragement of her intellectual interests:

> I lived ... on the west side of Chicago, the Lawndale district, which was a large area for Jewish immigrants at that time, and it was a very intellectual atmosphere there. And somebody who lived in that area, somehow I was in his [Sunday school] class. And he thought I was a bright kid, and so he gave me private lessons. He taught me Hebrew and he taught me calculus. And I think I was about twelve or thirteen years old. (Pless, 1)

In this particular case, the Sunday school teacher was a graduate student at the University of Chicago who went on to become a famous mathematician: Samuel Karlin.

For many of these women, mathematics was just one among many interests they had as children; it was not necessarily identified or developed at an early age, and certainly not to the exclusion of other interests. Moreover, as young girls they were able to freely imagine the possibility of a future career apart from marriage and motherhood. Perhaps not surprisingly, many of the women indicated that the first aspiration they had was to be a teacher:

> I've always been interested in teaching. Now, that was for a very good reason. My dad started life, his adult life teaching, and so did my aunt, [who] took care of me when my mother died. (Bates, 1)

> [No] matter which grade I was in—first, second, third—among the things I wanted very much to do was to teach at that level. (Weinstein, 3)

For Herta Freitag, the love of mathematics and the desire to teach mathematics emerged together at around the age of twelve:

> [As a child I] kept a diary, which I still have. It is, of course, in German. And I was twelve years old, and what the diary says is, "School is sort of all right, but it seems to be the case that getting an education is equated with memorization, which I find simple but boring. But I have finally found a subject where I don't have to memorize:

mathematics. I can just think it out." And then comes the next entry: "I like mathematics more and more from day to day, and I now know that I want to become a mathematics teacher." And then, the last entry, still at twelve, [which] I rather like: "I have changed my mind. I do not want to become a mathematics teacher. I want to become a *good* mathematics teacher." (Freitag-1, 1)

Teaching was not, however, the only thing one could aspire to. As noted earlier, Tilla Weinstein freely entertained a variety of career ambitions, with her mother's encouragement, although teaching remained continually among the options. Jane Cronin Scanlon recalls having an early interest in chemistry and particle physics, while Barbara Beechler aspired early on to be "a professor of physics."

A good many of these women grew up in environments where their intellectual development was taken seriously. It was crucial to their future success that they had support for, and encouragement of, their intellectual interests and professional ambitions during these formative years. That their specific talents in mathematics were not identified and developed early seems to have had little effect on their later success as mathematicians.[4]

High School and College

Very few of these women identified a particular interest in mathematics prior to high school, and some did not form the interest until they reached college. It is important to note, however, that few of the women interviewed had been actively discouraged from studying mathematics prior to college, and most had had at least one teacher who encouraged them in their mathematical studies.

Growing up in rural Manitoba in the thirties and forties, Margaret Marchand did her first two years of high-school work by correspondence course. For her final two years of high school, she attended a boarding school in the town of Teulon, sixty miles from home. The principal of the school was also her mathematics teacher, and it was he who first praised her for her mathematical talent and, perhaps more importantly, gave her the idea of attending university in the first place. She went on to the University of Manitoba on a scholarship and knew she would be a mathematics major from the first.

For many of these women, however, the choice of mathematics took some time in coming. Some, like Anne Lewis Anderson and Jane Cronin Scanlon, knew that they enjoyed science and did well at it, but it was not until college that a specific interest in mathematics began to emerge:

> I had an awfully good high school math teacher, and I did well in it and liked it. And then in college—I went to Randolph-Macon Woman's College—I was going to major in math and/or biology, but I decided to do the math and not the biology. And my sophomore year, one of the freshman students had an appendectomy or something like that, and the math teacher asked me, after she got back, if I would help her catch up. And so I found I liked that, teaching somebody, and ... after I finished the job with her, I got to tutoring other students, and I liked it and so I started thinking in terms of graduate school and college teaching. And I was encouraged in that by the two main math professors, Miss Gillie Larew and Miss Evelyn Wiggin, both of whom were Chicago Ph.D.'s. (Anderson-1, 1)

> I became interested in science, I guess when I was maybe ten or eleven.... I got a *serious* interest in it when I took chemistry in high school. And from that I got interested in particle physics, and so I thought of majoring in physics in college, and it wasn't until junior year in college that I realized I was more interested in the mathematics than the physics. (Cronin Scanlon, 1)

For Anne Lewis Anderson, two college mathematics teachers—both women—served as catalysts for the emergence of mathematics as her dominant interest. Indeed, it was not uncommon for a particular high-school or college teacher—sometimes female but often male—to offer the encouragement and mentorship that led a young woman to the choice of mathematics. For Mary Ellen Rudin, R. L. Moore was an extremely powerful and influential mentor:

> I attended the University of Texas, and there, I met, on the first day I was there, a mathematician, R. L. Moore, with whom I ended up writing a Ph.D. And I was in a class with him every year—usually *two* classes with him every year, from the time I entered the University of Texas in 1941 until I got my Ph.D. in 1949. So that was the thing that interested me in mathematics, that pushed me toward mathematics. (Rudin, 1)

Jean Rubin's earliest interest in mathematics was sparked by a talented high-school mathematics teacher:

> Well, I think [my interest in mathematics began] when I was in high school. In my junior or senior year in high school, I had a very interesting instructor. He had a Ph.D. in math, and I think he turned me on. I really became interested in mathematics after that. (Rubin, 1)

Later on, as an undergraduate at Queens College, another teacher provided the impetus for a major change in plans. In college she prepared for a career in mathematics teaching but reports that the education courses "really turned me off." Meanwhile, the most exciting mathematics course she took as an undergraduate—and the one she found most difficult—inspired her subsequent choice of research field:

> I remember a teacher who taught a course on logic—Nagel? And actually that was the only course in math that I didn't get an A in! I only got a B in his course. But logic is my field of research now, so that really started me off in logic. I became interested in logic because of that class. (Rubin, 3)

While many of the women were positively encouraged by high-school and college teachers, several experienced obstacles of various kinds to their continuing in the subject. In the 1930s, while a student at Cazenovia Seminary, a private boarding high school in New York State, Grace Bates had to petition the state board of education for permission to take advanced mathematics courses:

> I pulled the strings to—I was taking the usual elementary algebra and then geometry, and I wanted to go on in my senior year with intermediate algebra, and they said there that I'd have to take a history course. And I squawked and I wrote my dad, and he got the commissioner [of education] to write and say that [if] some young person that was really interested in mathematics, [then] they could take history ... another year, but don't try to deter [them from taking mathematics]. So I got to take mathematics! (Bates, 3)

Later on, at Middlebury College, which was then divided into a men's college and a women's "coordinate college," she had to petition to take advanced mathematics once again. She recalls that all of the women's math courses were taught by one female professor; enrollments in these courses declined steadily from the freshman to the sophomore to the junior year. Finally,

> I had to petition the trustees at Middlebury to get into a course in differential equations my senior year, because it was only taught in the men's side. (Bates, 3)

Her petition was granted and she was the only woman enrolled in this course during her senior year in college.

Although she did not experience the same barriers to enrolling in advanced mathematics courses, Jean Walton reports that as a student at George School, a private high school in Pennsylvania, during the 1930s, she was the only girl taking advanced mathematics:

> [W]hen I got into high school I was taking mathematics. I took an advanced class—in those days, advanced high school math was solid geometry and trigonometry—and I was the only girl in the class. (Walton, 1)

She reports having had the distinct impression that certain messages she heard in her mathematics classes were not intended for her, but rather for the boys only:

> I mentioned this advanced class in high school, in math, [where] I was the only girl. And I remember very vividly a class session, during that senior year, when the teacher said, "Now, any of you who are going on to college and planning to go on in mathematics, I want to urge you to buy a slide rule and to get familiar with using it." And, as you probably know, in any case, in those days there were no calculators. There were certainly no computers, there weren't even any calculators. And the slide rule played a very important role. But the thing that I remember so vividly was the clarity of my conviction that "He's not talking to me. Because girls don't take math! I of course won't be doing that when I get to college. I'm doing it now because it's kind of fun, but that won't be what I will do, and I don't need to get a slide rule and I don't need to learn how to use it!" (Walton, 2–3)

She goes on to add that she does not know whether the teacher actually communicated this to her, directly or indirectly, or whether it was a message that came from within herself:

> Whether he really gave me any clues that he wasn't talking to me—
> whether he gave me the high sign, "You don't need to bother about
> this"—I don't know. All I know is, I heard what he said and I took from
> that, "I do not need to get a slide rule. I do not need to learn mathe-
> matics." The next year I went to the college, I enrolled in freshman
> mathematics, and I never, I never got a slide rule, and I never learned
> how to use it. And before very long I became embarrassed over not
> knowing, and I tried to hide the fact that I didn't know. And I was able
> to do this; I got along perfectly well. I used tables, and I guessed, and
> I never used a slide rule.... I was also, at that stage in my life, very
> aware of the fact that men were the people who knew things and men
> were the authorities, and I was not a person who had a mind of her
> own at all at that stage of my life. (Walton, 3)

The irony here is that she had done very well in mathematics at George
School and proceeded, with her teachers' encouragement, to Swarthmore
College, where she had decided early on to major in mathematics. Despite
the apparent clarity with which she chose mathematics, she discounted her
authority and her potential as a mathematician. Perhaps this was partly the
result of having been the only girl studying mathematics in her high-school
years.

Tilla Weinstein's path to mathematics is an extremely interesting one.
She is the youngest of the women in this study and attended college in the
early 1950s. Unlike the other interviewees, she started college as a major
in English and philosophy at the University of Michigan, without any particular interest in mathematics or even in the sciences. She took college-
level mathematics courses but found them something of a struggle. She
reports:

> Well, I had taken calculus my freshman year, I took what they
> thought of as their better calculus course because it incorporated
> analytic geometry.... Hans Samelson, who is a geometer, taught the
> honors calculus course. Oh, he was wonderful. Nonetheless, I wasn't
> particularly taken by it. I worked very hard; I got an A. I felt I didn't
> understand anything, and in retrospect, I *didn't* understand very
> much! But I suppose the only thing that shows I was *potentially* a
> math student is that I understood that I didn't understand. Ah, then
> I had a third semester [of calculus] ... and I didn't want to go on in

a regular mathematical track. I knew I hadn't enjoyed the calculus. (Weinstein, 7)

Though still an English and philosophy major, she nevertheless decided to take some more math at Michigan. Although at this point she had no intention of changing her major, a course in foundations with R. L. Wilder made a deep impression on her:

My cousin [also a student at Michigan] suggested that I might like Wilder's course. It was a course in foundations.... [Even though] it was a graduate course, it wasn't a high-pressure course at all. Wilder taught by the R. L. Moore method. He was extraordinarily gifted at getting the students to participate. And it was *perfect* for me—you needed no knowledge. He threw out an axiom, gave you a few models for the axiom, gave you a few definitions involving undefined terms, and suggested one or two things that could be proved, and let us loose. The whole ... content of the course, when you looked back, was on a stack of index cards: axiom, definition, theorem. I enjoyed it enormously. It was self-contained and beautiful.... [Y]ou didn't learn many facts. You didn't learn many skills. But you came away with a sense of how things actually came together, and how very *much* you get out of very *little*. (Weinstein, 8)

At the end of her sophomore year in college, she married a man from her old neighborhood in New York and transferred to New York University, where her initial intention was to resume her major in English and philosophy. But this inclination was tempered by two considerations:

I looked at the [NYU] catalog. There were two courses [in English] I could take that I hadn't already had. On top of that, I was marrying someone who intended to go on and get a Ph.D. in English. And it was not comfortable for me to be in the situation of being in the same field as my husband. There was the discomfort of possibly competing; wives didn't compete with their husbands in those days. (Weinstein, 7)

The desire to avoid competition with her husband, coupled with the paucity of interesting English courses, combined to make her reconsider her choice of a major. She looked first at the course offerings in philosophy and was not impressed. Finally, she consulted an advisor:

> I remember asking, "What's good here?" And the advisor said, "Oh, there's mathematics." And he never got farther on the list, because I had just had the wonderful course with Wilder at Michigan, which I truly enjoyed. (Weinstein, 7)

When she began coursework as a mathematics major at NYU, she captured the attention of her professors. But she reports with some certainty that she did not have natural talent for the subject and discounts her professors' interest in her:

> My junior year I took advanced calculus from [Jean] van Heijenoort, who was remarkably attentive to any of the students he thought of as having any ability whatsoever. He was very encouraging, even though I don't think I could have seemed terribly good to him at the time.... I had a great deal of general intelligence. Mathematically, I really worked hard to understand things. The questions in calculus were never the ones that I would have posed. They didn't come naturally. I got an A, but I'm sure I didn't get an A+. I was not what I called a mathematical animal. There were two other undergraduates at the time who were much more mathematically gifted.... I think one reason he [van Heijenoort] paid attention to me was that he needed three people for a Putnam team. And *we* were it; there weren't others who were gifted mathematically at the time. (Weinstein, 8)

She elaborates a bit on the term "mathematical animal":

> [T]he term "math animal" was one coined by my then-husband. We'd meet each other's friends, and he tagged certain of the people he met as "math animals," and I thought it was a wonderful word. They were creatures who by nature had an affinity for the subject, and it showed in the way they spoke, the way they looked at things, and even if they had varying personalities. (Weinstein, 12)

In particular, it would seem that a mathematical animal was someone— usually male—who conformed, at least early in life, to the pattern set forth in the myth. Though she consciously recognized that she was *not* a "math animal," she nevertheless continued in mathematics—realizing, perhaps, that there is more than one route to mathematics.

Transition to Graduate School; Luck and Timing

In the thirties, forties, and fifties, it was relatively unusual for a young woman to major in mathematics and still more unusual for her to decide to pursue a Ph.D. in the subject. In this section, I consider the transition from college to graduate school in some detail. Here the women in this study seem to fall into four broad groups. First, there are those fortunate women who attended college in the 1930s and proceeded directly to graduate school without a break, starting work toward the Ph.D. before the United States entered the war. Second, there are those women who received undergraduate degrees in the 1930s but whose work toward the Ph.D. was delayed or postponed for several years, often due to circumstances largely beyond their control. This group includes American women who, affected by the depression, were unable for financial reasons to proceed directly from college to graduate school. It also includes women who began their university studies in Europe; the war imposed upon them an educational hiatus of several years. Women in both of these groups are generally somewhat older, having completed their undergraduate educations by 1940.

The third and fourth groups comprise women who began undergraduate study in the mid-to-late 1940s and 1950s. Women in the third group began work toward the Ph.D. during the latter years of the war or shortly after the war's conclusion, when the period of explosive growth in higher education and federal support of research was just beginning. Their graduate experiences are marked by signs of the social and cultural transition going on about them. Women in the fourth group, by contrast, began their graduate educations in the late 1940s or thereafter, after the intensity and chaos of the immediate postwar period had begun to settle down a bit.

While it is impossible to make neat divisions among the four groups, examples will help to illustrate the significance of the differences between them. To begin, I will consider the women in the first group, who entered college in the 1930s and experienced a relatively seamless transition to graduate school.

In the mid-1930s, Dorothy Maharam Stone attended Carnegie Institute of Technology (now Carnegie-Mellon University) in her home city of

Pittsburgh. The daughter of a rabbi, the fifth of six children, her college education was paid for by scholarships. She studied mathematics because she enjoyed it but initially had no intention of going to graduate school. She says that she always expected to continue doing mathematics after college, but only as "an amateur at home, or ... possibly taking night school courses or something like that" (Maharam Stone, 4).

The chair of the mathematics department at Carnegie Tech encouraged her to go on to graduate school and recommended Bryn Mawr, where he had a friend on the faculty. Bryn Mawr College had a small graduate program in a very small but highly regarded mathematics department chaired by Anna Pell Wheeler, who had received a Ph.D. in mathematics from Chicago in 1910 (Green and LaDuke 1990, 131). "Mrs. Wheeler," as she was known to her students, became Dorothy Maharam Stone's dissertation advisor. For a variety of reasons—including Wheeler's illness and Maharam Stone's propensity to work on her own—she did most of her research independently of Wheeler. She was, as she puts it, "a homemade product" (Maharam Stone, 7). She acknowledges, however, that Wheeler was instrumental in getting her the Emmy Noether Fellowship, which gave her a year's postdoctoral study at the Institute for Advanced Study at Princeton after she completed her Ph.D. in 1940.

For Anne Lewis Anderson, the decision to go on to graduate school grew out of the enjoyment she experienced as an undergraduate mathematics major at Randolph-Macon Woman's College. She went directly from Randolph-Macon to the University of Chicago in 1940 and received a Ph.D. there in 1943. It is interesting to note the lack of hesitation, the lack of questioning of her own ability, as she describes her decision to go to graduate school. She speaks only of the encouragement offered her by two women professors at Randolph-Macon who clearly served as role models and encouraged her to follow the path they had taken:

> I was encouraged in [my desire to go to graduate school] by the two main math professors, Miss Gillie Larew and Miss Evelyn Wiggin, both of whom were Chicago Ph.D.'s.... Miss Larew was head of the math department and also became dean of the college my second or third year there. And Miss Wiggin was another one of the professors there. So when I started thinking in terms of graduate school, I was sort of aimed toward Chicago. And some of the men that those two

ladies had worked with were still there, so I sort of had an entrée. (Anderson-1, 1–2)

Interestingly, Larew and Wiggin had done their dissertation research in calculus of variations with Gilbert Bliss. Anderson did her research in the same field, working with Magnus Hestenes, who himself had been a student of Bliss. In a manner of speaking, Anne Lewis Anderson was passed on via the "old-girl network" to the University of Chicago. She remembers her graduate student days (1940–1943) as particularly congenial:

> The relations between the faculty and the graduate students, and the relations among the graduate students, were just marvelous. The older graduate students would take the young ones under their [wing], you know, and help them out in rough spots, and the professors were, almost without exception, just very warm and helpful. Well, Mr. and Mrs. Reid [one of the professors and his wife] used to have teas frequently on Sunday afternoons for the graduate students, and the graduate student group would often take one of the professors out to lunch, this sort of thing. It was a very congenial, happy group. (Anderson-1, 5)

During her student years at the University of Chicago, the effects of the war were felt in a variety of ways. First of all, the mathematics department was moved to temporary quarters from its home in Eckhart Hall, which was occupied by the Manhattan Project. Her dissertation advisor, Magnus Hestenes, left the campus to undertake war work before she completed the Ph.D., and W. T. Reid presided over her dissertation defense. Finally, she was encouraged by the university to remain on the faculty as an instructor during the years 1943–1945, when the shortage of faculty was most keenly felt. The university was running educational programs for military personnel in addition to its own undergraduate and graduate programs, while many of its own faculty were, like Hestenes, engaged in war work off-campus.

Both Anne Lewis Anderson and Dorothy Maharam Stone discovered mathematics as a "calling" while in college and were able to continue from college to graduate school without a break thanks to the encouragement of undergraduate mentors and a combination of scholarship and fellowship support. Domina Eberle Spencer, by contrast, came from a family in which the education of the children—both girls—was a high priority. Both Domina and her older sister, Vivian, earned Ph.D.'s in mathematics. Vivian, twelve years Domina's senior, experienced several interruptions in her work toward the Ph.D., which she earned at the University of Pennsylvania in 1936. Domina, by contrast, earned all of her degrees at MIT during the years 1937–1942. Although she was able to get some scholarship support, it was her family's financial and moral backing and her own determination that provided the momentum and the wherewithal to pursue an uninterrupted path to the Ph.D.

The women of the second group experienced a delay between undergraduate study and the Ph.D., some due to extenuating circumstances such as the depression and war, some because they needed a certain amount of life experience before they could be sure that graduate school was what they wanted. Four of the interviewees—Winifred Asprey, Grace Bates, Margaret Willerding, and Jean Walton—held jobs in teaching or educational administration before they completed the work for a Ph.D. Two European-born interviewees—Herta Freitag and Maria Steinberg—experienced lengthy interruptions in their education because of the dislocations of World War II. The stories of Margaret Willerding and Herta Freitag serve as but two illustrations of the variety in experience of the women in this group.

A native of St. Louis, Missouri, Margaret Willerding graduated from high school in 1936. "I was very ambitious," she says. Her parents had very little education and had not attended college themselves; while they did not oppose her educational ambitions, they were not particularly supportive of them, either. She reports that she was undaunted by their lack of interest: "I was the kind of person that was going to go [to college] come hell or high water." But finances were a problem:

> I graduated from high school in the depth of the Depression. And there was no chance, nobody gave scholarships like they do now, you know. So I went to the city teacher's college [Harris Teacher's College], which was completely free.... Incidentally, they gave a very good education. I didn't want to go there, but I didn't have any choice. (Willerding, 1–2).

Her undergraduate major was in education, with a minor in mathematics. She enjoyed mathematics and decided to go on to graduate school in the subject. Her parents' only child, they wanted her to live at home with them, so she limited her consideration to graduate schools in St. Louis. At the time of her college graduation in 1940, there were two: Washington University and St. Louis University, the latter having the better mathematics department in those days. After a year of apprentice teaching in the St. Louis city schools (1940–1941), she enrolled as a graduate student in mathematics at St. Louis University. From 1941 through 1946, she lived at home with her parents and taught full-time in the city schools to support herself and pay for graduate courses, which she took in the late afternoons and evenings. She earned a master's in 1943 and continued on for the Ph.D. while working full-time.

To meet the residency requirement for the doctorate, she took a leave of absence from the city school system in the last year of her doctoral program. It was only in her last semester at St. Louis University that she obtained financial support from the school:

> I quit [teaching] in forty-six, January of forty-six. And then took my year off, and I went to St. Louis University full-time.... [The] second semester, the last semester before I got my [Ph.D.] degree, I taught two classes. I was the first woman who got a fellowship in the math department. (Willerding, 3)

At St. Louis University, she took a course in number theory with Arnold Ross and developed a liking for the subject and the teacher. This led her to work under his direction on a dissertation in number theory, which was eventually published in the *Bulletin of the American Mathematical Society*. She was hired by Washington University in 1947, at a time when they—like many other universities—were intent on improving the research quality of their faculties.

Herta Freitag's educational hiatus was both the lengthiest and the most dramatic of any of the interviewees. She studied mathematics at the University of Vienna in the late twenties and early thirties. In 1934, at the age of twenty-five, she earned the degree of *Magister rerum naturalium* after seven years of coursework and practice teaching in the Gymnasium. Many years later, when she entered graduate school at Columbia University, she was told that her Vienna degree was "the equivalent of their Ph.D. with respect to coursework" (Freitag-1, 9).

The job market for mathematics teachers in Vienna in 1934 was not good; she recalls:

> There was, in fact, in Vienna at the time—possibly before—a fantas-tic overproduction of academic workers. In other words, as we went into the study of mathematics, I think we were all clearly aware of the fact, that, as to a job [teaching Gymnasium], we'd never get one.... And we were so idealistic: "But we [want to study] mathe-matics. As to a job, we can always scrub floors." I remember so well that we kept saying that to each other. (Freitag-1, 12)

She and her classmates earned their living not by classroom teaching, but by tutoring students from the Gymnasium and university. She was em-ployed as a tutor from the time of her graduation until March 13, 1938—the day that Hitler marched into Vienna.

That event began a six-year sojourn that took her from Vienna to En-gland—where she worked as a housemaid, governess, waitress, and teacher—and finally to the United States in 1944. There, after two years of teaching at a private boarding school in upstate New York, she began grad-uate work in mathematics and education at Columbia University at the age of thirty-seven. Like Margaret Willerding, she was employed full-time as a teacher throughout much of her graduate education—first at Greer School in New York, later at Hollins College in Virginia. She took most of her graduate coursework in the summer, spending exactly one full semes-ter in residence at Columbia during the academic year. In the latter years of her work toward the Ph.D., her energies during the academic year were more than occupied with the responsibility of teaching the entire under-graduate mathematics curriculum at Hollins College. Under these unusual circumstances, she completed a dissertation under Howard Fehr in the spring of 1953.

The women of the third and fourth groups earned their doctorates under circumstances that, by comparison, were less stressful and more relaxed. But these women, who entered graduate school in the postwar years, had their own unique set of challenges and opportunities. The third group—which includes Anne Whitney Calloway, Mary Ellen Rudin, Jane Cronin Scanlon, Violet Hachmeister Larney, Margaret Marchand, and Augusta Schurrer—consists of those women who attended gradu-ate school during the dramatic and often chaotic expansion of the early postwar period. The fourth group—including Joyce White Williams, Barbara Beechler, Jean Rubin, Joan Rosenblatt, Vera Pless, and Tilla Weinstein—attended graduate school in the later postwar period, a time of more carefully managed change, during which mathematical research gained in status and significance in colleges and universities throughout the United States.

Both Augusta Schurrer, who began graduate work in 1945, and Tilla Weinstein, who began work toward the Ph.D. at New York University about ten years later, shared the perception that it was mostly a matter of luck and timing that allowed them comparatively easy access to graduate study. It is interesting to note the extent to which they attribute their success in graduate school to having been in the right place at the right time.

Augusta Schurrer entered Hunter College in January 1941 at the age of fifteen. Her early entry to college came as the result of steady progress through the "rapid advance system" of the New York City schools. She was attracted first to statistics, which she saw as a lucrative field; coming from a poor family, her decisions were often colored by the practical issue of earning a living. But it was mathematics that proved more interesting to her, and she changed her major to mathematics. She developed an interest in the possibility of teaching, preferably at the college level. Her desire to go to graduate school emerged slowly, influenced somewhat by the presence of C. C. MacDuffee, a visiting professor from the University of Wisconsin during her junior year:

> I thought I might go to [graduate] school; I thought it might be in physics or astronomy or mathematics. I didn't really worry about it too much. Nor did anybody direct me too much. I suspect, when I think about it, having had MacDuffee at Hunter at the time he was [there] made me think of the possibility of maybe going to graduate school. Just the fact that he was there and talked about students who had gone, you know. And there weren't too many men, so they were still seriously considering women. (Schurrer, 9)

She graduated from Hunter in January 1945, worked for several months as a "computer" at the Office of Scientific Research and Development, and was awarded a teaching assistantship for graduate study at the University of Wisconsin at Madison the following fall.

She attributes the ease with which she was admitted to graduate school to a shortage of available men at the end of the war. By the late forties, she maintains, women were far less highly prized as graduate students:

> I think my timing has been unusually good. If I had not finished when I did finish [college], I probably would not have gotten a TA ... at Wisconsin. You know, three years, four years later—no. Because I saw what they did with women. I mean, women got cut at the master's very fast at that time. They were not encouraged to go on. . . . It was a more competitive situation, I guess. It's that you had to be really something *special* at that time, to make it through or to have anybody be willing to work with you. Because there were enough men. When I went, there weren't enough men. There weren't enough *anything.* (Schurrer, 29)

She connects the devaluation of women graduate students with the fact that university mathematics faculty were increasingly expected to do a large quantity of high-quality research:

> [A few years after I started graduate school] there was already a shift in what you had to do to survive [as a university faculty member]. . . . My sense was it became much more competitive, and it became very important, now, who you surrounded yourself with. And you wanted people who were going to stay with you a long time. You didn't want people who were going to get married off and leave. (Schurrer, 30)

Put another way: graduate students serve to carry on the research program and the research legacy of their advisors. If women are perceived as likely to abandon the field, why bother training them to become research mathematicians? In fact, the situation Schurrer describes offers evidence for the increasing power of the myth. In the postwar years, the myth first exerted its pull upon faculty members, eventually to be passed on through their example to the next generation of Ph.D. mathematicians.

It took seven years from her entrance into graduate school for Augusta Schurrer to earn the Ph.D., a delay she attributes to several factors. First, she says that she had not really mastered the art of theorem-proving while at Hunter College. Second, she selected an advisor, Morris Marden, who was actually on the faculty of the University of Wisconsin at Milwaukee. He worked in complex analysis, a field of mathematics where, when she first encountered it at Hunter, "the fires lit up—I thought that was the greatest thing I ever saw!" (Schurrer, 6). Working with Marden offered certain advantages, but there was the logistical disadvantage of having an advisor at a distance:

> Morris Marden came down from Milwaukee and gave a course on zeroes of polynomials, and I thought that was neat stuff. That was complex again, and Morrie was a *super* teacher. And I got interested.... And Morrie was very patient with me, and didn't have any other graduate students. He let me come up to Milwaukee and drink beer with him and talk math.... He was on the faculty [at Madison] for a semester, on leave, and then he went back to Milwaukee. And I commuted. (Schurrer, 17)

Third, she came to Madison at an early age and it was her first time away from home, so she had some catching up to do socially, and some maturing to do mathematically. Despite these obstacles, she reached "the write-up stage" of her dissertation by 1950. In that year, she decided to take a job at Iowa State Teachers' College. Employment slowed down her progress somewhat, but she received the Ph.D. in 1952.

While Augusta Schurrer felt fortunate to have entered graduate school when she did, the changes in the graduate school environment during her tenure may have had a negative impact on her self-confidence as a mathematician. During her early days at Wisconsin, the graduate program was small. At first, there were very few graduate students—two other women, but not that many more men. But it was not long before the graduate program received an influx of mostly male students on the GI Bill:

> [P]eople were beginning to come back from the war. And ... they were coming to school with less preparation than I had. Which was good! I was in a safe position: people were filing in as graduate students who had definitely less academic ability than I, and less training, basic training. So I was able to be of help to others. (Schurrer, 14)

But toward the latter part of the forties, when graduate school became more competitive, she became increasingly aware of her limitations and less conscious of her assets.

Tilla Weinstein began her graduate studies at the Courant Institute of New York University in 1955, having spent her last two undergraduate years as a mathematics major there. While Augusta Schurrer ascribes her success to a shortage of *students*, Tilla Weinstein attributes her success to a shortage of university *faculty*. By the time Weinstein got to graduate school, the importance of higher education to national security was a widely accepted fact, and the growing population was exerting additional pressure on the universities to expand. She argues that she entered graduate school at a time when any qualified applicant would be welcomed with open arms:

> [I]t was a time when math students were encouraged to go on. There was a great need. There was no sense that some terrible mistake would be made if you turned out someone who was not *great*. There were expanding schools all over the country; they needed faculty members. (Weinstein, 9)

For Tilla Weinstein, general intelligence, diligence as a student, and the mentorship of her advisor, Lipman Bers, were the key factors in her success:

> I'm much better at being able to see that something is wrong, than to be able to do something that takes cleverness. My general intelligence was just much greater than my particular ability in mathematics.... Of course, I was a professional, I was a *good* student. I was out to learn whatever was in front of me; and even if I didn't have a particular affinity for the material—as was true for calculus—I still wanted to know and I wanted to understand. I think when I got to complex variables it was much more enjoyable material; Lipman Bers was an extraordinary lecturer. And he was going to be encouraging no matter what. I did not have to be as good as I was for him to be encouraging. He was just generally encouraging. (Weinstein, 10)

It is true that Weinstein entered graduate school under extraordinary circumstances. It was, as she was so clearly aware, a propitious time for a talented young person to undertake graduate study in mathematics. She worked toward the Ph.D. at the Courant Institute during an exciting period of growth and development (see Morawetz 1989). But it is nonetheless remarkable that she received one of the first NSF graduate fellowships, which even included an allowance for her husband and infant son:

> It was just pre-Sputnik, but NSF was funding money, and I had an NSF fellowship. And it was granted just a few weeks before the baby was

born. And one of the things that made it so clear that I was going to finish college and go to summer school and do whatever I had to do to start the following September was that I had a fellowship. That fellowship was renewed three years running, and since I somewhat accidentally had a dissertation early on, I got a fourth year as a postdoc. My degree was granted in the middle of that postdoc year, because the work was finished.

NSF financed my education. I was impressed by the fact that they were as helpful to me as they were in a time when I don't think other institutions took the same chances on women.... I think if you were married there was an extra allowance, simply because you were married. And there were dependency allowances for children. I'm not sure of the language, but it was extra money. And in other places it was so clearly understood that the extra money was for a wife, that only husbands needed to support children, that for instance, at the Institute for Advanced Study at the time, visiting members would be given a different sum if they were married, if they were male—not if they were female. And this changed in the seventies. (Weinstein, 11–12)

In short, the progressive policies of the NSF were fifteen to twenty years ahead of their time.

In the nearly twenty years between 1940, when Dorothy Maharam Stone earned her Ph.D. at Bryn Mawr, and 1959, when Tilla Weinstein earned hers at New York University, the terms and conditions of graduate education in mathematics in the United States had changed radically. In some ways it had become easier, but in other ways more difficult, for women to obtain the Ph.D. Many women, as Augusta Schurrer observed, did not make it. But for those who did, the Ph.D. was only the beginning. The problem before them was to figure out how to weave mathematics into the fabric of their lives.

Interweaving a Career and a Life

In any life lived according to the myth, mathematics is at the center, the single most important activity; the mathematical career begins early and unfolds seamlessly from early youth through advancing age. For many men

in the postwar era, it was possible to live a life that conformed closely to
the myth, because the prevailing social and political forces facilitated such
a life with, for example, the growth of the universities and of federal funding for education and research, and the social pressure upon women to stay
home and work as supportive wives to their husbands, mothers to their
children, and caretakers of the home.

For women, however, the demands of motherhood and the broader
social limitations placed upon them made single-minded devotion to mathematics difficult if not impossible. What is more, many women who loved
mathematics and wanted to make it their life's work did not believe that
mathematics was meant to be served so exclusively. The women mathematicians of the postwar era had to create their own "mathematical life-
course," and they did so in a wide variety of ways.

As in the years before World War II, there were those women who
pursued careers in mathematics with relatively few interruptions because
they remained unmarried. Even so, they faced obstacles and challenges as
their careers progressed. Margaret Willerding, though briefly engaged to
a fellow academic in the 1940s, values her independence and has never
married. "I'm perfectly capable of taking care of myself," she says
(Willerding, 10). After receiving the Ph.D. from St. Louis University in
1947, her career got off to a promising start: she was awarded an instruc-
torship at Washington University. But she felt that she was never taken as
seriously as the men:

> I remember when I was at Washington University we had a big meet-
> ing there, the American Mathematical [Society] had their meeting
> there. And one of the wives called me up, the faculty wives, and
> wanted me to pour at one of the teas they were having. And I said,
> "I don't intend to pour at one of the teas you're having. I'm one of
> the faculty." (Willerding, 11)

In fact, Margaret Willerding left Washington University after just one
semester on the faculty "because the head of the department told me I
couldn't go up as fast as a man, even if I did as much or more work than
they did" (Willerding, 7). In 1946 she had taken a leave of absence from the
St. Louis city school system to complete her Ph.D.; in 1948, she returned
to the school system, which granted her request to be assigned to the faculty of Harris Teacher's College, her undergraduate alma mater. At Har-

ris, she was relieved to find that "they didn't care whether I was a man or a mouse" (Willerding, 11). The return to Harris brought a shift in focus, from mathematical research to the education of teachers. Mathematics education became her primary focus, first at Harris Teacher's College and later at San Diego State University.

Margaret Willerding expresses some ambivalence about mathematical research. As a graduate student she spent a great deal of time with Arnold Ross and his colleagues:

> And all they did was eat, drink, and sleep mathematics, and I said, "There's more to life than this." And that's why I went to a state university, where they didn't expect me to do research in mathematics, and do nothing but research. (Willerding, 5)

At a very early stage in her education, she rejected the single-minded devotion to the subject that a career in mathematical research seemed to require. On the other hand, as she looks back over her life, she can imagine how things might have been different. Had she not felt compelled to stay in St. Louis, had she been born a bit earlier, "if I could have gone to Bryn Mawr and studied with Emmy Noether, I might have been quite a famous mathematician now" (Willerding, 12).

In other words, a strong female role model might have convinced her of her ability to persevere in research. Had she not felt so alienated, so unable to fit in and be taken seriously at Washington University, might she have pursued a different path? It is interesting to note that in her subsequent career in mathematics education, she wrote and published thirty-one textbooks. It is clear that she possessed tremendous creative energy, and one can only wonder what she might have created had she not felt deterred from traditional mathematical research. She has, however, led a life filled not only with mathematics, but with friendship and travel. She has lived a broader, fuller life than she might have thought possible in her graduate student days.

Winifred Asprey, who received a Ph.D. at the University of Iowa in 1945 and spent a long career at Vassar College, never gave serious thought to the possibility of marriage: "I was so busy doing so many other things! It certainly wasn't a vital part of my life" (Asprey, 46). She had been an undergraduate student in mathematics at Vassar, earning a bachelor's degree in 1938, and she was invited back to join the faculty upon completion of her Ph.D. Her career was one of service to Vassar and to the mathematical profession; never especially inclined to engage in research, she was more interested in teaching and popularizing mathematics for a variety of audiences. Hers is an entrepreneurial spirit, and the greatest peril she faced in her career was the possibility of boredom:

> By the time that I was in [my mid-forties], a very wise friend pointed out to me [that I was in a rut]. What was I going to do? I had been chairman of the department; I'd been on the most important committees, college committees; I'd done national things; I was lecturing all over the [country] and even abroad. Was I simply going to repeat these experiences until I retired? (Asprey, 44)

Her rut ended when she immersed herself in the emerging and exciting field of computing. Inspired by the example of her former Vassar professor, Grace Murray Hopper, Winifred Asprey left the Vassar campus and traveled across town to the Poughkeepsie IBM plant. Thus began a collaboration between Asprey, Vassar, and IBM that would continue for thirty years. In early 1967, Asprey became the founding director of the computer center at Vassar College:

> The trustees had approved, much to our astonishment, [an IBM] 360: brand-new, most powerful computer at the time. Only one other liberal arts college in the country—Pomona College in California—was getting one, and Vassar was the second college to get one.... And it, as I tell my friends nowadays, was a state-of-the-art machine. It was a 360 Model E, with capacity, memory capacity of *thirty-two K!* Now, today, you pick up the tiniest little computer or calculator, it outdoes that. (Asprey, 38)

In many respects, her single status afforded her the freedom to immerse herself in the new world of computing, to bring her knowledge back to Vassar, and to act as a goodwill ambassador for both Vassar and computing, as she had done for mathematics in earlier years. She traveled widely to IBM sites across the country and lectured on computing at numerous colleges and universities. Although she worked for the same college throughout her career, holding a professorship in the department of mathematics throughout, she created and carried out varied and challenging jobs. Her work influenced generations of students and faculty alike.

In retirement, she remains active in the life of the college and the mathematical profession, broadly understood.

The challenges faced by those women who wished to combine marriage and mathematics were daunting ones, then as now. These challenges were met in a wide variety of ways. By choice or by circumstances, many of the interviewees who married did not have children. Herta Freitag, whose life was dislocated in so many ways by World War II, married in 1950 at the age of forty-one. Her husband, Arthur, left a promising career in educational administration in Chicago to join her in Roanoke, Virginia, where she was on the faculty of Hollins College; he became a teacher in the Roanoke City schools. They had no children, devoting their energies to work and to their shared life as a couple. Herta Freitag has this to say about him:

> Well, he was exceedingly good and felt that I, being a college teacher, would have very much more work to do than he. So he just set himself to take everything away from me that he possibly could. In those olden days, we also taught on Saturday at Hollins; and he, of course, in high school did not. He used that Saturday to do the cleaning, the washing, the ironing, the grocery shopping, and everything else. (Freitag-3, 15)

Other women who married but had no children worked out other kinds of dual-career accommodations with their husbands. Maria Steinberg married a research mathematician, Robert Steinberg, whom she met in the early fifties at UCLA. She made a conscious decision to subordinate her career to his:

> I took second spot, because I do realize he's a far better mathematician. He's done a lot of research, and, well, we've seen the world because of it. Which is the nice part. And I see no harm in being a woman and taking second place—or taking first place. I feel it should be so, but it is a good idea to ... let one person ... fashion the life, because otherwise you go [in separate directions], and it's not a good idea.... So, say, [on] all sabbaticals I've gone with him, and always have taken a leave of absence [from my job], and always have been rehired. (Steinberg, 18)

She readily acknowledges that in today's more competitive academic job market, it might not be so easy for a woman to take such leaves of absence.

There can be no question that a married life with children poses the greatest challenge to the pursuit of a mathematical career. Mary Ellen Rudin, for example, raised four children, held part-time faculty positions, and maintained a continuous and active involvement in mathematical research and publication with consistent NSF support for nearly twenty years. At the same time, her husband, Walter Rudin, held tenured positions in mathematics at the University of Rochester and the University of Wisconsin, building his own research program in real and complex analysis. For the Rudins, in contrast to the Steinbergs, it was not the case that one member of the couple was acknowledged to be the superior mathematician. At the same time, it was Mary Ellen Rudin who took primary responsibility for household and children.

Despite numerous and often daunting logistical and personal difficulties faced along the way, Mary Ellen Rudin characterizes the period in which she balanced research, teaching, parenthood, and household responsibilities in positive terms. At each university where her husband held a regular faculty position,

> [t]hey sort of asked me, "How many courses do you want to teach this semester, and what would you like to teach?" I really had the best of all possible worlds. I wasn't on any committees. I taught what I wanted to, when I wanted to, the amount I wanted to, and I had four children. (Rudin, 14–15)

It is by no means clear that Mary Ellen Rudin's experience is typical of married women with children in her generation of women mathematicians. Her positive experience came about through an unusual confluence of personal and professional circumstances. She has an extraordinary capacity to work with a high level of distraction and frequent interruptions; Walter Rudin was supportive of her need to remain active mathematically; and, above all, the Rudins had the financial means to make Mary Ellen's unusual combination of mathematics and motherhood possible:

> [Working] was never a matter of financial necessity; I never even tried to have it come out even. I spent more money than most on child care. It would have been cheaper for me to stay home. I paid more

than I got. I mean, I just got a thousand dollars for teaching a course or something. I didn't get a big salary. But [Walter] got a good salary, and so it was really never a problem. (Rudin, 17–18)

Like Mary Ellen Rudin, Jane Cronin Scanlon received her Ph.D. in 1949, married in 1953, and had four children. Her husband was a physicist whose career took precedence; child rearing was her responsibility. Despite her talent for mathematics and her enjoyment of the subject, once she had begun to raise a family she did not think explicitly in terms of a career:

[W]e were not in debt, but we had no [financial] backing [from our families] at all. And, you know, one begins to think in terms of buying a house someday, or something like that. There was no possibility of anything like that unless I did some work.... It seemed to me that I had certain responsibilities. If I had any time left over after the discharging of those responsibilities, then I'd do mathematics. But, you see, I didn't think of mathematics—well, I didn't think of it in terms of, you know, *career* or anything like that. (Cronin Scanlon, 23–24).

Jane Cronin Scanlon cites a variety of obstacles to her continued employment and involvement with mathematics: her desire to take responsibility for and care for her own children; the difficulty of obtaining reliable and trustworthy child care; the ambivalence of her husband about his wife's working; the social stigma attached to any attempt to deviate from the traditional female role. Many other women I interviewed experienced these same obstacles, and overcoming them was only possible through a combination of creativity and good fortune.

The greatest good fortune for many of the women with whom I spoke was the support of a loving family. Tilla Weinstein—then Tilla Klotz—was married and had a child while still an undergraduate student. In the early years of her first marriage, both she and her husband were graduate students. They shared equally in child-care responsibilities and had the benefit of supportive families close at hand. Domina Eberle Spencer gave birth to her only child at the age of forty-four while on the faculty of the University of Connecticut, where she still teaches; her mother was living with her family at the time and provided child care on an as-needed basis. In later years, when her sister was semiretired from her position with the federal government, she served as a tutor to Domina's son.

Women who were married, had children, and worked on college and university faculties often had to worry about the perceived effect of their family lives upon their careers. Jane Cronin Scanlon was very careful to keep her personal and professional lives separate. She was a faculty member at the Polytechnic Institute of Brooklyn in the late fifties and early sixties, where she was perhaps the first woman to be awarded tenure in 1958. She says, "[A]t Brooklyn Polytech ... I realized it would be a good idea not to mention the fact that I had two small children. I think that was a good, a very sensible conclusion." Moreover, she adds, "I don't think anything has changed" (Cronin Scanlon, 39).

Tilla Weinstein met similar concerns head-on at UCLA, where she was hired as an instructor after completing her Ph.D. in 1959. During her second year there, the department deliberated over whether or not to offer her a tenure-track assistant professorship:

> [The department head asked,] would I please make them aware of my research plans, and he probably asked me at that point whether I intended to have more children. And I said, "Well, I might, but you can look at my record and see whether having one child in any way caused me to stop in my career. And if I have a second child, I'm in a better position now to finance the care of the child and continue."
> (Weinstein, 23)

Ultimately, the matter was resolved in her favor:

> [T]hey very quickly decided to make me an assistant professor, and the moment they decided to make me an assistant professor on a regular tenure-track line, it was as if they took a deep breath and said, "We're not going to notice, one way or another, whether this person is a woman or not a woman. Let's, for goodness sake, make her an assistant professor." And from that moment on, I never sensed the slightest bit of awkwardness in the department. Now, for all I know, one or two members of the department were uncomfortable with it, but so what? It ... just wasn't there anymore as an issue.
> (Weinstein, 23)

She went on to become the first tenured woman in the mathematics department at UCLA.

For some of the women I interviewed, it was either impossible or undesirable to attempt to pursue marriage, motherhood, and mathematics simultaneously. Joyce Williams earned a Ph.D. from the University of Illinois in 1954. She had married just prior to graduate school, and when she finished the degree, she followed her husband to Massachusetts, where he had a job with Raytheon. During the years 1954–1959, she gave birth to four children and was occupied with child care on a full-time basis. She taught briefly at Lowell Technological Institute (now the University of Massachusetts Lowell) when her youngest child started school; but she did not take up teaching full-time until 1973, by which time she had endured the death of one child and had given birth to another.

During her years of child rearing, she was not actively involved with mathematics; but in 1973 she picked up where she had left off almost twenty years before. In the late seventies she published her dissertation research, and shortly thereafter she was made a tenured associate professor at Lowell, a position from which she retired in 1996.

Anne Lewis Anderson similarly pursued mathematics, marriage, and motherhood in separate stages, but in a more dramatically segmented fashion than most. From 1945 to 1965 she was on the faculty of the Woman's College of North Carolina (later the University of North Carolina at Greensboro), earning tenure and advancing to the rank of professor and department head. In 1965 she retired upon her marriage to D. B. Anderson, the vice-president for academic affairs of the Consolidated University of North Carolina. Upon her retirement from teaching, she says, "I had a second career, as the vice-president's wife and helpmate" and as stepmother and friend to his grown children (Anderson-2, 7).

All of the women mathematicians of this generation—married or unmarried, with or without children—shared the common problem of determining how to balance their mathematical and personal lives. This task was often made more difficult by the intensified pressure to conform to traditional female roles. Adding to this difficulty, within the mathematical community itself there was heightened tension over the relative importance of teaching and research. Women felt this conflict most acutely, for teaching and research—not unlike marriage and career—often stood on opposite sides of a chasm widened, if not defined, by gender.

Teaching and Research

The doctoral dissertation is the key characteristic that distinguishes recipients of the Ph.D. in mathematics from other students of the subject. Everyone who has earned a Ph.D. in mathematics has, at least once in his or her life, made an original and creative contribution to the field by discovering and proving at least one significant and original fact that adds to the body of mathematical knowledge.

Teaching and research have always been the main responsibilities of college and university mathematics faculties. From the earliest years of the American mathematical research community on into the 1930s, the majority of Ph.D. recipients did not engage in any significant research beyond the doctoral dissertation; for most, the Ph.D. was a union card of sorts that granted them admission to the college and university mathematics faculties (see Richardson 1989). Although change was in the air even earlier, World War II brought an increased sense of the primary importance of mathematical research (see Rees 1980). In the years following the war, conscious effort was made—first at the major private and public universities, spreading later to the smaller colleges—to foster and encourage the research activities of mathematics faculty. Mathematics had gained in status and power during the war, and basic research in mathematics was increasingly seen as essential to national security and technological preeminence. While teaching remained a necessary activity for mathematicians, research was increasingly viewed as their raison d'être.

Many women (and men) who pursued Ph.D.'s in mathematics during the 1940s (and on into the 1950s) did so with a career in college-level mathematics teaching as their primary objective. Many were successful in realizing their goals and had satisfying careers devoted almost exclusively to teaching. But even those for whom teaching was a primary goal—and who had succeeded in finding a position at a school where teaching still held primacy—could not help but be affected by the increasingly privileged place of mathematical research in the constellation of mathematical activity. Moreover, many women who aspired to careers in mathematical research—for which they demonstrated real creativity and talent—found it difficult to secure employment that made full use of their talents or to have their contributions adequately acknowledged. Research, having gained in status and significance, was primarily the province of men.[5]

What role did mathematical research play in the lives and careers of women who received Ph.D.'s in mathematics during the 1940s and 1950s? With a view to obtaining at least a partial answer to this question, we will consider the experiences of several women in detail.[6]

For Anne Lewis Anderson and Violet Larney, a career in postsecondary mathematics teaching had always been the primary objective. Although Anderson's twenty-year teaching career in Greensboro seems to have brought her considerable personal and professional satisfaction, she still expresses regret that she did not do research beyond the Ph.D.:

> I was kind of sorry I didn't try to pursue some more research than I did, but as I said, I loved teaching and working with the students, and I was on a lot of committees.... I just think I didn't, perhaps, live up to my potential, ... what I was trained for. The examples I had of my professors at Chicago and so on—I feel like maybe I let them down some. (Anderson-1, 9–10)

For Violet Larney, the matter seems a bit more complicated. The bulk of her teaching career was spent in Albany, New York, at an institution whose changing name—it had been the New York State College for Teachers when she arrived but was transformed into the State University of New York at Albany—reflected its changing identity. She could not help but be affected by the transition from a faculty primarily focused on teaching and the training of teachers to a faculty expected to contribute significantly in quantity and quality to the body of mathematical research.

Though teaching was the primary activity of her career, she did serve as interim head of the mathematics department at Albany during a crucial transitional period. She eventually published a textbook in abstract algebra, though she never published her dissertation. Her relations with new, research-oriented colleagues were better than most; she was allowed to continue teaching graduate courses and held other administrative posts in the department. She says, "I had some responsibility. I wasn't shunted to the corner to the extent that some of the others were" (Larney, 20).

Her thoughts and feelings about research are somewhat contradictory. On the one hand, she questions whether she was given the kind of support in graduate school that would have enabled her to develop momentum in research. On the other hand, she seriously doubts whether women are naturally capable of research productivity in mathematics:

I didn't have, really, any great fervor for research. And I think it was because of the training I had or the faculty I worked with. I mean, [C.C. MacDuffee, my advisor at the University of Wisconsin,] he's gone now, bless his soul, but I didn't find what he would do or set me on particularly helpful. I didn't seem to have—I think I didn't have as much guidance along the way as I could. There weren't professors sitting around you brimming with ideas, and [saying], "Oh, yes, why don't you try this!" or something. You had to search things out more or less for yourself....

I still have a sneaking feeling that men are better at mathematical research than women. I mean, if one did a complete analysis of this, say, all the women, even right now, that are teaching in colleges— what percentage, as opposed to the number of men, and compare that with the number of pages of research published for women as compared with men, I think that the percentage for women would be a lot less than that for men. (Larney, 11)[7]

At the same time, she expresses regret that she didn't pursue a different field of study, one in which the standards for research might have been less rigorous, where she might have made a contribution.

Grace Bates aspired to be a teacher from a very young age. She taught mathematics and English at the elementary and secondary level before entering the Ph.D. program in mathematics at the University of Illinois in 1944, with a view to teaching college. Working on a doctoral dissertation with Reinhold Baer was a transforming experience for her:

[T]he one thing about getting a doctorate I had dreaded was this original thesis you were supposed to write.... I didn't think I could do it, and I [thought] it would be all drudgery. Well, it wasn't that way at all with Baer....

I have it [the dissertation] here—it's on free loops and nets. He gave me the definition of a loop, of which I'd never heard before, and [the] idea of using a graphic approach to some of the theory he had [believed] ought to be true, and said, "Oh, go ahead now, let's see what you can do." And I'd fumble around, and I didn't think I had much. I'd go into the study room we graduate students had, and he'd be in the very next day to see. And he'd say, "Miss Beets!" He never did get my name right. And ... after I'd give him something that I'd done ...

he'd say, "Well, this is all wrong. This theorem is all wrong. I don't think it's true." ... I thought, "I'm going to stay up all night till I find a counterexample!" And I really worked like a dog, and I got into my study place there the next day, and sure enough he came in and said, "Ah, Miss Beets, I found a counterexample!" And I said, "So did I!" And that was the first [time], really, that I began to have confidence in myself. (Bates, 13–14)

Working with Baer and meeting his frequent challenges enabled her to overcome her fears and develop an enjoyment of and appreciation for research.

Upon receiving the Ph.D. in 1946, Bates obtained a teaching position at Mount Holyoke, where she remained until her retirement in 1979. Although her responsibilities there left her little time for research, she published her dissertation and continued to work on problems in algebra, the field of her doctoral research, for a few years. She corresponded with Baer and published a paper with a colleague at Mount Holyoke.

At Mount Holyoke, however, a remarkable thing happened:

It was a tradition everywhere that statistics-probability was given to the youngest person. Nobody wanted to teach it! And so I was given a course in probability and a course in statistics at Mount Holyoke. And I worked like a dog. And I found I was getting really interested in it. My predecessor was a famous mathematician, [Antoni Zygmund,] who went to the University of Chicago from Mount Holyoke. Well, he had taught [probability and statistics before me]. And I'd come in after him and struggled along as he did.

But [Zygmund] came back for a social occasion [some] time later. And I was telling him how interested I was getting in the subject, but I really needed more education in it. And he said, "Well, I'll write to my friend out in California, Neyman, Jerzy Neyman"—a Polish mathematician. "I think maybe he could help you." And he apparently did, and I got this letter offering me an assistantship for the summer session there at the University of California at Berkeley. (Bates, 16–17)

On Zygmund's recommendation, Bates worked for several summers in the 1950s with Neyman at Berkeley, coauthoring a number of research articles with him. In the 1960s she turned to the writing of elementary instructional material on probability. While she cannot be said to have had a "research career" by contemporary standards, Grace Bates found that teaching led her to research and back again.

There were many women who received their Ph.D.'s before, during, and after the war who identified themselves primarily as researchers and who have made substantial contributions to mathematical knowledge. Dorothy Maharam Stone, who earned her Ph.D. from Bryn Mawr in 1940, proceeded directly from Bryn Mawr to the Institute for Advanced Study as the first recipient of the Emmy Noether Fellowship. She continued her work in measure theory there, where, she says, "I felt very much like a very small dog in very tall grass!" But she profited from her interactions with other mathematicians there:

> I talked with other junior people, and learned a lot from them. And once in a while, in a blue moon, I would take all my courage and ask [John] von Neumann a question. In fact, I actually set him to work. I asked a question [on which] he actually spent some time, and apparently he turned out two fallacious proofs before he got the correct one! And it took him all of about three weeks. Now von Neumann was just *fantastically* fast. (Maharam Stone, 7–8)

Her stay in Princeton was extended for a second year thanks to a grant from the Institute. By the end of her time there, she had married a fellow mathematician, Arthur Stone; from that point onward they made most of their career moves together. One career did not clearly take precedence over the other; in fact, after many years on the faculty of the University of Manchester in England, they were hired together by the University of Rochester in 1961.

Dorothy Maharam Stone served as an example for Jane Cronin Scanlon to follow. Both women were primarily motivated by the desire to do research, viewing teaching as secondary. Cronin Scanlon actually completed the work for her Ph.D. at the University of Michigan during the summer of 1948, although the degree was not awarded until 1949. As she was completing the Ph.D., she decided that she would try to obtain a postdoctoral research fellowship. Before the war, such fellowships had been uncommon; although they were more widely available in the late forties, obtaining one was still relatively novel.

I had applied the preceding spring—I decided I would [apply for] a postdoctoral fellowship.... I went to the library one day, and there was a new journal. And I looked at the table of contents, and there was an article by Dorothy Maharam. So I looked it up; you know, it was something written by a woman. And there was a footnote at the bottom of the title page that said that this work had been done while she was supported by some kind of a postdoctoral fellowship. And I thought, "Well, *she's* a woman, *she* got a postdoctoral fellowship. *I'm* a woman; *I'll* try it." And I did get one. (Cronin Scanlon, 16)

In fact, Cronin Scanlon got a postdoctoral fellowship at the Institute for Advanced Study, just as Maharam had done. This postdoc was followed by a succession of other research positions: a year of sponsored research back at Michigan in 1949–1950, a postdoctoral fellowship at the Courant Institute in 1950–1951, and a position at the United States Air Force Cambridge Research Center from 1951 to 1954.

Dorothy Maharam Stone obtained her fellowship at the Institute for Advanced Study with the assistance of her advisor, Anna Pell Wheeler, and the encouragement of a Bryn Mawr professor, John Oxtoby. Similarly, Jane Cronin Scanlon obtained her earliest research posts with the support of her advisor, E. H. Rothe, while taking inspiration from her teacher, Warren Ambrose:

I wanted to go to Princeton because Ambrose used to talk about it. You know, all the graduate students thought Ambrose was wonderful.... [H]e would describe what a wonderful place Princeton was, and ... he was *really* interested in mathematics. He was *really* interested in rigor. I think he probably influenced all of us, one way or another. So I decided I would—if I could—I would go to Princeton. (Cronin Scanlon, 16–17)

With her marriage in 1953 and the birth of her first child just over a year later, Cronin Scanlon sought out teaching positions for the first time since receiving her doctorate. This marked the end of her exclusive focus on research. But in those early years she had gained valuable experience, which gave her the confidence and the momentum to persevere in research through many years of juggling the responsibilities of marriage, mother-hood, and teaching.

It is curious that the United States Air Force Cambridge Research Center played an important role in the formative years of another research mathematician. After earning bachelor's and master's degrees from the University of Chicago, Vera Pless completed her Ph.D. at Northwestern University in 1957 with a dissertation in algebra. She had met and married Irwin Pless in 1952 while still at Chicago; he had gone on to earn a Ph.D. in physics there. Even before she finished the doctorate, Vera Pless moved to the Boston area with her husband, who had a position in physics at MIT.

For five years she held unsatisfying temporary teaching positions while caring for her two small children. Finally, she decided to seek full-time employment in the Boston area—not for the money, but for the intellectual stimulation she badly missed.

> I did find a position with an Air Force laboratory, which was right in our neighborhood. I thought [it] was better [than an academic job], actually, for taking care of children, because you didn't have to be there at any certain hour, so if the kids needed you ... maybe you could ... take off.
>
> [At the research lab] I was consulting on things that ... anybody had an interest in. And then I was working on this new area called error-correcting codes, which I had never heard about. There were some people there who were interested in it, and they were quite pleased to get me—they couldn't get a Ph.D. in algebra for a place like that! (Pless, 13)

The work in error-correcting codes that she did at the research lab formed the basis of her subsequent research career. In the thirty-five years since, Vera Pless has become perhaps the foremost authority on error-correcting codes in the world. On the strength of the research she had begun at the Air Force Research Center, Pless obtained her first regular faculty position in 1976, as a tenured full professor of mathematics at the University of Illinois at Chicago.

Research success, for this generation of women mathematicians, came as a consequence of serendipity, good fortune, judicious use of personal contacts, and the careful management of personal and professional responsibilities. It is perhaps not surprising, given the competing demands of family and career, that the research output of many of these women came to full flower later in life—contrary to the myth. Mary Ellen Rudin offers this viewpoint:

> I think that my mathematics became best when I was about sixty....
> Among many of the women that I know, their mathematics got sig-
> nificantly better when they were somewhat older. I think it's that they
> were somewhat distracted when they had little children at home.
> They had succeeded in continuing to do mathematics, but they did
> not quite do it at the same level of competency that they would have
> at some other time. And therefore this was built up in them, ready to
> come out a little later. While with most men, it isn't broken up in
> quite that way. (Rudin, 26)

Tilla Weinstein, who believes that her own work as a geometer came to maturity only recently, offers a somewhat different explanation:

> If you're lucky enough to be very brilliant, young, and be able to do
> extraordinarily good work, maybe you can burn out, and even if you
> keep going, never quite attain the heights of your initial work. But if
> you start out with nowhere but up to go, and you're bound and de-
> termined to keep living, then you have every reason to expect that
> you're going to get better. It's only if you're already at the top that
> it's very hard to keep getting better. And I do think a good many
> women, if not of my generation, let's say, *near* my generation, did
> improve with time. (Weinstein, 39)

Mary Ellen Rudin fears that for many women even today, the opportunity to do mathematics can be lost when other responsibilities became too great. But Herta Freitag offers the hope that it may, indeed,
never be too late to engage in creative mathematical activity. Herta Freitag's research in elementary number theory began in the early 1960s—
when she was already in her fifties—and continues to this day. She maintains a lively correspondence with mathematicians all over the world; her
work is published, presented, and discussed at international conferences.
Although she claims to work only on "little problems," her results have
found application in cryptanalysis. At this writing, Herta Freitag is ninety
years old.

The Question of Identity

What does it mean to be a mathematician? And what does it take to come to identify oneself as such? Paul R. Halmos, who earned a Ph.D. at the University of Illinois in 1938 and went on to a distinguished career in research, teaching, administration, and writing, offers the following stringent requirements for would-be mathematicians in his popular book, *I Want to Be a Mathematician:*

> I spent most of a lifetime trying to be a mathematician—and what did I learn? What does it take to be one? I think I know the answer: you have to be born right, you must continually strive to become perfect, you must love mathematics more than anything else, you must work at it hard and without stop, and you must never give up. (Halmos 1985, 400)

It is interesting and instructive to contrast Halmos's view—which, he confidently asserts, would be shared by many, if not most, of the outstanding creative mathematicians of this century—with the thoughts and feelings of the women who received Ph.D.'s from American universities in the forties and fifties.

Jane Cronin Scanlon's contributions to mathematical research have been substantial. She has published nearly seventy articles and books and made substantial contributions to differential equations, nonlinear analysis, and mathematical biology. She has continued to do mathematics almost daily since her retirement in 1991—proving theorems, writing papers, attending conferences. Despite her ongoing involvement with the subject, she has always viewed mathematics as an activity, rather than a central part of her identity:

> I don't think I ever identified myself as ... an *anything....* I'm pretty sure that I never think that I *am* a mathematician. Sometimes I *do* mathematics. Now, do other people think this way? I don't know. Certainly, I think some people—mercifully not too many—use mathematics to the pleasure of their egos. You know, they need to show off; sometimes, there are a few people who are really unpleasant—mercifully few. [But I do mathematics because] I like it. (Cronin Scanlon, 44–45)

Unlike Jane Cronin Scanlon, most of the women of this generation do readily identify themselves as mathematicians. For Tilla Weinstein, a colleague of Jane Cronin Scanlon's for many years at Rutgers University and also a prolific researcher, being a mathematician is part of her core identity. But her process of becoming a mathematician was slow:

> I didn't even think of myself as a mathematician—I didn't think of that word for myself—until quite recently. I'd say the first time that I felt that the mathematics I was doing was somehow, finally, flowing from inside of me, was right around 1980.... [B]efore that, I *wanted* to be doing mathematics. I kept working; every now and then I really *found* something. But it was from plugging away and plugging away, and it was never seeming to come from inside of me. (Weinstein, 19)

In other words, one has not become a mathematician until mathematics has been internalized—until it becomes a part of oneself.

Many of my other interviewees not only identified themselves as mathematicians, but stated that they had been mathematicians for a long time. Mary Ellen Rudin, who first identified herself as a mathematician when she entered graduate school, says, "For as long as I can remember, I've always considered myself a mathematician" (Rudin, 18). Moreover, identity as a mathematician is not necessarily tied to research activity. Margaret Marchand, who did substantial research early in her career but was primarily a teacher of mathematics, connects her identity as a mathematician to her ability to do what mathematicians do. Although she began to think of herself as a mathematician in graduate school, she asserts:

> I've been a mathematician all my life.... [At this point I asked her: Do you know what it was that made you feel, finally, that you were a mathematician, in graduate school?] Well, the fact that I had success in it. You know, I could do what was considered as mathematics. What else? I mean, it always came easy to me, and so I figured, that's the way I am! There's a lot of things I can't do that I wish I could do! But this is one thing that I could do; it came easily. So that's what I am. I've been a mathematician all my life, and that's all I can say. (Marchand, 22)

Maria Steinberg, like Margaret Marchand, was quite active in research early in her career but eventually concentrated on teaching. She retired early, at the age of fifty-six, in 1975. Since retirement, she has maintained contact with the mathematical community—particularly through her husband, long on the faculty of UCLA. Although she has not engaged in mathematical activity per se in over twenty years, she, too, is still a mathematician:

> [Y]ou don't want to provoke [a negative] reaction. I keep it a secret as long as I'm not among mathematicians or something.... [But] yes, I'm a, I've always been a mathematician. *Ja.* Because I also live among mathematicians. But, you know, it's something to be proud of! (Steinberg, 18)

In short, mathematics need not be an all-consuming passion, more important than anything else, in order to be a significant part of one's identity and something in which to take pride.

Can mathematical identity be lost? For Jean Walton, the answer is yes. Her career is distinguished from those of the other interviewees by the fact that, even before she began work toward a Ph.D. in mathematics at the University of Pennsylvania in 1944, she had worked as an assistant dean at Swarthmore College. Early on she had the option of pursuing a career in teaching or in administration; when she completed the Ph.D. in 1948, she was considered for jobs in both. She landed a job as dean of women at Pomona College, but for several years she taught mathematics courses there as well.

Jean Walton remembers clearly the day that she finally said goodbye to mathematics. It was in the early 1960s; she was by this time dean of students at Pomona, and had finally given up teaching:

> I came home, and ... got my mail and I started going through it. And there was a copy of a mathematics journal, which I was still subscribing to for sentimental, nostalgic reasons. And I took one look at that journal, and I said to myself—clearly, it was a very strong, clear moment—"Gosh, I'm glad I'm where I am, and not doing mathematics." ...
>
> [In my job as dean] I was so much alive, because it took all that I am.... My image of myself as a mathematician was somebody who was playing interesting and fun games, unrelated to the rest of my

life.... But what I felt when I looked at that math journal was an image of the kind of narrow focus which would have been much more central in my life had I gone that route. And, in a certain sense, my goodness, I was focused, I was focused on these issues of all the challenges that students were facing, and it was tapping every skill that I had. And it was exhausting....

I thought it [mathematics] was fun, it was a great game. I liked it. But I stood there, tired as I was, looking at that mathematics journal, and said, "Okay, dears," and I cancelled my subscription. I thought, "I might as well face it. That's gone." And that was the moment that I said goodbye to math. I learned a lot from it all, and I loved it, and certainly the teaching was always ... a positive. I will never know what I might have done had I gone to a college—the option that was there—as an instructor of mathematics.... But ... I don't mind not knowing, really. (Walton, 24–25)

Mathematics had never really become an integral part of Jean Walton's life. Unlike Jane Cronin Scanlon, Jean Walton never reached the point where mathematics was a fascinating and compelling activity. Unlike Tilla Weinstein, she never felt that mathematics was internal to herself. Unlike Margaret Marchand, she never developed a strong sense of mathematical competence, despite having completed an excellent dissertation. Unlike Maria Steinberg, she never felt immersed in a sense of mathematical community. Finally, she lost her sense of identity as a mathematician.

Remarkably, however, this loss of identity was a very long time in coming. Involvement with mathematics at the level of the Ph.D. has a lasting impact on a woman's life and sense of herself.

Conclusion

In this essay I have considered the wide variety of ways in which women who received Ph.D.'s in mathematics during the 1940s and 1950s pursued careers in the field and developed a sense of mathematical identity. I have allowed the women to speak for themselves as much as possible, in order to come to a fuller understanding of their relationship to mathematics.

Although these women have had an affinity for mathematics for most of their lives, the early detection and development of their mathematical talent was not particularly crucial to their future success. What was considerably more important to their future development was the opportunity to explore their natural intellectual interests and develop their own aspirations; to grow up in an environment where education was valued; and to be taken seriously as a student by family, teachers, and peers.

It was crucial that, as young girls, they were not actively discouraged from taking mathematics, so that mathematics always remained among the options available to them. Once they had decided to make mathematics the focus of their studies, it was important to have key role models and mentors. The experience of working toward the Ph.D. formed the foundation of their future sense of themselves as mathematicians.

Their lives and careers stand in striking contrast to the dominant image of the mathematical life-course. They often had to juggle competing interests, needs, and responsibilities. They experienced numerous interruptions in their mathematical careers, but as long as they were able to maintain some sense of connection to mathematics, they eventually returned. Contrary to the folk wisdom that mathematics is an activity for the young, many of these women have done their best work in their forties, fifties, sixties, and beyond.

These women, to the extent that they were successful in pursuing the mathematical careers they sought, succeeded through persistence and diligence, making wise use of both setbacks and opportunities. Their experiences can serve as models for how women can survive and thrive in male-dominated professions, particularly when society at large is ambivalent about their ambitions.

Appendix 1: Interviewees

What follows is a list of the twenty-one women who were interviewed for this study. The list is chronological by the year in which the Ph.D. was awarded. Each listing includes the interviewee's year of birth, and a brief summary of educational background and employment history. This information has been compiled from the annual list of degrees awarded in the *Bulletin of the American Mathematical Society;* the biographical entries in *American Men of Science* and *American Men and Women of Science;* and the partial listing of women mathematicians compiled in the 1970s by Amy King and Rosemary McCroskey (King and McCroskey 1976–77). In each case, the information has been corroborated and supplemented by the interviewee. Finally, each entry notes the interview date and location and the approximate length of the interview transcript in pages.

I have referred to interview transcripts by the surname of the interviewee and the page number(s) of the interview transcript from which quotations are taken. In two cases, more than one interview was conducted; so, for example, the first and second interviews with Anne Lewis Anderson are distinguished from one another by the designations "Anderson-1" and "Anderson-2," respectively.

1940

Dorothy **Maharam Stone,** born 1917—B.Sc., Carnegie Institute of Technology, 1937; Ph.D., Bryn Mawr College, 1940. Professional positions include Institute for Advanced Study, Purdue University, University of Manchester, University of Rochester, Northeastern University. Interview: Boston, Massachusetts, 28 August 1996; 15 pages.

1942

Domina E. **Spencer,** born 1920—S.B., MIT, 1939; M.S., MIT, 1940; Ph.D., MIT, 1942. Professional positions include American University, Tufts College, Brown University, University of Connecticut. Interview: Boston, Massachusetts, 26 August 1996; 42 pages.

1943

Anne Lewis **Anderson,** born 1919—A.B., Randolph-Macon Woman's College, 1940; S.M., University of Chicago, 1941; Ph.D., University of Chicago, 1943. Professional position: Woman's College of North Carolina/University of North Carolina at Greensboro. Interviews: by telephone, 18 April 1995; 13 pages. In person, Chapel Hill, North Carolina, 20 November 1995; 8 pages.

1945

Winifred **Asprey,** born 1917—A.B., Vassar College, 1938; M.S., University of Iowa, 1943; Ph.D., University of Iowa, 1945. Professional position: Vassar College. Interview: Poughkeepsie, New York, 24 August 1996; 56 pages.

1946

Grace **Bates,** born 1914, died 1996—B.S., Middlebury College, 1935; Sc.M., Brown University, 1938; Ph.D., University of Illinois, 1946. Professional positions include Sweet Briar College, Mount Holyoke College. Interview: Newtown, Pennsylvania, 13 June 1996; 24 pages.

1947

Margaret F. **Willerding,** born 1919—A.B., Harris Teacher's College (Missouri), 1940; M.A., St. Louis University, 1943; Ph.D., St. Louis University, 1947. Professional positions include Washington University in St. Louis, Harris Teacher's College, San Diego State University. Interview: LaMesa, California, 26 May 1996; 13 pages.

1948

Jean B. **Walton,** born 1914—B.A., Swarthmore College, 1935; M.A., Brown University, 1940; Ph.D., University of Pennsylvania, 1948. Professional positions include Swarthmore College, Pomona College. Interview: Claremont, California, 24 May 1996; 37 pages.

1949

Anne Whitney **Calloway,** born 1921—B.A., Swarthmore College, 1942; M.A., Columbia University, 1947; Ph.D., University of Pennsylvania, 1949. Professional positions include Goucher College, Carleton College, Kalamazoo College, Michigan Department of Transportation. Interview: Kalamazoo, Michigan, 21 October 1996; 23 pages.

Mary Ellen Estill **Rudin,** born 1924—B.A., University of Texas, 1944; Ph.D., University of Texas, 1949. Professional positions include Duke University, University of Rochester, University of Wisconsin–Madison. Interview: Madison, Wisconsin, 17 July 1996; 28 pages.

Jane **Cronin Scanlon,** born 1922—B.S., Wayne University (Detroit), 1943; M.A., University of Michigan, 1945; Ph.D., University of Michigan, 1949. Professional positions include Institute for Advanced Study, U.S. Air Force Cambridge Research Center, Wheaton College (Massachusetts), Stonehill College, American Optical Company, Polytechnic Institute of Brooklyn, Rutgers University. Interview: Highland Park, New Jersey, 12 June 1996; 49 pages.

Maria Weber **Steinberg,** born 1919—*Licence,* University of Geneva, 1940 (mathematics), 1941 (physics); Ph.D., Cornell University, 1949. Professional positions include Goucher College, California Institute of Technology, UCLA, Hughes Aircraft, California State University at Northridge. Interview: Pacific Palisades, California, 25 May 1996; 21 pages.

1950

Violet Hachmeister **Larney,** born 1920 — B.Ed., Illinois State Normal University, 1941; A.M., University of Illinois, 1942; Ph.D., University of Wisconsin, 1950. Professional positions include Kansas State College, New York State College for Teachers/State University of New York at Albany. Interview: Mesa, Arizona, 21 May 1996; 24 pages.

Margaret Owchar **Marchand,** born 1925 — B.A., University of Manitoba, 1945; M.A., University of Minnesota, 1947; Ph.D., University of Minnesota, 1950. Professional positions include Southwest Missouri State College, Manitoba Cancer Relief and Research Institute, Bemidji State College, University of Denver, Lakehead University, Superior State College (Wisconsin), Adrian College. Interview: Adrian, Michigan, 22 October 1996; 25 pages.

1952

Augusta L. **Schurrer,** born 1925 — A.B., Hunter College, 1945; M.A., University of Wisconsin, 1947; Ph.D., University of Wisconsin, 1952. Professional position: Iowa State Teachers College/State College of Iowa/University of Northern Iowa. Interview: Cedar Falls, Iowa, 20 July 1996; 34 pages.

1953

Herta Taussig **Freitag,** born 1908 — *Magister rerum naturalium,* University of Vienna, 1934; M.A., Columbia University, 1949; Ph.D., Columbia University, 1953. Professional position: Hollins College. Interviews: Roanoke, Virginia, 28 October, 11 November, and 2 December 1995; 23, 25, and 19 pages.

1954

Joyce White **Williams,** born 1929 — B.A., University of Minnesota, 1949; M.S., University of Illinois, 1951; Ph.D., University of Illinois, 1954. Professional position: Lowell Technological Institute/University of Lowell/University of Massachusetts Lowell. Interview: Lowell, Massachusetts, 27 August 1996; 20 pages.

1955

Barbara **Beechler,** born 1928 — B.A., University of Iowa, 1949; M.S., University of Iowa, 1951; Ph.D., University of Iowa, 1955. Professional positions include Smith College, Wilson College, Wheaton College (Massachusetts), Pitzer College. Interview: Claremont, California, 23 May 1996; 51 pages.

Jean E. Hirsh **Rubin,** born 1926 — B.S., Queens College (New York), 1948; M.A., Columbia University, 1949; Ph.D., Stanford University, 1955. Professional positions include Queens College, Stanford University, University of Oregon, Michigan State University, Purdue University. Interview: West Lafayette, Indiana, 15 July 1996; 16 pages.

1956

Joan Raup **Rosenblatt,** born 1926 — A.B., Barnard College, 1946; Ph.D., University of North Carolina at Chapel Hill, 1956. Professional positions include National Institute of Public Affairs, United States Bureau of the Budget, United States Bureau of the Census, National Bureau of Standards/National Institute of Standards and Technology. Interview: Gaithersburg, Maryland, 2 October 1996; 23 pages.

1957

Vera Stepen **Pless,** born 1931 — Ph.B., University of Chicago, 1949; M.S., University of Chicago, 1952; Ph.D., Northwestern University, 1957. Professional positions include Boston University, U.S. Air Force Cambridge Research Center, Argonne National Laboratories, MIT, University of Illinois at Chicago. Interview: Oak Park, Illinois, 16 July 1996; 29 pages.

1959

Tilla Savanuck (Klotz Milnor) **Weinstein,** born 1934 — B.A., New York University, 1955; M.S., New York University, 1956; Ph.D., New York University, 1959. Professional positions include UCLA, New York University, MIT, Boston College, Douglass College/Rutgers University. Interview: Metuchen, New Jersey, 11 June 1996; 44 pages.

Appendix 2: Women Mathematics Ph.D.'s of the 1940s and 1950s

I have attempted to compile a list of the women who received Ph.D.'s in mathematics from American colleges and universities during the years 1940–1959. I have obtained the names by consulting the annual listing of Ph.D.'s awarded in the *Bulletin of the American Mathematical Society* during the years 1941–1960 and by consulting an incomplete listing of American women mathematicians compiled by Amy King and Rosemary McCroskey in the 1970s (King and McCroskey 1976–77). I have verified more than half of the names with the appropriate graduate school alumni offices.

To date, I have been able to locate 83 women who received degrees during 1940–1949 and 103 women receiving degrees during 1950–1959. This list is not yet complete, but it is close: the National Research Council statistics compiled in table 1 list 87 female recipients of the Ph.D. in mathematics during the forties, 109 during the fifties.

Based on this admittedly somewhat incomplete tabulation, it is interesting to note those colleges and universities that produced the greatest number of women mathematics Ph.D.'s during the forties and fifties. The following is a list of those institutions producing five or more women mathematics Ph.D.'s during the 1940s or 1950s; the number of women in each case is listed in parentheses.

1940s	1950s
Illinois (9)	NYU (10)
Michigan (8)	Brown (6)
Catholic (8)	Michigan (5)
Harvard/Radcliffe (7)	Minnesota (5)
Chicago (6)	Illinois (5)
California/Berkeley (5)	

Only Illinois and Michigan are found in both lists. The decline in production of women Ph.D.'s at Chicago is especially dramatic. In the 1920s, 13 women received Chicago mathematics Ph.D.'s, and in the 1930s the number rose to 24 (Judy Green, private communication, April 1997). In the 1940s, the last Chicago Ph.D. awarded to a woman was in 1946; in the 1950s, Chicago awarded three Ph.D.'s to women.

The appearance of NYU in the second list is especially noteworthy. The graduate program at the Courant Institute was coming into its own in the 1950s and for many years was considered a particularly hospitable place for women. Many of the women who earned Ph.D.'s at NYU in the early years worked with two advisors in particular: Wilhelm Magnus and Lipman Bers. (For further information, see Morawetz 1989, and the interview with Bers in Albers et al. 1990.)

Notes

I want to express my thanks to the Center for Programs in the Humanities at Virginia Polytechnic Institute and State University whose financial assistance was indispensable to me in the early stages of this work. I am also deeply grateful to the Alfred P. Sloan Foundation and the Spencer Foundation for their generous financial support of this research. Finally, I would like to acknowledge my professional and personal debt to Judy Green and Jeanne LaDuke, whose work on the women who earned Ph.D.'s in mathematics from American universities prior to 1940 has been both an inspiration and a resource for the present study.

1. Curiously, Columbia University did not subsequently award large numbers of Ph.D.'s in mathematics to women. After Winifred Edgerton (Merrill) earned her degree in 1886, the next woman to receive a Ph.D. in mathematics from Columbia did so in 1901; altogether, during the years 1901–1930, seven women received Ph.D.'s in mathematics from Columbia (personal communication with Jeanne LaDuke, April 1997). In the years 1931–1959, only three women received Columbia mathematics Ph.D.'s, in the years 1941, 1942, and 1953, as gleaned from the listings published annually in the *Bulletin of the American Mathematical Society* and the partial (and somewhat inaccurate) list of women mathematicians published in 1977 by Amy King and Rosemary McCroskey (King and McCroskey 1976–77). It should be noted, however, that the Columbia Teachers College, distinct from the mathematics department, awarded a good many doctorates in mathematics education to women in this century.

2. It is interesting to note that throughout the 1960s and early 1970s, the numbers of Ph.D.'s awarded continued to increase dramatically, with the largest percentage increase in the latter half of the 1960s. It is impossible to give a simple reason for the changes observed in the late 1970s. It seems reasonable to speculate, however, that the increases in women's participation during this period are due in no small part to the antidiscrimination legislation of the early 1970s, most notably Title IX of the Educational Amendments Act of 1972 (see Rossiter 1995). It is also curious to note that the numbers of men receiving the Ph.D. in the years 1975–1984 actually *fell*. The only other time this had happened was during the years 1935–1944, coinciding with the late Depression and World War II.

   Patricia Albjerg Graham has written a provocative history of women in higher education in the United States, which addresses more broadly many of the social and political issues touched on in this essay (Graham 1978).

3. I am grateful to Jeanne LaDuke and Judy Green for the statistics on the University of Chicago prior to 1940 (see Green and LaDuke 1990, 129, 144n. 52).

4. In fact, Tilla Weinstein, who entertained so many career options as a child, did not decide to major in mathematics until she was halfway through college; yet she is among the most productive mathematical researchers of her generation.

5. The sociologist Christine Williams has done a comparative study of men and women in nontraditional occupations. She observes:

> Some have argued that women are excluded from male-dominated occupations because men are "territorial": they perceive women as unwanted competitors for their jobs and construct barriers to them in order to preserve their monopoly over the desirable occupations. Women in female-dominated occupations have the opposite incentive: many believe that allowing more men in will bring higher salaries and greater social prestige....
>
> However, ... in addition to economic self-interest, there is something even deeper and more fundamental involved in the asymmetry of men's and women's experience in nontraditional occupations: job segregation by sex allows men to maintain their masculinity in contradistinction to femininity. Men have historically used the occupational realm not only to secure economic advantages over women, but also to establish and affirm their essential difference from—and personal sense of superiority over—women. (Williams 1989, 132–33)

It can be argued that mathematics as an occupation has never really been closed to American women in this century. But the profession has been stratified into a male-dominated section—research—and a female-dominated section—teaching. It is curious to note that movements intended to bring more (male) research mathematicians into mathematics education are generally applauded by the mathematical community, while efforts to increase women's participation in research have met with far greater resistance.

6. In the 1950s and 1960s, the psychologist Ravenna Helson conducted a landmark study of the personality profile of creative women research mathematicians (Helson 1971). Many of the women in the present study told me that they were among Ravenna Helson's subjects.

7. In 1973, Violet Larney published a paper in the *American Mathematical Monthly* expressing similar concerns; this paper has recently been reprinted (Larney 1973).

Bibliography

Albers, Donald J., Gerald L. Alexanderson, and Constance Reid, eds. 1990. *More Mathematical People: Contemporary Conversations*. San Diego, Calif.: Academic Press.

Duren, Peter, Richard A. Askey, and Uta C. Merzbach, eds. 1989. *A Century of Mathematics in America*. Parts 1–3. Providence, R.I.: American Mathematical Society.

Fenster, Della Dumbaugh, and Karen Parshall. 1994. "Women in the American Mathematical Research Community: 1891–1906." In *Images, Ideas, and Communities,* vol. 3 of *The History of Modern Mathematics,* ed. E. Knobloch and D. Rowe, 229–61. San Diego, Calif.: Academic Press.

Graham, Patricia Albjerg. 1978. "Expansion and Exclusion: A History of Women in American Higher Education." *Signs: A Journal of Women in Culture and Society 3*, no. 4: 759–73.

Green, Judy, and Jeanne LaDuke. 1987. "Women in the American Mathematical Community: The Pre-1940 Ph.D.'s." *Mathematical Intelligencer 9*, no. 1: 11–23.

————. 1989. "Women in American Mathematics: A Century of Contributions." In *A Century of Mathematics in America,* ed. Peter Duren, Richard A. Askey, and Uta C. Merzbach, part 2, 379–98. Providence, R.I.: American Mathematical Society.

————. 1990. "Contributors to American Mathematics: An Overview and Selection." In *Women of Science: Righting the Record,* ed. G. Kass-Simon and Patricia Farnes, 117–46. Bloomington: Indiana University Press.

Halmos, Paul R. 1985. *I Want to Be a Mathematician: An Automathography in Three Parts.* New York: Springer-Verlag.

Harmon, Lindsey R., and Herbert Soldz. 1963. *Doctorate Production in United States Universities 1920–1962.* Washington, D.C.: National Academy of Sciences / National Research Council.

Hartmann, Susan M. 1982. *The Home Front and Beyond: American Women in the 1940s.* Boston: Twayne.

Helson, Ravenna. 1971. "Women Mathematicians and the Creative Personality." *Journal of Consulting and Clinical Psychology 36*, no. 2: 210–20.

Jones, L. M. 1990. "Intellectual Contributions of Women to Physics." In *Women of Science: Righting the Record,* ed. G. Kass-Simon and Patricia Farnes, 188–214. Bloomington: Indiana University Press.

Kass-Simon, G. 1990. "Biology Is Destiny." In *Women of Science: Righting the Record,* ed. G. Kass-Simon and Patricia Farnes, 215–67. Bloomington: Indiana University Press.

King, Amy C., and Rosemary McCroskey. 1976–77. "Women Ph.D.'s in Mathematics in USA and Canada: 1886–1973." *Philosophia Mathematica* 13 / 14:79–129.

Larney, Violet H. 1973. "Female Mathematicians, Where are You?" *American Mathematical Monthly* 80: 310–13. Reprinted in *A Century of Mathematics through the Eyes of the Monthly,* ed. John H. Ewing, 281–83. Washington, D.C.: Mathematical Association of America, 1994.

MacLane, Saunders. 1989. "Mathematics at the University of Chicago: A Brief History." In *A Century of Mathematics in America,* ed. Peter Duren, Richard A. Askey, and Uta C. Merzbach, part 2, 127–54. Providence, R.I.: American Mathematical Society.

Morawetz, Cathleen. 1989. "The Courant Institute of Mathematical Sciences." In *A Century of Mathematics in America,* ed. Peter Duren, Richard A. Askey, and Uta C. Merzbach, part 2, 303–7. Providence, R.I.: American Mathematical Society.

National Research Council. 1996. *Survey of Earned Doctorates.* Unpublished tables. Washington, D.C.: National Academy of Sciences.

Parshall, Karen V. H., and David E. Rowe. 1994. *The Emergence of the American Mathematical Research Community 1876–1900: J. J. Sylvester, Felix Klein, and E. H. Moore.* Providence, R.I.: American Mathematical Society.

Rees, Mina. 1980. "The Mathematical Sciences and World War II." *American Mathematical Monthly* 87: 607–21. Reprinted in *A Century of Mathematics in America,* ed. Peter Duren, Richard A. Askey, and Uta C. Merzbach, part 1, 275–89. Providence, R.I.: American Mathematical Society, 1989.

Richardson, R. G. D. 1989. "The Ph.D. Degree and Mathematical Research." In *A Century of Mathematics in America,* ed. Peter Duren, Richard A. Askey, and Uta C. Merzbach, part 2, 361–78. Providence, R.I.: American Mathematical Society. Reprinted from *American Mathematical Monthly* 43 (1936):199–215.

Rossiter, Margaret. 1995. *Women Scientists in America: Before Affirmative Action 1940–1972.* Baltimore, Md.: Johns Hopkins University Press.

Solomon, Barbara Miller. 1985. *In the Company of Educated Women.* New Haven, Conn.: Yale University Press.

Williams, Christine L. 1989. *Gender Differences at Work: Women and Men in Nontraditional Occupations.* Berkeley and Los Angeles: University of California Press.

Strategies for Teaching "Female-Friendly" Science to Women

Using History and Research to Guide Instruction

Valerie N. Morphew

While it is commonly accepted that women have been underrepresented in the sciences, it is not so evident that some women have made important contributions in various scientific disciplines. The nature of science and the nature of women are, and have been, sometimes even harmonious and complementary. By analyzing historical accounts of successful women in science and applying what research says about teaching female-friendly science, I have attempted to increase women's interest in the practice of science. The results have been encouraging and exemplify how, as educators, we may increase women's interest in science and science careers.

Science has not always been unfriendly to women. Indeed, there have been times and situations in which women's roles in society were compatible with their role in science. For example, in early-nineteenth-century England, combining family and botany in the home as part of the family routine made work in science accessible to women. At that time, taxonomy—the collecting and categorizing of flora—dominated botany and could be carried out by women in the home. This compatibility, however, began to wane later in the nineteenth century when botany shifted to empiricism and the laboratory, toward "science on a male model" (Shteir 1987, 43).

Sometimes attributes typically associated with women also helped women mark a place in scientific society. In the nineteenth and twentieth centuries, the "wait on nature" approach to medicine made the profession "especially vulnerable" to entrance by women (Morantz-Sanchez 1987, 46). Here, woman's intuition, her way of knowing, were professionally acceptable. Although today women are entering medicine in record numbers, the way women "do science" in contemporary medical practice is, again, science on a male model.

Women sometimes found acceptance and opportunity in the sciences through their relationships. For example, Marie Curie was provided with laboratory space and contacts with male scientists through her husband, Pierre. After Pierre's death, however, Marie had to prove herself worthy of acceptance by the scientific community. Indeed, in 1911, Marie won a second Nobel Prize, solely on her own merits (Pycior 1987). Margaret Huggins also found a place in the scientific community as a collaborator with her astronomer husband, William, in the late nineteenth and early twentieth centuries. Still, Margaret was considered a subordinate part of this astronomy team (Ogilvie 1987). Maria Mitchell was deeply influenced in her astronomical studies by her father, William, who taught her how to use a telescope at an early age. Mitchell was not only a pioneer female scientist but also a promoter of women in science in the late nineteenth and early twentieth centuries (Kohlstedt 1987).

Despite the positive environment some women scientists enjoyed, in general attitudes were stifling. Even though women made contributions to botany, for example, this was often in the compilation of county flora rather than in the more visible work of presenting papers and presiding over major institutions (Shteir 1987). Being among the uninitiated in a male-dominated domain also impeded women's acceptance and recognition. For example, unfamiliar with the rules of scientific circles, Dorothy Wrinch intruded upon another's territorial field and stepped on the toes of prominent scientists by claiming discovery of protein structure. As a result, Wrinch was all but muted for a number of years (Abir-Am 1987).

Sometimes women's contributions were suspect for their methodology. Take, for example, Margaret Mead's contributions to the social sciences in the early twentieth century (1928). The validity and reliability of her qualitative methods were questioned. Indeed, some accused her of having made up some of the data she collected from the native Samoans. Had she conducted her studies using quantitative measures instead, one wonders whether her contributions would have been suspect at all.

Later in the twentieth century, Rachel Carson increased public awareness by writing about the devastating effects of DDT (1962). Carson's concern for the natural world also stirred up suspicion. This should come as no surprise: those she criticized were the same ones who were operating successfully in the empirical, male-dominated world.

Accounts of successful women in science demonstrate that women do have a place in science and that science has a place in women's lives. By analyzing these accounts and infusing them into what we understand about women's ways of knowing, it is possible to establish what Sue Rosser calls a "female-friendly science" (1990).

According to Rosser, there are steps educators can take to establish and enrich the science learning environment for female students. For example, by increasing the number of observations in laboratory settings and by remaining longer in the observational stage of the scientific method, educators can provide an experience that capitalizes on the strengths and attributes of women. Also, by undertaking investigations more holistically, the same result can be achieved.

Similarly, Rosser believes there are methods of science investigation that benefit women in science. For instance, teachers can use a combination of qualitative and quantitative methods in data gathering. Also, teachers can increase the use of interactive methods, which may shorten the distance between the observer and the observed.

Rosser contends that the conclusions and theories drawn from data gathering can be approached in a female-friendly way as well. She encourages teachers to be open to critiques of conclusions and theories that differ from those that the traditional male scientist has drawn from the same observations. She also encourages the development of theories that are relational, interdependent, and multicausal rather than hierarchical, reductionistic, and dualistic. Rosser also believes that the practice of science can be female-friendly. She supports the use of models that are less competitive and the use of discussion to help students see science in its social context.

Considering these lessons and recommendations, I have attempted to improve science education for my female (and male) students. I encourage descriptive science in the classroom and emphasize observation. I encourage the sharing of personal experiences related to the science that students are learning. I employ qualitative and quantitative methods in scientific inquiry. I also promote cooperative learning. I believe the results of my efforts are noteworthy and exciting.

My faculty appointment at Longwood College from 1996 to 1999 was in education and science. The botany and zoology science classes I taught were for liberal studies majors who were preparing to teach at the elementary school level after graduation. The majority of my students were women. I asked both female and male students from a fundamental zoology class I taught during the spring of 1997 to write about what they found different about this science presented in a female-friendly way and what they thought about my teaching methods. The students' responses confirmed that I was practicing female-friendly science.

Some of my female students experienced success in science for the first time:

> [This] method of teaching has been the only one that has worked for me. A professor I had in the past would simply put a typed overhead of the notes up every day. Then he would read exactly what was on the overhead while we copied it down. So, when you're trying to listen and write at the same time for a certain amount of time you don't retain the information. On the other hand, Dr. Morphew writes on the chalkboard and we copy it as she is writing. She will then stop and explain what she has written. She uses examples that we can relate to, which helps me hold in the information.

Several other students also responded well to the class discussions and favored this method over a straight lecture format. Rather than inundate students with a lot of facts and figures, I choose instead to engage students in discussions relating to the topic of study. For example, when Dolly the lamb was cloned, we discussed the differences and similarities between twinning and cloning and deliberated on the ethics and implications of cloning animals and humans.

The explanations and group discussions helped students grasp the science concepts I was teaching:

> I am a woman and I have had more difficulty in other science classes. I think this is because things were not explained as well. Things were just introduced, then we were expected to know all about it.... Being a girl, class has been very interesting to me, and I want to attend every

class. Things seem to be more intriguing. Other times in other classes I would just sit there and copy notes. I would get nothing out of it.

I feel I have learned more in this class than in previous classes. In previous classes with male professors, I felt as though facts were simply thrown at us with hardly any discussion. We, as students, would copy key words from the overhead only to later look at them and think "what did this mean?" It was almost as if the male professor simply wanted us to memorize the information and not learn it. This was difficult for me, and I did horrible in his class.

Instead of memorization I feel as though I learn the information and even am able to apply it to things in my everyday life. Hands-on learning is the best for me as a female. It makes science fun and interesting.

Flexibility and emphasizing the relevance of the concepts complement the way our students think:

Past science classes were strictly run and never varied from the schedule, so there were never really opportunities to ask questions or to elaborate on certain topics. Finally the information presented was not really practical and the labs were not related to anything we might encounter out of class.

[In this class,] we are allowed to ask questions and that helps to get a better and more complete idea of what we are discussing. The information is directly related to school and/or teaching knowledge, so we aren't wasting time. Finally, we are able to get help if we need it without being treated like we don't know anything.

The implications that my teaching methods have for traditional gender roles were not lost on the students:

I have always looked at science as a male-oriented class and occupation, but ironically the girls in my classes often seem to do the best. Dr. Morphew's approach to science gives females a feeling of accomplishment. I feel that most of my girlfriends and I deal much better with things when we understand how they might really interact with our lives. The relation between real life and science keeps my interest.

I am encouraged by what I have learned from my students. They have confirmed my belief that women can succeed in science and that there are ways that we, as educators, can help achieve this end. I anticipate further improvements in my classroom practices as more research is conducted to determine the optimum learning environment for women in science. My students, future teachers, will impact the lives of girls and boys not yet born. I hope and trust that my female-friendly practices will extend to these classrooms of tomorrow.

References

Abir-Am, P. G. 1987. "Synergy or Clash: Disciplinary and Marital Strategies in the Career of Mathematical Biologist Dorothy Wrinch." In *Uneasy Careers and Intimate Lives: Women in Science, 1789–1979,* ed. P. G. Abir-Am and D. Outram, 239–80. New Brunswick, N.J.: Rutgers University Press.

Carson, R. 1962. *Silent Spring.* New York: Houghton Mifflin.

Kohlstedt, S. G. 1987. "Maria Mitchell and the Advancement of Women in Science." In *Uneasy Careers and Intimate Lives: Women in Science, 1789–1979,* ed. P. G. Abir-Am and D. Outram, 129–46. New Brunswick, N.J.: Rutgers University Press.

Mead, M. 1928. *Coming of Age in Samoa.* New York: William Morrow.

Morantz-Sanchez, R. M. 1987. "The Many Faces of Intimacy: Professional Options and Personal Choices among Nineteenth- and Twentieth-Century Women Physicians." In *Uneasy Careers and Intimate Lives: Women in Science, 1789–1979,* ed. P. G. Abir-Am and D. Outram, 45–59. New Brunswick, N.J.: Rutgers University Press.

Ogilvie, M. B. 1987. "Marital Collaboration: An Approach to Science." In *Uneasy Careers and Intimate Lives: Women in Science, 1789–1979,* ed. P. G. Abir-Am and D. Outram, 104–25. New Brunswick, N.J.: Rutgers University Press.

Pycior, H. M. 1987. "Marie Curie's 'Anti-natural Path': Time Only for Science and Family." In *Uneasy Careers and Intimate Lives: Women in Science, 1789–1979,* ed. P. G. Abir-Am and D. Outram, 191–215. New Brunswick, N.J.: Rutgers University Press.

Rosser, S. V. 1990. *Female-Friendly Science: Applying Women's Studies Methods and Theories to Attract Students.* New York: Pergamon.

Shteir, A. B. 1987. "Botany in the Breakfast Room: Women and Early-Nineteenth-Century British Plant Study." In *Uneasy Careers and Intimate Lives: Women in Science, 1789–1979,* ed. P. G. Abir-Am and D. Outram, 31–43. New Brunswick, N.J.: Rutgers University Press.

Successful Strategies for Teaching Math to College Women

Ruth O'Keefe

After several years of working for a large corporation as a mechanical engineer, I became critical of the manner in which my children were learning mathematics and of the insufficient amount of time—in some cases—that was being devoted to the subject. In retrospect, I suspect their elementary school teachers may have been victimized by "math trauma," just as are many of my present students.

My educational background—primarily in math and psychology—and my real-world experience have been the basis for my love of learning, which helps me not only to stay on top of things but also to have certain insights into the relationships between the learning and teaching of math and into the cognitive models currently in vogue regarding how students learn mathematical concepts. As an adjunct professor I have taught at a number of colleges in Grand Rapids, Michigan, including a junior college, a business college, a liberal arts college, and an art and design college. Students at these colleges have had diverse academic backgrounds, interests, and goals. While this alone can be a challenge pedagogically, there is the additional problem that, within each college, the students are generally specializing in a variety of academic disciplines. For this essay, I shall focus primarily on my experience at one of the liberal arts colleges.

For a number of years, graduates at this liberal arts college could successfully complete their program without ever having passed the doorway of a math class. This is very often the case at small liberal arts colleges throughout the United States. We in the math department, as well as the college accreditation organization, became concerned about this state of affairs. Therefore, within the past several years, if a student has taken no math course during her or his course work at this college, she or he is required to take a math proficiency test. If the student's score falls short of expectation, she or he is required to take an elementary math course (MS110), which I teach. Incidentally, many of these students have teaching as their goal; however, they are not necessarily pleased to be told of the math requirement to achieve it. Some of them are very ingenious in developing avoidance strategies, but most acquiesce for a positive, rewarding personal experience.

The students at this college may be majoring in criminology, theology, criminal justice, teaching, Christian philanthropy, music, art, communication, or special education, in addition to many other fields. Their status in life—as a sampling—may be in law enforcement or social work, as housewives, educators, or religious, at traditional age or continuing education (older adults). Many have established careers and have returned to college for a variety of reasons. Obviously, many of these students are successful in an administrative capacity outside the college. This elementary math course (MS110) is seen as a threat, a painful reminder of their past experience with mathematics buried deep within their subconscious.

The college advising team prepares the students through advance explanation of the course, and students are encouraged to contact me for support. Still, the math phobias of these students are apparent and overwhelming to many of them. I have taken it upon myself, through this class, to collect many of the stories about what induced their math phobias that these students, in their own words, have shared with me through the years. Having faced close to a thousand students over the past ten years, I have accumulated three binders of these stories, and it was a moving experience for me to review them en masse for this paper. What follows is but a small sampling of the stories that students have shared with me that illustrate what they believe lies at the heart of their difficulties and fears surrounding the learning of mathematics.

> 1. Let's call 5, "x" and call 6, "y" ... why? The teacher didn't take time to make sure my "why" was answered. Life became complicated when I was forced to deal with negative numbers, integers (what are they really?), and (can you believe this!) ... imaginary numbers ... to graduate from college and teach literature. I could not understand why a negative number existed (a "not" number to me) and even more unreasonable to me was why a requirement to teach English?

2. I could rapidly examine number problems and solve them without hesitation. When I entered algebra, things changed. I was very bitter for being confused in math classes—from that point on—math became a monster which I wished to avoid. Problems arose when I could not see the connection between my life and the numbers—when there was no real "reason" behind a problem, my mind left me to stare blankly on a white page. In my opinion most people are terrified of math because they are blind to its uses, or in many cases, unable to do it because of previous experience. I remember having a horrible math teacher, he was very critical, which led me to have a low self-esteem. They [math classes] have left you feeling stupid or unqualified.

3. I studied two years in high school; one year geometry, one year of algebra and didn't do well. I never took another math course again. I believe I was the product of a male math teacher who catered to the male engineering-bound members of the class, and the feminine "Barbie doll" syndrome of "math is hard."

4. My family frequently moved around during the time I was growing up. My [math] teacher insisted I was not intelligent, though I had good grades in my other classes. I eventually dropped the class, never to take another high school math class again.

5. As far as I can remember I have been a math illiterate. I think the problem started in grammar school, where the thought of numbers brought a chill to my bones. As a child I equated math with frustration and envy for children who understood the concept. I used to think I was retarded when asked a question at the chalk board.... Math became my dire nemesis, and since I figured they had me beat (the teachers, math, and the class), I spent most of math class doodling or day dreaming. It seemed most elementary school math teachers had one thing in common: they were out to get me and keep me from passing to the next grade. But I had a plan to foil them—I would cheat. I had to be kind of slick about it though, since they knew I was a rotten student. I would make it so I would just get by. Getting an "A" would be suicide; I would be caught. Also, I would have to become a master cheat. Math teachers tended to be pretty observant.

My shortcomings in math have cost me entrance into colleges, jobs, and almost every day I get short-changed since I can't count money fast enough. I am twenty-two years old and I still count on my fingers. I know that if someone took some time with me when I was younger and explained math in a practical language I would be a lot better off. So now, at my age, I have to teach myself multiplication tables at night. The thing I can't understand is why teachers never caught on to me. Many times I wish I had gotten caught, but I never did. I am paying for it now.

6. High school demanded I meet certain requirements for graduation. So on to Algebra I and II. The teacher was fresh out of college, tall and blonde—every high school girl's dream. Unfortunately, he knew it; this and coaching football seemed to be the only reason he was there. I gained little from his class and barely passed. The final straw was geometry and Mrs. Swanson. Ready for retirement, void of a sense of humor, geometry was her whole life. Unable to live up to her expectations, I dropped out after six weeks, vowing never to take another math class. With the exception of basic formula calculations in nurse's training, I've managed to keep this vow.

7. I have always had a difficult time understanding math. For as long as I can remember, I have tried to avoid math. In ninth grade I had an algebra teacher who insisted math was for guys. This man tried to prove that females were not as good at math. Of course I could not prove this, but I would say 90 percent of all his students felt the same way. Each day before class I felt like I had a knot in my stomach. One day stands out in particular. Each student was assigned a problem to solve on the board. Needless to say, I was very nervous. We began solving the problems with the first three male students that volunteered. They worked their problems correctly and took their seats. Three more guys did the same and then Mr.—— announced, with a smile, that it was just a little boring watching all right answers and that this would be a good time for a few girls to go to the board. Of course, after hearing a teacher say such a thing, it somewhat breaks down any confidence a student may have had. He instructed the class to pay close attention and added that they may witness a new way of learning algebra altogether. Of course, this brought a roar of laugh-

ter from all the male students. This is one thing Mr.——— loved, to feel like he was popular with his students, at least his male students. It must have taken me approximately five minutes to complete the problem, but it felt much longer. I felt like I was under so much pressure that it was hard to concentrate. I did not come up with the right answer, therefore I had to stay at the board and try another problem. All of that was so humiliating to me. I honestly feel that if I would have had a different teacher when I was first starting to learn math, I would have liked it a lot more and I probably would have taken more math throughout high school. It's a very good feeling to work a long problem and come up with the right answer.

Both my students and mathematics are very important to me, and, as these few examples show, the many accounts of students' experiences with math phobia have made me very aware of the baggage they have carried through the years. An unfair, thoughtless action has become a tragic, prolonged burden for them. I have only a fragile opportunity to promote the soothing balm of a successful closure of the past, followed by opportunities with the tools of mathematics to establish the goals of the future. Determined to make a contribution in reversing some of these negative attitudes that students have regarding learning mathematics, I constructed the elementary math course with the conditions that they had complained about in the forefront of my planning ideas.

My first task is to create a nonthreatening environment for the students. Each student has a "history envelope," containing an account such as those I quoted previously, that she or he steadfastly guards as private. To reveal the contents is too dangerous (at least for the first three weeks of class). An open-forum atmosphere is essential. This is not to say the class lacks structure—on the contrary, these students demand structure. They want, and need, to know what is expected of them. We have a text, and we adhere closely to the syllabus. However, from time to time, when I sense an opportunity to elaborate on a situation the students are concerned with, I do so without hesitation. In this way I show interest and understanding. This method seems to work well. Whenever possible I make use of information students may be interested in or bring to class.

Abraham Maslow's "hierarchy of needs" is the foundation upon which I build my program. I endeavor to create a comfort zone for my students.

Over the past few years I have studied the different learning styles of individuals. I have been exposed to the ideas of many professionals who have spent, in some cases, the better part of their lives researching how people learn; these professionals include experts from the fields of neurology, psychiatry, and related fields of medicine that deal with the organ of the brain and the secrets of its role with regard to "the learning process." Employing strategies learned from this exposure, I am often able to recognize a way of understanding my students' learning agendas. I reinforce my students' comfort zones by allowing them to be accepted as they are.

Force does not enter my classroom. Only once did I "force" a student to take a test. One evening when an exam had been planned, as I entered the classroom I was met by a bright student who had low self-esteem. I asked her where she was going, and she quickly let me know she was going to "fail the test," therefore she was "leaving." I linked my arm in hers, and we returned to the classroom. I then persuaded her to remain for the test by reassuring her that she would do well or we would find a way to solve the problem if she failed. In other words, there was no way she could fail unless she worked at failing. Fortunately, after a few minutes of trauma, she completed the first test successfully. Later, in an evaluation, this student stated that I was the first person to visibly indicate a faith in her ability to succeed in math. Once she felt comfortable with herself in this discipline, she literally thrived. She also became the driving force in the class. "If I can do it, you can too!" she would repeat during the semester. She had partnered with my efforts and was proud of that.

Students are accepted as they are when they enter my class. My history of teaching assures me that improvement will come, if not necessarily complete success (passing). I have a nonjudgmental attitude, which takes a great amount of patience. In teaching these students I take the attitude that they are allowed to succeed or fail, whichever is the most comfortable to them. It is their choice, and I will not judge their choice. I will do everything in my power to help them succeed; however, if they choose to fail by nonparticipation, they may do that! I am very clear on this matter.

Acceptance among their peers (the middle need in Maslow's hierarchy) is also very crucial. Since my students have, for the most part, been unsuccessful in the study of mathematics, my syllabus is a combination of traditional math and written papers, which also must be presented orally to the class. The traditional math may vary, depending on the student's major, but it generally consists of algebra, geometry, statistics, quantitative studies, business applications, and related topics (fractals, patterning, the golden mean). This balance between testing and written papers gives comfort to the student who freezes at the mere mention of a test. The feeling of pride after having successfully written a paper also gives the confidence needed to do well with traditional math. Our math is strong in application of the traditional tools of algebra and geometry. Students are encouraged and challenged to find math in their daily activity, no matter how obvious and irrelevant this may appear on the surface. I am initially deluged with requests for me to choose topics for them to research. My reaction is to ask them first about themselves—hobbies, interests, course of study, and so forth. I encourage them to become selfish in their selection of a topic *they* wish to pursue because of their interests. The class as a whole will benefit from their presentations.

After about three weeks into the semester, my students' papers can be astounding. The four-page written report (with bibliography) often is supplemented with videos, charts, slides, and musical presentations. The interest and curiosity among the students is aroused, and many times the uniqueness of the presentation results in visible and audible praise from classmates. Acceptance at last—in a math class, of all places! Presentations occasionally can be so overwhelmingly professional that I have requested permission from the student to use the material in one of my other (not math) classes.

Sports enthusiasts view the playing field from a new perspective, noticing the actual geometry of the playing field, the scoring procedures, and so forth. The manager of the meat department of a large grocery chain vehemently denied the use of math in his daily activity. After we had talked about probability and statistics, he realized that when he is asked to predict the number of cases of meat he will sell in response to a holiday ad, he truly is involved in mathematics. Actually, upon reflection, he subsequently realized his constant use of mathematics on an hourly basis. One of my students realized her interest in photography was filled with ratios and proportions as she explained the significance of f-stops on her camera relative to many other ingredients required for the perfect photograph.

During a Christmas holiday break, I received a card from the president of the college where I teach this class. As I opened the envelope I was attracted by the mathematical images shown on this beautiful card. I searched for the name of the artist who had created this elegant work of art and found the name of one of my former students. I contacted the student, and her comment was: "The proportions of the painting *were* based on the golden mean." While a student in my class, she had researched and written a report on the golden mean, an example of pleasing proportions in the work of an artist. Receiving the card was an amazing and rewarding experience for me. I am grateful to have the opportunity to help people change the way they "see" mathematics.

Most important, I've learned from this teaching experience that the pedagogy of college mathematics at an elementary level for those who are not math majors is more a function of structure and class environment than it is of content. For math phobic individuals, the first hurdle is always going to be teaching them how to overcome their fears. This can only be done, I am convinced, in an atmosphere similar to the one I've described here. This revelation and the impact that it can have on leading students to pursue more studies in math, as well as to learn to apply mathematical concepts to their daily lives without fear, have wide-ranging implications for all types of math teaching.

Factors That Increase Persistence of Female Undergraduate Science Students

Michelle Smoot Hyde
and Julie Gess-Newsome

Introduction

Women in the United States have long been underrepresented in science-related disciplines across college campuses and in industry. Recent statistics show that more women are declaring majors in science and engineering fields, but they are not necessarily graduating from those fields (NSB 1993). Statistics from the National Science Board (NSB) reveal that during 1975, women represented 18 percent of mathematics, engineering, or science (MES) majors. As of 1995, women in science-related fields account for 26.7 percent of the college MES majors, an increase of 0.05 percent per year. Despite this increase, women still only represent 16 percent of the science and engineering work force (NSB 1995), indicating a loss of women MES majors during the college years (Astin, Astin, and Dey 1992).

Attrition—of both male and female students—from MES majors has been a historical problem in undergraduate education. Students studying in MES fields are not always prepared for the demanding curriculum, which may include numerous no-credit laboratories and usually takes a minimum of five years to complete (Hyde 1997). Persistence rates for women in science-related fields, however, are significantly lower than those of their male peers (Seymour 1995). Strenta et al. (1993) found that the persistence rate of men in MES majors was as high as 61 percent at highly selective institutions, with an average of 39 percent for national samples, compared to 46 percent and 30 percent, respectively, for women. Thus, the initial

underrepresentation of women in MES is compounded by their disproportionate loss during their course of study and suggests possible gender
inequities within MES cultures.

The college years can be a crucial turning point in a woman's decision-
making process. Ehrhart and Sandler argue that institutions of higher education are in a "unique position to facilitate and encourage women's involvement in mathematics, science, law, and business because they educate
future professionals in these fields and serve as gatekeepers to the professions" (1987, 2). Postsecondary institutions can offset the decline in female
science enrollment by insuring opportunities for women and providing
special programs to facilitate women's participation in traditionally male
programs, as well as by encouraging the recruitment of women to these
programs (Ehrhart and Sandler 1987; Tobias 1990). For these reasons, investigations into the college MES experience are crucial to our understanding of female persistence.

This research investigated high-achieving female science students who
were pursuing their academic endeavors at a large research institution (referred to here by the pseudonym Western University). They were enrolled
in Project Access, a program dedicated to providing female science students
with support and assistance in attaining their science degree. The purpose
of our study was to define and clarify critical factors within the institutional
context that contributed to the persistence and graduation of 32 female MES
majors at Western University. Questions addressed included: What charac-
terized the experience of the women who stayed in science and graduated?
What types of interactions and events impacted their decision to persist?
What types of relationships were meaningful to their experience, and did
those associations help them to persist in their academic pursuits? What was
the nature of the university context? Did the university's special programs
for female MES students make a difference in persistence?

While many researchers have examined the issue of female science attrition during the precollege experience (Alper 1993; Kahle 1990; Kahle and
Lakes 1983; Pallas and Alexander 1983; Sadker and Sadker 1985b; Tobin
and Gallagher 1987; Vockell and Lobonc 1981), only a few gender studies
have focused on the female undergraduate, especially those who choose
to major in science, engineering, or mathematics. The college-level literature that does exist has concentrated on the reasons why women have not
succeeded in science programs and has emphasized observed disparities in

classroom interaction (Seymour 1995). In contrast, the examination of successful female students in MES provides a different research perspective, allowing for the understanding of success factors in educating and retaining female MES majors.

Methods

Theoretical Framework

Traditionally, issues of gender diversity in science classrooms have been studied using quantitative procedures. By providing statistical evidence for factors contributing to female science attrition, the problem has been substantiated, but causal mechanisms remain elusive. As more women enroll in previously male-dominated science-related classes, new research approaches and methodologies are needed to consider new and existing questions and explore territories that are outside the traditionally prescribed frameworks.

Erickson (1986) proposed that research should adopt an interpretive methodology when the substantive focus is on human meaning and social life. Our belief that classrooms and teaching are by nature socially and culturally organized environments for learning guided our research toward a cultural analysis. Interpretive methods of data collection allowed us to analyze several factors: (1) what was happening in a specific social setting; (2) what the actions meant to the actors involved; (3) how the culturally learned principles of conduct affected one's meaningful actions; (4) how events in one setting related to other events outside the setting; and (5) how everyday life in one setting compared with life in a wide range of other settings. Positivistic methods would not have provided us with the details of social occurrences that we needed to understand. For example, causal linkages cannot be determined by quantitative methods. As Miles and Huberman discuss, "with qualitative data one can preserve chronological flow, see precisely which events led to which consequences, and derive fruitful explanations" (1994, 1).

Our use of symbolic interactionism within the interpretive paradigm was well-suited to our examination of the day-to-day interactions of female MES majors. This approach allowed us the flexibility to understand how female science students make sense of and contend with institutional, instructional, and personal interactions, as well as conflicts and hierarchies.

Through documentation of concrete details of specific behaviors and practices we gained an understanding of female persistence in the sciences.

Project Access Program and Participants

The participants for our study were drawn from Western University's Project Access program. Project Access recruited approximately twenty top female science students during their senior year of high school and, after admission, brought them to campus for an eight-week session during the summer prior to their freshman year. During the summer workshop a different subject was taught each week by a professor committed to the goals of Project Access. Despite the academic orientation of the workshops, the primary purpose of the summer program was not the expansion of scientific knowledge but the development of beneficial relationships. The program also provided these students with a $2,000 scholarship during their first year. Additional assistance, through scholarships, cohorts, seminars, lab research, mentors, help sessions, and support groups, was offered to encourage graduation in their intended field of study. The objective of the program was to acclimate the female students to college life and introduce a support network of peers, professors, counselors, and staff.

The program, developed at Western University in 1991, was initially funded by the National Science Foundation. Following the grant period, the university elected to fund the program as part of its commitment to policies of nondiscrimination and affirmative action. At the time of this study, the program was administered through the office of the dean of the College of Science, who devoted considerable amounts of time and money to insure the program's success. As of 1997, the program involved over 120 students.

Twenty-two Project Access students were accepted as freshmen in 1991, followed by twenty-one students in 1992. It is from this original population of forty-three that our participants were drawn. At the time of this study (1995–1996), seventeen of these students were juniors, twelve seniors, and three had graduated. Eleven of the original students had discontinued their education at Western University; some to attend another institution, others to temporarily postpone their university studies. All of the students originally admitted to Project Access were contacted by letter and/or phone and asked for their assistance in this study. All twenty-nine of the students who remained at Western University and the three graduates agreed to participate in interviews about their experiences at the university and in Project Access. In addition, twenty of these students further participated in a roundtable discussion of the findings synthesized from interviews of the larger group.

Data Collection and Analysis

Data collection consisted of three phases, engaging both qualitative and quantitative methods. In phase 1, we collected and analyzed academic and demographic information on the forty-three students originally accepted into Project Access during 1991 or 1992. The data included current status in science, changes in declared majors, high school performance records and the science courses taken, scholastic achievement test scores, AP test scores, high school class rank and GPA, high school achievements and awards, college academic history, laboratory assistantships, college GPA, and total credit hours earned. The data were analyzed quantitatively and qualitatively to elicit demographic patterns such as average GPAs, numbers of majors declared, specific science field chosen, academic year of attrition, and science success rates.

In phase 2, we spent over two months investigating the personal and academic relationships and events that shaped the experiences of the thirty-two women who remained at Western University. All the women were interviewed at least once, and several as many as five times, in order to help us determine critical factors in MES persistence. The women were urged to speak candidly and reflect upon the details of their lives as they related to their college career. Adhering to symbolic interactionism, we sought to understand the day-to-day interactions and events that impacted their decisions to persist. We were interested in their interpretations of the academic context and their perceptions of the personal and academic relationships that were important to their success. By using a constant comparative analysis of the interview transcripts, we devised a coding system for variables related to female MES achievement. These variables were then clustered into three broad categories: school factors, personal factors, and external factors (see appendix).

In phase 3, we conducted a roundtable discussion with twenty of the students who were willing to participate further in the study. The roundtable was designed to allow the participants, in a group forum, to discuss again their experiences as female students in an MES undergraduate program and as participants in Project Access. In addition, the roundtable allowed us to seek confirming or disconfirming evidence for our emerging hypotheses. The participants were presented with the results of our interview analysis (phase 2; see the appendix) and asked to organize and weigh the importance of the various factors. The roundtable discussion was recorded, transcribed, and used to substantiate or call into question our previously formed categories of variables.

Although intelligence, motivation, and family support were all important factors in female MES success, we have selected to highlight factors that were found to have an immense impact on the participants' academic success and persistence (as revealed in phase 3) and have a high degree of potential for intervention by educators and administrators. Specifically, in this essay we address three broad categories of variables, synthesized from the factors identified in phases 2 and 3 of this study, that impacted female MES persistence: personal associations, pedagogy, and related work experiences.

Results and Analysis

We were surprised by the positive attitudes that the participants shared with us concerning their education. We heard very few complaints or experiences of sexism, gender discrimination, or overt bias. One student reported: "It's been fairly positive. At some point there has been indifference. But we have not found real opposition anywhere." The review of the literature may have predisposed us to believe that our group would experience significant barriers to these historically male-dominated fields. The positive disposition of our population may have also been related to their successes—they had less reason to criticize the system. On occasion a few of the participants complained of fellow students who were sexist; however, the evidence led us to conclude that the MES field was generally encouraging toward women at Western University.

The analysis of the academic and demographic information about the Project Access students revealed a consistent pattern of backgrounds and accomplishments. Both the total group of forty-three and the subgroups that were interviewed in phases 2 and 3 were found to be intelligent and achievement-oriented, with no statistical differences among the groups. Their average scores included a 3.9 high school GPA, a 29 on the ACT, and a 3.5 college GPA. A significant aspect of the participants' academic profiles was their extensive involvement in high school science and mathematics courses, suggesting that high school course work and grades may be a good indicator of MES success in college. Of the thirty-two participants in phase 2, twenty-five students (78 percent) eventually graduated in an MES field, while six elected to change to a major outside this area. Of these twenty-five graduates, seven (28 percent) expressed the intention to pursue a graduate MES degree. These persistence statistics are higher than those reported for men and women at highly selective institutions (61 percent and 46 percent, respectively; Strenta et al. 1993) and suggest that participation in Project Access and other factors at Western University potentially impacted the persistence of these women.

Through phases 2 and 3 we identified and confirmed various aspects within the environment and culture of MES disciplines that benefited the participants' persistence. The women provided consistent descriptions and reactions to their environment that confirmed the need for personal associations, the incorporation of collaborative teaching methods, and the establishment of internships and work-related programs supported by the curriculum. Each of these variables will be discussed in detail.

Personal Associations

One of the primary goals of Project Access was to acclimate the program participants to the university context. An important part of that acclimatization was the establishment of relationships among these young MES majors and with members of the university community. The participants in this study overwhelmingly agreed that the most beneficial aspect of Project Access, and a critical component in their MES persistence, was the fostering of relationships. Primary among these relationships were those with the other female MES majors, as noted by Robyn: "I think that having study groups with friends was probably the most valuable part about the Access program. I've kept a lot of those relationships. It's really nice when you're in a class struggling that you have some other people to help you out." Nancy agreed:

> It really helped to get into the math classes and already know other
> girls in the class and have someone to study with for the first couple
> of years. Because there will be maybe two girls in the whole class,

out of fifteen or twenty. I mean you could feel like you're all alone,
but we get together and study and we're all in sciences and it was nice
to have some friends.

The women we interviewed relied heavily on the emotional support
that came from knowing other women MES majors. This support, often
in the form of study groups, also provided academic assistance. For instance, Karen's strategy was to form a study group with the smartest member in the class: "I'm a bit slow, so I like to find someone that is really bright
to study with. That way I have two chances to pick up the material." Betty
also relied heavily on her peers for conceptual understanding: "I think one
of the best things is getting to know people in your class, because that can
make a big difference. When you don't understand something, to be able
to call somebody up." While most of the students involved with a study
group became associated with the group through their own initiative,
many of the groups were formed through Project Access associations.
Those students not fortunate enough to have participated with a cohort or
study group struggled with feelings of isolation and frustration. As Betty
noted, "I would have to give the credit for my graduation to my friends
[study group]."

In addition to the use of study groups, these women used fellow female MES majors as peer mentors. Although there was no formal program
established to bring all female MES majors together, these women often
informally exchanged comments on teacher and laboratory preferences or
discussed career issues. Annie's strategy was to ask a lot of questions, especially of friends who had already been through a particular course: "I
found it very helpful to ask questions about different classes and teachers.
I would even ask the group ahead of us if we could get their notes for comparison." When asked what advice she would give to a future science major, Bernice responded, "I'd have her first try and talk to a lot of the people who may be seniors or upperclassmen and get an idea of how to plan
and schedule and what to expect and ask as many questions as they can
think of about that field, about job outlooks."

An inventive idea of the Project Access participants was to establish the
use of e-mail as a means of communication and a form of peer mentorship.
The students were given each other's e-mail addresses at the conclusion of
the summer workshop and encouraged to keep in touch. For some students,

daily correspondence on a variety of issues acted as an important source of emotional and academic support from women in similar situations. The point is, regardless of the method, these women viewed support and common association as a prerequisite for success—taking advantage of support systems offered or creating systems when they did not exist.

In addition to relationships with peers, Project Access provided the students with the much appreciated opportunity to get to know university faculty and personnel. As Maria stated:

> I think the biggest benefit to me from the Access program was the self-confidence it gave me as far as you worked with these department heads and just with professors and realized, "Gosh, they're really nice people." I don't think I was as apprehensive to talk to them as I might have been had I just been in the class with 300 and never had that experience.

A key success strategy of the Project Access students was the purposeful development of relationships with their professors. The majority of the participants were unyielding in their commitment to succeed in their courses, made a conscious effort to get to know their professors, and would risk rejection in order to pursue a relationship that they felt could offer them assistance. As Mary explained: "I think it's important for students to get to know their teachers. I always liked the professors that would make themselves available and who were willing to work through the problems with you in their office. I always did better in their courses."

The professors involved with the program were willing to engage themselves with the students and were willing to dedicate extra assistance. Michelle said: "I think the biggest support for me came from the fact that there were professors and teachers that were interested in my success. That really impressed me and gave me confidence that I could do it." Bev attributed a professor's encouragement as a factor in her decision to persist: "Dr. Jones was there when I was ready to give up. He convinced me I could do it and that I was as smart as everyone else. He worked with me the entire quarter to help me get through calculus." Ricky agreed: "I think ... that they [Access professors] expected a lot, so we kind of had to fulfill their expectations and it kind of gave me a confidence that I could do it."

Associations were encouraged not only among the participants and professors but also with administrators, school counselors, and student service representatives as well. Bev noted: "I think the summer session helped me to get over my fear of college because I was really afraid that I was going to come from high school and not do well in college. They [Project Access] showed us where everything was and who to turn to when we needed help." In addition to learning the campus layout and the location of computers and library facilities, the Project Access students were introduced to a number of university programs and special services. Many of these programs were credited for lending support to the participants at critical points during their academic careers. For example, when Karen desperately needed a job, a campus organization called the Undergraduate Research Opportunities Program (UROP) came to the rescue: "I just about had to quit school because I couldn't keep my [off-campus] job and survive my class load. But then I heard that UROP hired students to work with faculty on their research.... It worked out really well." Minorities in Engineering, a program developed to foster the involvement of minorities and women in engineering disciplines, provided free tutoring, assistance in class scheduling, stress management and other weekly seminars, and assigned a mentor to each participant. It was this program that sustained Jane in her engineering endeavors:

> I wasn't making it in engineering. It was too tough and I was ready to give it up when I heard that the Minorities in Engineering provided assistance. So I enrolled and it literally saved me. I received hours of free tutoring and explanations, as well as a lot of encouragement and unconditional support. I give them all the credit for my survival.

The Access program also introduced the students to the Women's Resource Center during the summer workshop—a potential source of support if they ran into difficulty during their college career. Based on this awareness, a number of the participants turned to the center during trying times, including serious illnesses and cases of sexual harassment. Lori explained:

> During the second quarter of school I was having some serious medical problems and they were exacerbated by the stress of my classes. My professors were going to fail me because they didn't really believe that I was sick. It was lucky that I knew the director of the Women's Resource Center, because I called her and said, "This is the deal. You

know me, you know I'm not faking." So she called all my professors and took care of everything because I was so sick, I couldn't even do it. And it was such a big help that I didn't have to dig myself out of a failed quarter. And they would help me network with other people. They would say, "Oh well, I know this person at this office" and "You need to write this letter." They'd tell me exactly what I needed to do so that I didn't forfeit all my scholarships.

A primary benefit of Project Access and a critical factor in these women's MES persistence was the formation of positive personal associations within the university context. For example, prior to their freshman year—traditionally a lonely and rigorous time when attrition is particularly high (Alper 1993)—the students were assimilated, nurtured, and encouraged to develop important relationships with their peers, professors, and administrators. These positive associations added to their ability to collaborate as a community of learners, sustained them throughout their college experience, and often led to further opportunities in their field.

An important result of this study is the awareness by the women of the importance of and intense need for these personal associations in their current and future success. In fact, associations were so important that these students almost always availed themselves of programs that existed and created those that did not. The importance of establishing a firm support system as part of the undergraduate MES experience has been noted by others: Sadker and Sadker (1986) revealed the benefits that male students have long enjoyed from professorial attention and association, the Wellesley Report (Rayman and Brett 1993) emphasized the need for mentoring programs and role models, and Goldberger et al. (1996) highlighted the value of study groups, cohorts, and group collaboration, particularly for women.

Pedagogy

Most of the participants in our study stated that they learned more from professors who did not "just lecture." As Judy noted: "What doesn't work for me is when they stand in the front of the room and basically flip through the textbook. . . . They'll just . . . go page by page through the textbook, saying exactly what the text says." Karen concurred: "I think in a classroom, you get a lecture and stuff. But it doesn't really have meaning until you have a hands-on learning experience and see for yourself that this really works."

Our students referred to the need for practical and active learning experiences in the classroom. They agreed that interactive teaching methods and collaborative approaches promoted learning, while formal, didactic discourse or lecture formats were less effective. Nancy commented: "The best teacher I had was Dr. Lind. He was so interesting. He would involve the class in the discussion and teach us new knowledge using examples and real-life situations rather than just placing numbers on the board." Betty recounted a similar situation:

> I don't like memorizing. I like to learn. I took organic chemistry but I didn't even know what it was at first. I had no clue what was involved in it whatsoever. And it was so hard to get through it. The teacher made us memorize all these charts and stuff. He'd say, "Here is this chemical turning into this chemical." Okay, I'll memorize it, but what does it have to do with anything? And then later on I start working in labs and I realized I didn't know my organic chemistry and "this is what it's for" and man, I wished I knew it. I wished I could retake that class and learn it. When I heard about Dr. King's teaching and that it was very problem-based and problem-solution-based and that type of stuff, that's really why I decided to retake that class. This time I could remember, because I knew that these reactions are important and they're used all the time, and this reaction is in the body or whatever. I learned so much more just by the way he taught us.

Rogoff (1990), More (1992), and Geelan (1997) have discussed the benefits of collaborative teaching for both men and women. Interactive and collaborative teaching approaches increased the students' ability to understand the theories presented; they wanted teaching methods and lessons that involved them as learners. Our participants' persistence was positively influenced by experiential learning opportunities provided by laboratories and related work experiences. MES courses can be made more accessible to women by adopting problem-based learning models, interactive and collaborative styles of teaching, and group projects—all methods included under the umbrella of constructivist teaching methods (Rogoff 1990). Constructivism, "a major influence in contemporary science and mathematics education" (Mathews 1997, 5), encourages teachers to actively involve the learner in the construction of knowledge (Darling-Hammond and Snyder 1992). Social constructivist theory encourages teachers to recognize the situated nature of learning and the complexities of the classroom, where teachers and students are active meaning-makers who continually develop contextually oriented meaning, creating a community of learners (Rogoff 1990; Vygotsky 1978). Social constructivists support the tenet that the learning experience must be situated or contextualized and shared among the community of learners (Geelan 1997). The idea that learning is a social act and that meaning is worked out in the context of one's environment is consistent with our study participants' descriptions of how they best learned to understand scientific concepts.

Influenced by John Dewey, experiential learning has been promoted as an important tool in expanding knowledge through the use of interaction and the incorporation of practical activity. Dewey believed that it was only through experience that learning occurred, and that knowledge was gained through the "transformation of experience" (Dewey 1938). More (1992) has said that the advantage of experiential learning is that knowledge is derived through the analytical and synthesized efforts of the learner. Our participants claimed that they needed to understand the practical applications of the discipline's principles and that they learned more when they obtained hands-on experience, an idea consistent with the experiential model of learning.

Work-Related Experience

One of the more significant results of this study was the impact of related work experiences on the participants' decision to persist. Our interviews helped us realize the effective relationship between school and related work experience. Jane spoke of her self-initiated summer internship as the one saving aspect in her college engineering career: "Working in the field built my confidence because I realized that I could apply the principles I learned in school to real life and that they made more sense." Julie talked of the positive relationship between work and school: "I think that my work gave me an edge in my schooling because I had learned the material once in class and then I'd see the practical aspect of the principle applied to my work." Work-related internships provided the participants with the chance to apply their education in a new environment. Nancy claimed, "It [work] reinforces the basics." Annie agreed: "My job really helps me to kind of solidify my skills. I hear something in class and then it's kind of accentuated at work."

There was a high degree of correlation between those who had pursued involvement with their potential industry and the relative rate of persistence in MES. Thirteen of the twenty women who attended the roundtable discussion had been involved in related work experiences. Several of the students explained how these experiences encouraged them to remain in their MES field. Betty explained how the expertise she gained from the lab translated into greater motivation toward her discipline:

> I think that [working in the] lab has had a big influence on what classes I like too, because . . . it's really easy to relate back and forth [from lab to class], it's more practical. I don't think I would understand half as much as I do now after seeing how everything applies in the laboratory. And I know I wouldn't be applying to graduate school.

Karen agreed:

> I wouldn't have remained in chemistry, but working in this company has kind of shown that there is more than just the books. What's kept me in school is the fact that I can graduate and then I can go do something else. Because at work what I do makes more sense than what I see in the books, and it's important to me to see how everything is related to the real world.

The aspects of practicality and application as they apply to work situations were important to the women we studied. There was a certain urgency for them to see the outcomes and necessity of the concepts they were learning. While occasionally a student was able to find a job through the help of her department, the majority of these placements were self-initiated and pursued by the student without the aid of the career center or Project Access. Work-related programs promoted additional learning and knowledge of the subject matter by combining the practical and the theoretical, and they increased the confidence of these women in their chance of success in their chosen field.

The philosophy behind the idea of internships, apprenticeships, or any form of work-related experience is based on the experiential model of learning. Research on the benefits of internships has found that such work-related opportunities improve academic performance by encouraging the student to combine school knowledge and practical skills (Milstein, Bobroff, and Restine 1991). Prawat (1992) found that apprenticeship arrangements, where novices work directly with expert practitioners, are a more powerful learning experience than the classroom; in fact, the apprenticeship system has been put forth as the most effective way to foster learning (Dewey 1938). Daresh (1986) determined that field-based learning allowed students to experience the culture and test their commitment to their future career.

Research that suggests that women learn in experiential ways supports the incorporation of more work-related opportunities into the college curriculum. Feminists advocating a more holistic or humanistic education (Belenky et al. 1986) thus support the philosophy of experiential learning. Work-related internships provided the participants in our study with an opportunity to apply their school knowledge, to move from theory to practice. The practical application of their trade in a "real" situation not only confirmed the knowledge and theories they had been taught in college but also gave them the opportunity to experience how abstractions related to the concrete.

Discussion

The Traditional Culture of MES

Traditional MES programs have followed a sequential curriculum designed to prepare students on an individual basis for MES careers; that is, institutions were established to train the workforce. The system is automated and impersonal, with students progressing in stages from one course to the next and thus experiencing separate systems and fragmented pieces of knowledge. The classes are large, the curriculum is rigorous, and the labs are challenging. The process is linear in that little effort has traditionally been made to connect the academic world to the world of work until after graduation, at which point industry often believes that real job training begins.

Higher education gives center stage to disciplinary content and assumes that professors who research can teach in a formidable method that would provide knowledge to the standard learner. Traditional MES objectives have sought to transmit scientific knowledge and theoretical understanding through standardized lecture formats with subject-area criteria and norm-reference testing procedures. The behaviorist model of teaching has greatly influenced scientific pedagogical models: the student is considered to be "value-free" and thus accepts the knowledge as truth and learns through memorization of the objective, scientific truths. Pedagogical methods in science often emphasize the learning of fundamental principles, including scientific laws and their descriptions, classifications, generalizations, and quantifications.

The issue of quality teaching remains hotly contested. It has long been understood within higher education that a professor's reputation, tenure, and status are determined more by research than by teaching. Despite teaching awards and various initiatives to improve undergraduate education, the culture of higher education continues to reward research over teaching. Large institutions are often charged with unwillingness to change so-called institutional norms of pedagogy (Rosser 1990; Sadker and Sadker 1985a). The traditional methods of pedagogy that these institutions advocate and the "regularities" of schooling defeat "ambitious innovation," according to Biklen and Pollard (1993). Tobias (1990) has documented that traditional university pedagogy actually erodes interest in science among both women and men.

Cultures That Support Women

In contrast to traditional MES cultures, feminist theory encourages the development of a "community of learners" who share in the experience of learning (Goldberger et al. 1996). This model encourages professors to openly discuss their disciplines' principles and reject statements of "truth." Appropriate pedagogical techniques are interactive work assignments, reflective sessions, development of cohorts, two-way conversations, peer-reviewed papers, and shared learning experiences. The implementation of connected and collaborative teaching methods as proposed by feminist researchers and supported by this research would help female students to achieve higher levels of learning (Belenky et al. 1986) and understand the connection and rationale of the theories presented.

In domains where women represent the minority, it is particularly valuable to investigate female knowledge construction. Rosser (1990) argues that educators need to pursue alternative approaches to traditional androcentric pedagogical methods in order to advance competent women scientists. Research is establishing that women's modes of thought and women's methods of knowledge construction are different from those of their male counterparts (Belenky et al. 1986). Women achieve higher levels of learning through collaborative processes and experiential learning than through passive assimilation (Hollingsworth 1992). The idea that collaborative learning is beneficial to women is supported by cultural feminism, which emphasizes a holistic and collective orientation to the world and work (Gilman 1988), as well as feminist epistemology, which considers experience as knowledge (Belenky et al. 1986).

The historical development of higher education as a male institution has adversely affected female progress and has resulted in a gender barrier. When a woman enrolls in a college mathematics, engineering, or science course, her instructor is most likely a man. Historically, science has been dominated by men, their experiments, their achievements, and the benefits they provided to the development of our civilization. When one thinks of famous scientists, Galileo, Einstein, and Newton come to mind. With the exception of Marie Curie, all the heroes are men. The academic community (which was, after all, established by men for the purpose of educating men) has come under attack for not considering women's processes of understanding and for assuming that pedagogical techniques appropriate for men are suitable for women (Belenky et al. 1986; Gilligan 1982; Goldberger et al. 1996). Gilligan (1977; 1982) has called for an inclusion of women's voices in the educational process.

Feminist researchers have determined that traditional pedagogy has adverse effects on female college students. Tobias (1990) claims that capable female students reject science degree programs because of their competitive nature and lack of interactive learning opportunities. Deep-seated epistemological gender differences may make the science curriculum incompatible with the ways women think, which may account for women's lack of self-confidence in science-related subjects (Sonnert and Holton 1995). Rosser (1990) agrees that traditional science pedagogy is inherently more advantageous to men than to women, thus decreasing interest among female students who have science ability.

The Project Access Microculture

The participants in this study spoke of the need for a more involved education—one that considered their learning patterns and their need for interaction among the members of the MES community. Persistence was high among the Project Access participants because of the support system developed with professors and peers. Initially the Access participants used the structures provided by Access to develop associations that were determined critical to their continuation. Throughout the educational process, and based on their positive experience with Project Access, the participants were instrumental in designing an environment that enhanced their learning ability. They initiated work opportunities, furthered relationships with professors, developed study groups, sought role models, and created e-mail lists, all in an effort to enhance their educational experience. In developing an academic microcosm, Project Access fostered connections and the support system that furthered enabled the participants to modify the traditional MES environment to create their own community of learners.

Recommendations

The analysis of our data indicates that factors within the university context play an important role in female students' pursuit of a science-related degree. Our analysis identifies women's desire for a more holistic educational experience. Early intervention and encouragement can break the gender barrier to a career in science. The following are specific recommendations for changing the culture of higher education and MES pedagogy.

Most of our participants reacted positively to mutual association with professors, female friends, advisors, study partners, mentors, cohorts, administrators, and employers and to other beneficial relationships. The rigorous curriculum and academic challenge they faced motivated the women to seek positive support. Their endurance and sustenance depended on this network and the proximal relationships they developed. Thus it is critical that educators foster positive associations and support networks within the university setting (including involvement with the women's resource center and career center) in order to help female undergraduates pursue a more personalized and interconnected educational experience.

The student-professor relationship should further this personalization process. Professors—male or female—who were willing to devote their time to the development and growth of the student beyond the classroom setting were critical to the success of the female participants. Our research suggests that professorial associations are one of the most beneficial personal associations a student can enjoy—as a source of emotional support, knowledge enhancement, academic advising, added confidence, letters of recommendation, encouragement, and other support. Universities need to assist professors in the development of positive student association and provide them with effective mentoring methods. Recognition for such involvement would be a positive motivation for faculty who are reluctant to give of themselves outside the classroom. Administrators should encourage professors to extend their office hours, soften their approaches (to lessen the intimidation factor), and become interested partners in the educational process.

Those participants who engaged in study groups or cohort involvement credited them with their success. The development of study groups was enhanced through the use of required assignments and collaborative teaching methods that encouraged association among class members. Instructing faculty on effective methods of fostering student study groups and cohorts is important, as is providing an appropriate setting for informal study units to form. Structured assignments, with time frames and instructor-organized groups, accommodated those who had difficulty forming their own study groups and assisted them in the assimilation process.

Preparing MES professors to use constructivist teaching methods and mentoring would also greatly benefit the student population. The instruction in science, engineering, and mathematics courses could be improved with the adoption of interactive and collaborative styles of teaching. Professors need to evaluate their pedagogical techniques and the formal processes of MES education, consider female ways of knowing, and adjust their methods to incorporate female perspectives.

Related work experiences had surprisingly positive and significant effects on the development and persistence of all the Access students who had this opportunity. Those involved in their future trade as interns developed a broader perspective and understanding of their schooling experience. The practical aspects of their work or laboratory experience provided a needed balance to the theoretical knowledge stressed in college courses and contributed to their desire to continue. The development of work, intern, and laboratory opportunities within the university environment should be encouraged.

Conclusion

An important theme in the persistence of the participants in this study was directly related to their ability to connect personally and academically with their environment. These positive associations enabled them to more easily grasp and assimilate theoretically based knowledge. The students re-acted favorably to more personalized forms of education, such as intern-ships, professorial associations, collaborative teaching methods, study groups, and cohorts; these elements offered a more connected experience and were a catalyst for students' continuing their studies. It is obvious that female learners have distinct needs when it comes to MES education.

The traditional modes of MES education at the college level are often in conflict with the needs of the female MES population. Large classrooms, limited professorial office hours, lack of scholarship money, emphasis on research rather than teaching, few practical applications, and a general lack of connectedness and personalization are all contributing factors in the high attrition rate of female MES students. Our recommendations move from a linear model of student production to a holistic model that con-siders many aspects of education, including the cultural environment of the classroom, the university setting, and career possibilities, as well as the external and personal factors that impact the individual.

In evaluating our results we must remember that these women were considered high achievers and were recruited on the basis of their past per-formance. The factors we have identified, however, would potentially con-tribute to the persistence of any undergraduate woman who desired to pursue a degree in MES. In fact, we believe that marginal students would benefit the most from an academic support network, collaborative peda-gogies, and work-related experiences. While our recommendations target the specific needs of women, it is anticipated that their implementation may potentially decrease undergraduate MES attrition for both genders.

Appendix: Factors Affecting Female Persistence in Undergraduate Math, Engineering, and Science Majors

School Factors
positive association with professors
role models
curriculum plan—tracks, good labs, study groups
lab research—related to area of interest, professor available, support, co-ordinators as mentors
good teaching—good explanations, problem-centered, interesting

special programs (Project Access, Minorities in Engineering, Undergraduate Research Opportunities Program)

support agencies (Women's Resource Center, career services, financial aid)

scholarships

on-campus living—roommates, positive association with others in same major

high-school preparation—AP classes, honors, math foundation, science fairs, gifted program

secondary education teachers—mentors, academic foundation, confidence-building, advisors

External Factors

family support—science and academics valued, financial assistance, similar background, encouragement

work-related experience

study groups—crucial for freshman year

female friends—support network, emotional and academic

role model—family, advisor, boss, career-day speaker, or friend

multidimensional experience—well-rounded, balanced, good perspective, open-minded

Personal Factors

inclination

natural ability

confidence

determination

career outcome

References

Alper, J. 1993. "The Pipeline Is Leaking Women All the Way Along." *Science* 260: 409–11.

Astin, A. W., H. S. Astin, and E. L. Dey. 1992. *Undergraduate Science Education: The Impact of Different College Environments on the Educational Pipeline in the Sciences.* Los Angeles: Higher Education Research Institute, UCLA.

Belenky, M., B. Clinchy, N. Goldberger, and J. Tarule. 1986. *Women's Ways of Knowing.* New York: Basic Books.

Biklen, S. K., and D. Pollard, eds. 1993. *Gender and Education.* Chicago: National Society for the Study of Education.

Daresh, J. C. 1986. "Field-Based Educational Administration Training Programs." *Planning and Changing* 17: 107–18.

Darling-Hammond, L., and J. Snyder. 1992. "Curriculum Studies and the Traditions of Inquiry: The Scientific Tradition." In *Handbook of Research on Curriculum*, ed. P. W. Jackson, 137–50. New York: Macmillan.

Dewey, J. 1938. *Experience and Education*. New York: Collier Macmillan.

Ehrhart, J. K., and B. R. Sandler. 1987. *Looking for More than a Few Good Women in Traditionally Male Fields*. Washington, D.C.: Association of American Colleges.

Erickson, F. 1986. "Qualitative Methods in Research on Teaching." In *Handbook of Research on Teaching*, ed. M. C. Wittrock, 201–23. 3rd ed. New York: Macmillan.

Geelan, D. R. 1997. "Epistemological Anarchy and the Many Forms of Constructivism." *Science and Education* 6: 15–28.

Gilligan, C. 1977. "In a Different Voice: Women's Conceptions of Self and of Morality." *Harvard Educational Review* 47: 481–517.

———. 1982. *In a Different Voice: Psychological Theory and Women's Development*. Cambridge, Mass.: Harvard University Press.

Gilman, C. 1988. "The Home (1903)." In *Feminist Theory: The Intellectual Traditions of American Feminism*, ed. J. Donovan, 45–48. New York: Continuum.

Goldberger, N. R., J. M. Tarule, B. M. Clinchy, and M. F. Belenky. 1996. *Knowledge, Difference, and Power*. New York: Basic Books.

Hollingsworth, S. 1992. "Learning to Teach through Collaborative Conversation: A Feminist Approach." *American Educational Research Journal* 29: 373–404.

Hyde, M. S. 1997. "A Case Study of Undergraduate Female Students Majoring in Math, Science and Engineering: An Analysis of Persistence and Success." Ph.D. diss., University of Utah, Salt Lake City.

Kahle, J. B. 1990. "Why Girls Don't Know." In *What Research Says to the Science Teacher—the Process of Knowing*, 55–67. Washington, D.C.: National Science Teachers Association.

Kahle, J. B., and M. K. Lakes. 1983. "The Myth of Equality in the Science Classroom." *Journal of Research in Science Teaching* 20: 131–40.

Mathews, M. R. 1997. "Introductory Comments on Philosophy and Constructivism in Science Education." *Science and Education* 6: 5–14.

Miles, M. B., and A. M. Huberman. 1994. *Qualitative Research*. 2nd ed. Thousand Oaks, Calif.: Sage Publications.

Milstein, M. M., B. M. Bobroff, and L. N. Restine. 1991. *Internships Programs in Educational Administration*. New York: Teachers College Press.

More, D. T. 1992. "Perspectives on Learning in Internships." In *Internships: Perspectives on Experiential Learning*. ed. A. Ciofala, 11–20. Malabar, Fla.: Krieger Publishing.

National Science Board (NSB). 1993. *Science and Engineering Indicators*. Washington, D.C.: U.S. Government Printing Office.

———. 1995. *Science and Engineering Indicators*. Washington, D.C.: U.S. Government Printing Office.

Pallas, S. M., and K. L. Alexander. 1983. "Sex Differences in Quantitative SAT Performance: New Evidence on the Differential Course Work Hypothesis." *American Educational Research Journal* 20: 165–82.

Prawat, R. S. 1992. "Teachers' Beliefs about Teaching and Learning: A Constructivist Perspective." *American Journal of Education* 100: 354–95.

Rayman, P., and B. Brett. 1993. *Pathways for Women in Science: The Wellesley Report,* part 1. Wellesley, Mass.: Center for Research on Women.

Rogoff, B. 1990. *Explanations of Cognitive Development through Social Interaction: Vygotsky and Piaget.* New York: Oxford University Press.

Rosser, S. V. 1990. *Female-Friendly Science: Applying Women's Studies Methods and Theories to Attract Students.* New York: Pergamon Press.

Sadker, D., and M. Sadker. 1985a. "Is the Classroom O.K.?" *Phi Delta Kappan* 66: 358–61.

———. 1985b. "Sexism in the Schoolroom of the '80s." *Psychology Today* 66: 25–27.

———. 1986. "Sexism in the Classroom: From Grade School to Graduate School." *Phi Delta Kappan* 68: 512–15.

Seymour, E. 1995. "The Loss of Women from Science, Mathematics, and Engineering Undergraduate Majors: An Explanatory Account." *Science Education* 79, no. 4: 437–73.

Sonnert, G., and G. Holton. 1995. *Who Succeeds in Science? The Gender Dimension.* New Brunswick, N.J.: Rutgers University Press.

Strenta, C., Elliott, R., Matier, M., Scott, J., and Adair, R. 1993. *Choosing and Leaving Science in Highly Selective Institutions: General Factors and the Question of Gender.* Seattle: University of Washington Press.

Tobias, S. 1990. *They're Not Dumb, They're Different.* Tucson: Research Corporation.

Tobin, K., and J. J. Gallagher. 1987. "The Role of Target Students in the Science Classroom." *Journal of Research in Science Teaching* 24: 61–75.

Vockell, E. L., and S. Lobonc. 1981. "Sex-Role Stereotyping by High School Females in Science." *Journal of Research in Science Teaching* 18: 209–19.

Vygotsky, L. S. 1978. *Mind in Society: The Development of Higher Psychological Processes.* Cambridge, Mass.: Harvard University Press.

Perspectives from a Female Undergraduate Student on Successfully Integrating Learning and Researching Science with Leading Organic Chemistry Workshops

**Nermana Ligata and
Madeline Adamczeski**

Introduction

Although we realize that organic chemistry can be a major challenge and in some cases a stumbling block to students in achieving their career goals, [1] this subject also serves as a cornerstone to many scientific, technological, and medical advancements.[2] Conveying this message and teaching the subject matter in an interesting way, one that can be understood by both male and female sophomore organic chemistry students, is and has been a formidable challenge. Further, it is becoming increasingly clear that there exists a strong need to change the way science is taught in order to appeal to both male and female students. [3] Organic chemistry workshops offer students a novel approach to hone problem-solving strategies and develop effective communication skills in a nonintimidating atmosphere.[4] This approach offers new pedagogical techniques for reform of traditional teaching methods for a variety of related disciplines at diverse institutions (e.g., colleges, universities, and institutes of technology),[5] techniques that are potentially more "female-friendly,"[6] attracting and retaining women in chemistry, yet also retain their appeal for male students.

Organic chemistry workshops are one-hour weekly sessions in which eight or fewer students, facilitated by a peer group leader, actively engage in the learning process. These workshops offer students with a variety of learning styles a novel approach to honing problem-solving skills in a non-intimidating atmosphere. Workshops are viewed by students as a safe haven in which to engage in a collaborative effort to solve problems. Students learn to develop problem-solving strategies not only from their peer leaders but also in collaboration with their colleagues.[7] We have observed that the supportive atmosphere, due in part to the peer leader, plays a major role in allaying the feelings of being overwhelmed often demonstrated and documented by the students. In addition, workshop leaders inspire, instill student confidence, and promote and encourage speaking the language of chemists to foster interactions with and between students. It is also a time in which peer leaders serve as role models and have the opportunity to convey an appreciation, understanding, and enthusiasm for the subject matter.

The focus of this essay is to introduce and elaborate innovative strategies and new approaches in three areas—learning, teaching, and researching in chemistry-related disciplines—from the perspectives of a female undergraduate student (that is, Nermana Ligata), a peer leader, and a researcher, respectively, with emphasis on peer-led workshops in organic chemistry. We hope that these insights will encourage faculty to adopt and adapt similar initiatives in undergraduate courses they teach (e.g., chemistry, physics, mathematics, biology, computer science, environmental science, engineering, and geology), to assist both genders[8] in mastering all three areas, and to effectively emphasize breaking the gender barrier in science and technology. As a result of this perspective, we anticipate that the curricula and teaching techniques described herein may initiate new approaches and/or extend existing ones and thus make science more attractive to women.

It is our intention that, by assisting them to succeed[9] in these three areas, workshop participants, regardless of gender, race,[10] religion, nationality, socioeconomic background, and so forth, will benefit from these insights. The ultimate goal is that the science community reflect the diversity of backgrounds found in the general population.

Discussion

Both learning and teaching science-related courses can be intimidating, especially for female students. We believe that self-discipline and taking an active role in being responsible for one's learning, together with peer support and guidance, are essential tools for mastering important concepts in science. This, in fact, is the philosophy of the workshops that are proving to be an invaluable resource for students taking science courses such as organic chemistry. These workshops provide an opportunity to acquire other methods for solving problems, through the use of "peer brainstorming" or "think tank" panel discussions.

The intent of organic chemistry workshops is to enhance learning chemical concepts, problem-solving techniques, and verbal communication skills. Through collaborative efforts, workshop students solve problems. Together with the peer leader, students share different approaches to problem-solving and discuss organic chemistry concepts[11] and topics as they relate to everyday life experiences. Workshop participants have indicated through verbal feedback that both listening to their peers give a variety of methods to solve a single problem and explaining solutions to problems have enriched their learning experience and increased their repertoire of problem-solving techniques and strategies. Furthermore, the diverse nature of workshop participants provides a means for disseminating insightful learning techniques and sharing a wealth of knowledge beyond that discussed in the classroom. Responses from both students and peer leaders to surveys conducted at American University (AU) have been positive; such positive responses also have been noted by previous investigators using the workshop model.[12]

Workshop leaders take great pride in watching their students' knowledge and enthusiasm expand. For example, when a student says excitedly "I really understand this concept now," both the student and workshop leader feel a true sense of accomplishment.[13] From Ligata's perspective as a student workshop peer-leader, workshops have also proved rewarding, reinforcing her own knowledge of organic chemistry while enlightening her about new problem-solving techniques. Weekly sessions also provide the time and place to share advice on studying for course and national entrance exams, life experiences, or scholarly research and academic accomplishments and to discuss possible occupational opportunities in chemistry-

related fields—including information on co-ops, internships, work experience, and career-related matters. Summer research opportunities with local private or government-funded companies like the National Institutes
of Health (NIH), as well as contacts in the university career center and
other resources, may be suggested by peer leaders. Modes of compensation, whether through salaries or university credit toward academic degrees, are also discussed. However, the important focus is to motivate and
encourage those students who desire to pursue academic, laboratory vocations, and get firsthand experience conducting scientific research. An important factor to help students get in the door of a laboratory, especially
for female students, is to believe in themselves as scientists. This can be
achieved with self-confidence and competence, which we believe the workshop model encourages.

We are cognizant of the impact of gender issues on women and deeply
committed to the application of academic scholarship by women.[14] Participants in workshops led by women have agreed with Claude Bristol[15]
that women are naturally superb scientists because they are naturally analytical, have curiosity and observational powers, and have good communication skills. Female scientists who have made unique and significant discoveries and contributions to the field are discussed in workshops.
Workshop leaders encourage students of both genders to recognize their
abilities and to discuss the fact that women scientists continue to play a
positive role in scientific and technological advancements. As a peer leader,
Ligata found that these discussions about research and women in science
helped validate her own personal experiences and reinforce the idea that
women make good scientists, thus encouraging her own research pursuits
as a female scientist.

It is important to mention that the physical sciences remain professional
areas in which women still have not broken the gender barrier. A 1994 report from the National Research Council and references therein revealed
that even though women constitute 45 percent of the labor force, only 16
percent are employed as scientists and engineers,[16] with 12 percent in industry[17] and an even lower percentage of women scientists and engineers
in academics.[18] In addition, results of a 1991 study of 276 colleges and universities stimulated awareness that less than 40 of 400 recruitment and retention programs were aimed at female students or faculty in science or engineering.[19] Such statistics illuminate the facts that a gender barrier does

exist, with most scientists being male, and that learning, teaching, and researching in science may, indeed, reflect a masculine perspective.

As one would anticipate, female faculty and workshop leaders at AU have not been immune from experiencing gender bias, and some have had to conquer arduous obstacles in order to break through the glass ceiling in chemistry-related fields as students, teachers, and/or researchers. They readily share these experiences with their students. For example, as a workshop leader Ligata described for students her research experience at NIH and her enthusiasm for science, which escalated. She stressed that hands-on experience has many benefits and is a necessity for students interested in pursuing science-related careers. Such research experience provides a time in which students can put into practice and apply what they have learned. Students can gain firsthand insights through hands-on laboratory work, regardless of whether this is the career path they choose to pursue. These experiences also stress the importance of writing and communication skills for doing scientific research and being successful as a scientist.

After successfully completing the organic chemistry course, most peer leaders at AU pursue chemistry-related disciplines and successfully earn positions as scientific researchers in government, industry, and/or academic settings. Thus, peer leaders often share their excitement and research experiences with students during workshops. For example, leaders with research experience can address such student questions as, "How does one get hands-on experience as a scientist?" Responses vary greatly, but leaders stress that "It isn't necessarily whom you know but rather how you project yourself to the people you do know and the ones you meet." Other advice given is that "in science it is important to network since nearly every scientist's research involves collaborating with colleagues" and "an enthusiastic, articulate, and confident person is more likely to be asked to do an internship or get work experience than a nonchalant person, even though they know or have met the same person."

The workshop peer leader also helps students see science in its social context and connect what students learn to practical uses, everyday life experiences, and their environment. Thus students do not feel as detached from the material they are learning. This further helps to ameliorate the intimidation that students in science courses generally may feel. Students quickly learn that workshops involve group interaction and that everybody's input is a valuable contribution to everyone's overall learning.

Through workshops, we foster mutual respect and encourage students to listen to the way other students approach problems. For example, workshop participants believe that the workshop experience and curricula are invaluable and serve as vehicles for both learning and teaching the subject material.

Open communication also allows the students to share their fears and the learning blocks they experience with respect to learning organic chemistry. Their fears—usually feelings of being overwhelmed by the amount and nature of the material—are taken seriously. Through expressing these feelings that they may not be able to grasp it all, students are comforted to know that they all share similar fears, as did the workshop leader when he/she began his/her course of study. They are also comforted by the fact that each student's input during the workshops is part of a team effort in overcoming these fears. As workshop leaders, because we now understood what their fears are, we can find ways to respond to and eliminate them. Techniques such as visualization, tree diagrams, concept maps,[20] and so forth, are of great benefit in allaying these fears and addressing the learning of the subject matter. For example, tree diagrams and concept maps are initially constructed by the leader to demonstrate their format and utility. Next, each workshop student produces her or his own version. Such tools and other mnemonic devices have proved effective for both connecting the concepts and reactions and memory recall.

To avoid feeling overwhelmed by the sheer number of different reactions, reagents, and so forth, students are taught and encouraged to approach organic chemistry through effective organization of the material according to the fundamental similarities of reactions of individual functional groups and their mechanisms, rather than by compartmentalizing the information. Thus, from an understanding of the fundamental underlying principles of the properties of single atoms to the intricate complexities of intermolecular interactions of molecules containing a variety of functional groups, acquisition of a foundation of knowledge of organic chemistry becomes an exciting and thought-provoking subject.

Strategies and ideas discussed at workshops help visualize chemical concepts, which ultimately helps establish a solid foundation of knowledge. For example, describing a conceptual model of a group of negatively charged electrons as gray-colored dots flying in an octet formation around atoms represented by balls helps students see and feel the concept of resonance. Thus, students can gain an intuitive understanding using a visual approach that also enhances memory retention. Furthermore, as students' learning increases, higher-order thinking can lead to the understanding of more advanced chemical concepts.

Based on a working knowledge of the basic principles of organic chemistry, new concepts discussed in lecture are reinforced through practice by solving problems relevant to the newly introduced concept. Through workshop exercises and homework problems, problem-solving skills are enhanced. Students quickly learn that this approach is beneficial for a number of reasons, including the following:

1. A particular functional group found in many different compounds reacts similarly, so associations can be made.
2. Repeated problem solving allows for many of the reactions to become second nature. This builds confidence in learning abilities while simultaneously reducing the amount of time it takes to complete problems. This is particularly beneficial for making effective use of exam time, reducing the time required to complete the questions and therefore providing time to go back and check over the exam.
3. Working on the problems consistently and attending workshops has another advantage. By the time a student gets to the exam, it is like sitting down to do homework problems once more, which lessens the anxiety that exams can create. As a result of developing good test-taking strategies, a more relaxed atmosphere can be established, which then allows students to recall the material more quickly and easily. These efforts are rewarded with many benefits, including the reduction of time spent studying.

Overall, workshop experiences benefit both students and peer leaders in terms of success in learning, communicating, and applying chemical concepts. Additionally, workshop leaders' knowledge and confidence strengthen, which further benefits their research experiences and opportunities in science.

Conclusion

Participants of both genders find that the workshops are enriching, stimulating, and beneficial to their success in understanding and applying chemical concepts. The workshop leaders also feel that they benefit, in terms of applying what they have learned and engaging in scientific research. As well, peer leaders can share their research experiences and techniques of using mental pictures, tree diagrams, and so forth, to assist students in understanding chemical concepts. The students find such stimuli and interactions not only beneficial to their understanding but enjoyable. Students can form their own mental pictures and share them with the rest of the group, applying cartoon images and personalities to compounds and reactions as a way to understand and recall structures, reaction types, and mechanisms.

The workshops also include discussions of a variety of current topics covering chemistry and science. In general, students who have participated in workshops feel more confident with their abilities in organic chemistry. Confidence and competence are built from knowledge that arises from persistence in learning, with the assurance that there are a variety of tools and resources available to use in the process. During the course of the semester, students' fears about the course subside. Fear comes from not knowing about something and leads to insecurities about personal abilities. Through group brainstorming and reducing the material to manageable segments, the students can overcome their fears. They also can apply similar approaches to other courses. For example, several organic chemistry students who concurrently were taking courses such as genetics and cell biology formed their own workshoplike sessions. The organic chemistry workshops have proved to be beneficial not only for learning course material but also as effective vehicles to instill confidence about one's abilities to succeed in science.

Notes

We are grateful to Dr. David Gosser at the City College of New York, Pratibna Varma-Nelson at St. Xavier University in Chicago, Jack Kampmeier at the University of Rochester in New York, and the project evaluator, Leo Gafney, who provided invaluable assistance and support to the chemistry workshop project at American University. Currently, the workshop project at San José City College is supported by the National Science Foundation DUE-CCD through collaborations with Mark Cracolice at the University of Montana-Missoula, Jim Reed at Clark and Atlanta University, and Joseph Wilson at University of Kentucky; the University of California Santa Cruz-Education Partnership Center program with

Lisa Hunter; the San José State University-Math and Science Teacher Education Program; and a San José City College Partnership for Excellence grant.

1. E. Seymour, "The Problem Iceberg in Science, Mathematics, and Engineering Education: Student Explanations for High Attrition Rates," *Journal of College Science Teaching* 21, no. 4 (1992): 230–38.
2. M. D. George, S. Bragg, A. G. de los Santos, D. D. Denton, P. Gerber, M. M. Lindquist, J. M. Rosser, D. A. Sanchez, and C. Meyers, "New Expectations for Undergraduate Education in Science, Mathematics, Engineering, and Technology," in *Shaping the Future,* National Science Foundation publication no. 96–139 (Rockville, Md.: National Science Foundation, 1996).
3. For discussions on the masculine approach to the workshop that tends to exclude women, with an emphasis on the ways in which sciences is currently taught and practiced, see S. Harding and J. F. O'Barr, *Sex and Scientific Inquiry* (Chicago: University of Chicago Press, 1987); S. Harding, *The Science Question in Feminism* (Ithaca, N.Y.: Cornell University Press, 1986); and E. F. Keller, *Reflections on Gender and Science* (New Haven, Conn.: Yale University Press, 1985).
4. D. Gosser, V. Roth, L. Gafney, J. Kampmeier, V. Strozak, P. Varma-Nelson, S. Radel, and M. Weiner, *Workshop Chemistry: Overcoming the Barriers to Students Success* (New York: Springer-Verlag, 1996), 1430–71. This is also available in *The Chemical Educator* 1, no. 1, at <http://journals.springer-ny.com/chedr>. This work was supported by the National Science Foundation, NSF/DUE 9450627 and NSF/DUE 9455920. For more information on the Chemistry Workshop Project, please see <http://www.sci.ccny.cuny.edu/~chemwksp>; and D. Gosser and V. Roth, "The Chemistry Workshop Project: Peer-Led Team Learning," *Journal of Chemical Education* 75 (1998): 185–87.
5. P. McIntosh, *Forum for Liberal Education* 6 (1984): 2–4; M. Schuster and S. Van Dyne, *Harvard Educational Review* 54 (1984): 413–28; and M. K. Tetreault, *Journal of Higher Education* 5 (1985): 368–84.
6. S. V. Rosser, *Female-Friendly Science: Applying Women's Studies Methods and Theories to Attract Students* (New York: Pergamon, 1990); and S. V. Rosser, *Journal of General Education* 42 (1993): 191–220.
7. A. E. Black, "The University of Rochester Organic Chemistry Workshop Program: Summary Findings of a Pilot Program Evaluation," in *The Workshop Chemistry Project: Report to the National Visiting Committee,* 3rd meeting (Rockville, Md.: National Science Foundation, 1997), 182–201.
8. J. Gallos, "Gender and Silence," *College Teaching* 43, no. 3 (1995): 101–5.
9. Y. Lenzy and M. Adamczeski, "A Student's Success Story: Perspectives on the Peer-Led Organic Chemistry Workshop Model" (paper presented at the American Chemical Society 49th Southeastern Regional Meeting, Roanoke, Va., October 19–22, 1997); M. Adamczeski, K. Rositer, and P. Santos, "Preparing Future Science Teachers at San José City College through Peer-Led Chemistry Workshops: A Preliminary Study" (paper presented at the Math and Science Teacher Education Program Conference, Burlingame, Calif., November 13,

1999); M. Adamczeski, C. Graeber, K. Rositer, and P. Santos, "Preparing Future Science Teachers at San José City College through Peer-Led Chemistry Workshops" (paper to be presented at the American Chemical Society meeting in San Francisco, Calif., March 26, 2000).

10. W. E. Massey, "A Success Story amid Decades of Disappointment," *Science* 258, no. 13 (1992); C. West, *Race Matters* (New York: Vintage Books, Random House, 1994).

11. S. C. Nurrenbern and M. Pickering, "Concept Learning versus Problem Solving: Is There a Difference?" *Journal of Chemistry Education* 64, no. 6 (1987): 508–10.

12. D. Wedegaterner, "The University of Rochester Organic Chemistry Workshop Program: Surveys of Students and Workshop Leaders," in *The Workshop Chemistry Project: Report to the National Visiting Committee,* 3rd meeting (Rockville, Md.: National Science Foundation, 1997), 112–13.

13. M. B. Nakhleh, "Are Our Students Conceptual Thinkers or Algorithmic Problem Solvers?" *Journal of Chemistry Education* 70, no. 1 (1993): 52–55.

14. M. Rayner-Canham and G. Rayner-Canham, *Women in Chemistry* (American Chemical Society and the Chemical Heritage Foundation USA, 1998); N. M. Roscher and M. A. Cavenaugh, "Academic Women Chemists—Will They Be Major Players in the Twenty-first Century?" *The Chemist,* 1996, 33–36, and references therein.

15. C. M. Bristol, *The Magic of Believing: Women and the Science of Belief* (New York: Prentice-Hall Press, 1985), 132–55.

16. S. V. Rosser, *Women and Minorities in Science and Engineering: An Update,* National Science Foundation publication no. 92–303 (Washington, D.C.: National Science Foundation, 1992).

17. S. V. Rosser, *Women Scientists and Engineers Employed in Industry: Why So Few?* (Washington, D.C.: National Research Council, 1994).

18. N. M. Roscher and M. A. Cavanaugh, "Academic Women Chemists in the Twentieth Century," *Journal of Chemistry Education* 69 (1992): 870–73.

19. M. Matyas and S. Malcom, *Investing in Human Potential: Science and Engineering at the Crossroads* (Washington, D.C.: American Association for the Advancement of Science, 1991).

20. A. Regis, P. G. Albertazzi, and E. Roletto, "Concept Maps in Chemistry Education," *Journal of Chemical Education* 73, no. 11 (1996): 1084–88.

A Peer Mentoring Program for Underrepresented Students in the Sciences

Casey Clark, Ileana Howard, Sarah E. Lazare, and Doreen A. Weinberger

Background

In recent years, it has become increasingly apparent that the United States desperately needs to increase its scientifically literate workforce with new talent and expertise to compete in today's diverse and complex society. Despite this recognition, women and African Americans, Hispanics, and Native Americans continue to be significantly underrepresented in all science and mathematics fields, and particularly in the physical sciences and engineering. These individuals thus represent a critically underutilized national resource.

Federal government projections indicate that by the year 2000, the nation's workforce will be 47 percent female and 26 percent minority, and women and minorities will comprise 85 percent of new entrants into the workforce. Thus, women and African Americans, Hispanics, and Native Americans represent the largest single pool of candidates from which the nation can draw to meet the urgent need for a more diverse scientific and technologically literate workforce.[1] Presently women account for only 22 percent of scientists and engineers, although they represent the largest group of future workers. Most disturbingly, women of color comprise 18 percent of the U.S. labor force, yet represent only 6 percent of all employed scientists and engineers.[2]

Efforts to enhance women's and minorities' participation in technical fields over the past decades have yielded some positive results toward rectifying this imbalance.[3] However, it is well documented that women and underrepresented students take fewer upper-level mathematics and science courses in high school, and they earn far fewer bachelor's, master's and doctoral degrees in the sciences and engineering.[4] In the year 2000, one in three American students will be a minority, with African Americans, Hispanics, and Native Americans making up 90 percent of the nation's minorities.[5] It is thus imperative that ever more diligent efforts be made to address the deficit of people of color and women entering technical fields so that the education pipeline yields a larger and more diverse group of world-class scientists and engineers at all levels.

Women's colleges in general, and Smith College in particular, have historically demonstrated a special ability to train women scientists. Smith College, the largest private liberal arts college for women in the United States, has achieved national recognition for the caliber and diversity of students it attracts and for its high level of alumnae achievement. The college was founded in 1871 through a bequest from Sophia Smith, who envisioned a college where women would have the "means and facilities for education equal to those in our colleges for young men." Science has been an integral part of the curriculum since the college's founding, and Smith has had considerable experience and success in providing women with a supportive environment and inspiring role models for the study of mathematics and science. When compared to comparable coeducational institutions, Smith College has approximately three times the average number of women science majors, and almost twice that of other women's colleges. Smith also has had a distinguished record of sending graduates on for advanced degrees in science. According to the most recent *Baccalaureate Origins of Doctorate Recipients* (1993), Smith ranks in the top 3 percent of 925 private, four-year colleges in the number of graduates who have gone on to receive Ph.D.'s in science.[6]

The situation with regard to students of color is not so encouraging, however. In 1996, the student enrollment at Smith was 2,670, with 8.5 percent of this population African American, Latina, and Native American. Accordingly, the percentage of women of color majoring in the sciences is very low. Although this problem is not unique to Smith as a predominantly white institution, it is nonetheless a problem of serious concern. There are various reasons why these numbers are traditionally small: lack of role models; lack of interest in and misunderstanding of the sciences; inadequate advising; large introductory science classes in which students feel especially isolated; heavy course loads in the first few years; discouragement by low grades in the particularly difficult introductory courses; and students' being "over-encouraged to enter technical fields for which they were underprepared."[7]

Smith College is committed to rectifying this problem on its campus, and in the past several years, both faculty and students have taken steps to facilitate the recruitment and retention of underrepresented students in the sciences. In 1993, several faculty formed a Minorities in Science Working Group that organized a three-part series of workshops entitled "Beyond the Revolving Door: Students of Color in the Sciences." The workshops attracted thirty faculty members from seven science departments, in addition to several college deans and administrators. These sessions assisted faculty in understanding ethnic and cultural issues in the classroom, the experience of underrepresented students at a predominantly white institution, and the nature of mentoring relationships. In January 1995, Smith hosted the New England Conference on the Recruitment and Retention of Minorities in Science, a three-day event attended by ninety representatives from sixteen colleges and universities. This conference explored opportunities and strategies for faculty mentoring and presented strategies to improve the retention of minority students through dynamics that operate both inside and outside the classroom.

Simultaneously, student-led initiatives were developed and implemented, with the goal of creating vehicles through which women of color could begin to see themselves as an integral part of the scientific community. A student-run academic science group, the Union of Underrepresented Science Students (U.U.S.S.), dedicated to increasing the representation of students of color in the sciences, was established in 1994. Among other activities, U.U.S.S. sponsors a lecture series by women scientists of color, presents an information series on research opportunities for students, and works to foster better communication between faculty and students.

Program Description

In January 1995, the Peer Mentoring Program for Underrepresented Students in the Sciences was established at Smith College. The program was initially funded by a seed grant from the New England Consortium for

Undergraduate Science Education, and some college support. In the last several years, it has received partial funding from the General Electric Fund and from a four-year ongoing grant from the Howard Hughes Medical Institute. The primary goal of the program is to increase the participation of underrepresented students of color in mathematics and the sciences. The program offers a mentor (a more senior student majoring in math or science) for every underrepresented student of color who expresses an interest in the sciences. The program has grown each year since its inception: during academic year 1996–1997 there were fourteen mentors and twenty-five mentees as participants. The program's goals are to encourage more students of color to take science courses, and to ultimately major in the sciences; to raise the mentees' level of confidence and self-esteem; to introduce mentees to various campus organizations, resources, and research opportunities; and to facilitate communication with the faculty. It is important to note that the mentoring relationship does *not* have a tutorial component and that it is viewed as a partnership in which both mentor and mentee benefit and grow from their participation in the program.

Mentors are recommended by faculty and/or students. They must complete a formal application and are interviewed and subsequently selected by the program's administrators. The mentors are a diverse group including students of color, international students, and white students. One of the great strengths of the mentor group is its diversity and the bond that is established by coming together on a continual basis for a shared purpose. All mentors receive a modest stipend and participate in a six-hour training session in the fall of each year. A peer mentor is a nurturer, coach, advisor, role model, learner, advocate, and good listener. Each mentor typically has two mentees. The mentors meet at least once a week with each mentee and after each meeting complete a "mentor session report" that they share once a month with one of the program's administrators. These reports and monthly meetings help to document the progress and goals of each mentor/mentee relationship and enable the staff to get to know the mentors and to assist or intervene, if necessary, in problematic situations. The mentors also meet once a month as a group to share thoughts, concerns, and strategies for problem solving. These meetings are mandatory, and formal agendas are followed. The mentors also plan social activities for the entire group, such as bowling parties, picnics, informal dinners, or movie nights.

These gatherings enable the group to get to know each other in relaxed and informal settings and to develop and maintain ongoing contacts.

To alert first-year students of color to this mentoring opportunity, the program is presented at the annual Bridge Orientation Program for women of color, sponsored by Smith College in late August. All science faculty are sent information about the Peer Mentoring Program throughout the year and are encouraged to mention the program in their introductory classes in September. The first-year students who express an interest in being mentored attend an orientation meeting early in the fall where they learn about the goals of the program as well as the expectations and responsibilities of a mentor-mentee relationship. At this meeting the mentors give a brief presentation about themselves that includes a description of their academic and extracurricular interests, future career goals, and their reasons for participating in the program. An effort is made to pair mentors and mentees by preference and similar interests. We have discovered that this type of matching leads to greater success, although it is not always possible to honor every preference.

The program is too new to have any concrete statistics documenting the hoped-for improved retention of underrepresented students in the sciences, but mentor and mentee evaluations from academic years 1995–1996 and 1996–1997 have been positive. Out of a pool of twenty-three mentees in 1995–1996, eighteen stated that they intended to remain in the sciences, three were unsure, and two were interested in the humanities. In 1996–1997, from a group of twenty-four mentees, twenty-one remain in the sciences, two expressed an interest in a nonscience major before they entered the program and are still interested in the humanities, and one moved from a science to a nonscience major.

In light of these encouraging numbers, we believe that the Peer Mentoring Program has already had a positive impact on the college environment. The student mentees benefit from the encouragement, support, and guidance they receive to feel more prepared and comfortable at a predominantly white institution. The mentees gain the confidence needed to major in science and pursue their career aspirations while earning the respect of their peers. At the same time, the mentors take great pride in observing their mentees' growth and acquisition of new knowledge and understanding. Finally, Smith College benefits from increased retention and from a program that values and promotes diversity.

Mentor Training

There are five main goals of mentor training: (1) to develop a support network for the mentors; (2) to ensure that the mentors understand their role; (3) to alleviate mentors' anxiety regarding their role and responsibilities; (4) to build on the existing interpersonal skills and knowledge of the mentors; (5) to connect mentors to the available resources on campus. Training is an ongoing process that includes an initial in-depth training session, monthly group meetings, workshops, individual meetings with a program director, and weekly reports documenting the mentor-mentee relationship. During the training, mentors learn how they can provide each other with advice, information, and support. Mentors learn the most through sharing their experiences and developing their own approaches to problem solving by brainstorming ideas. Therefore, it is important for the mentors to contribute as much as possible, forming their own conclusions by using examples from one another's experiences.

Initial Training Program

In September, early in the fall semester, mentors attend a comprehensive six-hour training program at which they meet each other and the directors of the program. They are also introduced to their role, responsibilities, and resources. The training is broken into two sessions. The first three-hour session includes reading, writing, and role-playing exercises. These methods are all used as starting points for analysis and discussion, as well as for brainstorming approaches for intervention and resolution of problematic situations and encounters. The training draws on the experiences of each mentor and her perspective as a science student in her first year at the college. The participants discuss their role as mentors, the mentor-mentee relationship, racism and oppression, cultural differences, and responses to difficult problems. In recognition of the diverse backgrounds and experiences of the mentors, guidelines for respectful communication are discussed. These include active listening and patience, owning up to personal experiences and feelings, and asking questions of each other to clarify issues before making assumptions. In an initial exercise, mentors are asked to write out answers to questions such as: What would you have wanted as a first-year science student at Smith? What type of guidance and concrete knowledge would have been useful? What turned you (or a friend) away from the sciences? What worked well for you? How can we keep women of color in the sciences? This simple exercise serves as an ice-breaking activity that relaxes the atmosphere of training and immediately encourages a forum for interactive discussion. It allows the mentors to identify with one another's experiences, both positive and negative.

Next the explicit duties of the mentors are discussed. This is accomplished by posing to the group the question "What is mentoring?" In discussing their answers, the mentors themselves are able to piece together the responsibilities and expectations outlined in their job description, thereby gaining a clearer understanding of all the components of the mentor role.

The more general issue of "Why mentoring?" is then introduced. Using an article written by Adams and Adams (1993), underlying reasons for the low numbers of students of color in the sciences are addressed. The authors suggest that students lack access to important information and resources; they often have a fear of the unknown and a fear of failure; they lack network skills; they do not imitate the good habits and behavior of other students; they have more obligations outside of the science community than the average student; and they have limited contact with faculty.[8] After a discussion of the implications of these factors, the group ranks their importance as relevant to their own experiences. During the ensuing discussion, the mentors inevitably examine issues such as cultural and racial clashes that hinder communication between students and professors or peers, the lack of personal and familiar resources in the community, and the impact such clashes may have on self-esteem and motivation.

Other readings, including excerpts from "White Privilege: Unpacking the Invisible Knapsack,"[9] are used to help explore the ways society has influenced ideas of appropriate behavior and suitable professions for women and people of color. Mentors share how their self-esteem has developed in relation to internalized oppression and the pervasiveness of classism, racism, and sexism. They vociferously corroborate the findings of one study done by the Association for Women in Science on women of color who have had mentors: two of the most important outcomes of a mentor relationship are the enhanced self-image and self-confidence of the mentee.[10] This discussion and segment of training concludes with an examination of how each student views herself and her accomplishments: to whom does she attribute her successes and failures? Once a student begins to appropriately attribute responsibility for her performance, she is more able to recognize her abilities, further develop her skills, and ultimately change for the better.

The second three-hour session of the initial training focuses on more tangible advice. Mentors learn how to take care of themselves and learn more specifics of their roles and responsibilities as mentors such as problem solving, networking, and career strategizing. One important topic of discussion is the setting of boundaries. As occurs in any leadership position, demands are often placed on or asked of the mentor that she cannot fulfill. The training therefore presents strategies for time and stress management, including knowing when to say "no" and to reach out for help and advice before difficult situations arise. In this context, mentors advise each other on how to set clear boundaries for the mentor-mentee relationship. The available resources on- and off-campus are also discussed, so that when mentors feel they have reached their limit of effectiveness and ability, they are able to refer the mentee to a more appropriate person.

Within the mentor-mentee relationship several recurring problems often arise. These include: the mentee does not respond to mentor attempts to communicate (most common); the mentee loses interest in classes (often due to a variety of reasons—having difficulty with the material, feeling overwhelmed by expectations, experiencing feelings of isolation, or coping with an insensitive instructor); the mentee has difficult experiences outside of class (e.g., due to homesickness, roommate problems, insensitive community members, or harassment). The mentors are trained to be flexible in their responses and reactions to the above situations. In order to practice effective intervention, a large part of this training session involves role-play scenarios.

The role-playing is quite revealing and enjoyable, and it inevitably leads to the discovery of valuable insights for the mentors. During the discussions that follow the role-play, it has been productive to prompt the mentors to delve beneath the superficial responses. One-line answers are generally made more encompassing and exploratory by asking "why?" This helps to get at possible underlying and less obvious components of the situations acted out. Role-play situations used in training include: the mentee does not show further interest in the program after being paired with a mentor; the mentee and mentor do not seem to be well matched; the mentee experiences a hostile environment in class.

In the first of these scenarios, a mentee may not return mentor correspondence for a variety of reasons. These can include, but are not limited to, finding many other interests on campus; feeling intimidated by an upperclass student; feeling uncomfortable with a mentor younger than she (in the case of nontraditional age students); and not understanding the purpose of the program. In these situations, the mentor should attempt to initiate a conversation that will accomplish several things: bring the concerns of both the mentor and mentee out in the open; clarify the purpose of a support and advancement program; remind the mentee of the responsibility attached to the commitment she made; and address the issue of the mentee's workload and other commitments or activities in which she is involved, in order to help her balance her responsibilities with recreation and relaxation.

Occasionally the mentor-mentee partnership does not immediately "click." This can occur, for example, if the mentee's values and principles do not match those of the mentor, or if the mentor does not realize the scope of the mentee's experience or maturity and appears patronizing or unhelpful. This latter situation is especially of concern for mentors who mentor women significantly older than themselves. In such cases, it is important to do two things: discuss the situation with all the mentors—some may know the mentee and have helpful suggestions for working with her; and keep the conversation with the mentee directed to academics, time management, career opportunities, working with faculty, and any other concerns she voices. Although it is important for the mentor to plan activities and discussions for her meeting with the mentee, it is just as important to assess the mentee's position and preparedness to deal with specific issues and to follow her lead.

In the last scenario, a student may attribute an instructor's behavior to the way the instructor perceives the student ("My teacher doesn't like me because …"), and she will not continue to visit during office hours. When the student hears of positive interactions other students have had with the professor, in addition to blaming herself, she may blame her negative experience on assumptions about the professor's attitude toward whatever cultural group she belongs to. As a consequence, the student may start performing poorly, express feelings of isolation or dislike for the course, or even stop going to class. She tells the mentor she is uncomfortable with the professor, who she believes is biased in some way.

In role-playing this scenario, mentors are trained to look at how the mentee is responding to a situation in which she perceives that an individual (whether it be an employee of the college or another student) is racist, classist, sexist, or some other way biased. In this instance, it is most important to believe the student, and to validate her feelings, whether or not her conclusions of bias are in fact correct. The mentor should listen to the whole story and ask probing questions to get as thorough information as possible: What is it that makes the mentee believe she is being demeaned or dismissed? What are the explicit offensive behaviors (is it a direct attack or information presented in a lecture)? Has the mentee approached the offending individual about her feelings? After thoroughly assessing the situation, the mentor can work with the mentee to devise a plan to resolve the dilemma in a way most comfortable for the mentee.

If the severity of the incident is not too extreme, it may be appropriate for the mentor to present some alternative approaches for looking at the situation. This is sometimes difficult to do without appearing that she is dismissing the situation altogether; it is, therefore, usually more effective when included in follow-up meetings with the mentee. If, on the other hand, the incident seems quite serious, the mentor should make sure to include a discussion of the college's grievance procedure, the choices in referrals to college support systems, and a plan for coping and succeeding academically during the resolution of the situation. If the mentor does not feel comfortable in sorting through this information with the mentee, she can refer the student to one of the program directors. Follow-up meetings should take place regardless of the severity of the situation, and the mentor should report all progress to her supervising director.

During the role-play scenarios and subsequent discussions, the directors actively facilitate and guide the process. Special attention is given to the ways in which a mentor will look at a situation. It is crucial that the mentors learn to question the reasons for the behaviors of others before passing judgment or acting on a situation. The training session ends with a recap of the role of the mentor and a review of the structure of the program's events and meetings.

Monthly Group Meetings

Once a month, during both fall and spring semesters, mentors meet with each other and the directors as a group. This meeting has been integral to the development of a support network for the mentors. During the meeting, mentors primarily share concerns and accomplishments regarding the mentor-mentee relationships, share ideas for interesting activities, and advise each other on approaches to problematic situations. In addition, a forum for further mentoring and role modeling develops. The mentors are always asked to share their own personal accomplishments (presenting at a conference, completing a thesis) and struggles (searching for an internship, having a difficult time in class). Other mentors reply with praise, suggestions, and admiration. This results in a higher degree of respect for their peers and encouragement to continue through the more difficult times.

Workshops

During the academic year, further training is provided in the form of workshops, which are reflective of the needs of the current mentors and mentees. Workshop themes have included: how to use the internship room at the Career Development Office; how to use the Internet to find internships, grant money, fellowships, and so forth; how to improve study skills; and how to make more efficient use of time.

Monthly Individual Meetings with Directors

In order to ensure regular encouragement and guidance of the mentors, the directors meet individually with each mentor once a month. The directors coach the mentors in the mentor-mentee relationship and monitor their progress. Mentors file weekly session reports that track the activities, accomplishments, and concerns arising in the mentee relationship and that prompt the mentor to plan for future sessions. In addition to documentation, these session reports serve a second function in allowing the mentor and director to assess and plan for long-term goals. The directors not only monitor and give advice on the mentor's performance. They also make sure that she is managing her life in a way that will make her an effective mentor: by encouraging the mentor to pursue her own academic and career goals; by following the mentor's lead when it comes to discussing personal life; and by intervening if the mentor appears upset. The directors, in this way, serve as mentors for the mentors.

Looking Ahead

The obvious deficiency of the Peer Mentoring Program in its present guise is the lack of faculty involvement. We are intent upon expanding the current program to include science *faculty* mentoring of underrepresented students. Through a series of informal faculty gatherings, we are currently exploring ways to effectively accomplish this. Although there are a few standout schools that have formal and extensive faculty mentoring programs in place, these have been accomplished only with considerable institutional support—both financial and in terms of recognition of the substantial effort required on the part of involved faculty. The difficulty that many schools face is that there is limited institutional financial and administrative support, and limited acceptance of mentoring as an activity worthy of a faculty member's time. In addition, many science faculty are already heavily involved in directing thesis and independent study students during the academic year and research students during the summer (some of whom are underrepresented students of color), as well as devoting a substantial amount of time to their other academic duties and college responsibilities. In our postpresentation discussion with Sweet Briar conference participants, many voiced frustration with the academy "system" whereby "extraneous" activities (like student mentoring and outreach activities) are given little or no weight in making tenure decisions. Nonetheless, we are committed to finding ways for faculty members to have meaningful mentoring relationships with underrepresented students that will be an integral part of their faculty role.

As we have discussed at length, it is desirable and essential to target for mentoring those students who tend to drop out of the sciences disproportionately. While maintaining our focus on underrepresented students of color in the sciences, we would like to ultimately expand the peer mentoring program to other students who are thinking of majoring in the sciences. More often than not, women in science encounter similar difficulties and obstacles, regardless of their ethnic or cultural backgrounds.

Smith College is also proceeding with the development of a nascent engineering program. We have procured outside funding for summer research engineering internships, which have a faculty mentoring component during the period of the internship. As the number of engineering interns grows over the next several years, we will incorporate the more senior students as engineering peer mentors during the academic year, who will be trained along with the mentors in the current Peer Mentoring Program.

During the informal discussion following the presentation of this paper, we were reminded of an important fact. The demographics of the academic community in which the student finds herself can affect the degree to which she receives "natural" mentoring. Mentoring relationships with peers (or faculty) may occur more readily in some environments, and not at all in others. Thus, it will be necessary to consider the demographics and specific needs of the institutional community when planning a peer mentoring program. Finally, while it is true that a student may be able to fend quite well for herself, a peer mentoring program ensures that she does not miss out on all the opportunities available to her. She needs access to a campus network, which has traditionally been difficult for many women of color in the sciences to develop, and she needs at least one person who continually reminds her of her worth.

Reflections on the Peer Mentoring Program by Ileana Howard, Peer Mentor

"Mentoring," an important process that can enable students to succeed, especially in scientific fields, seems to be the recent buzzword in discussions of education. Much attention has been paid to the benefits of mentoring in the sciences, particularly in regard to the pairing of professionals with students in order to encourage and support them throughout their studies. One thing we have discovered in our group, however, is the value of peer mentoring. With a formalized program of structure and support in place, students can learn to form networks and assist each other.

I became involved in the Peer Mentoring Program two years ago as a mentee in my first year of college. At that time, the program was still in its first year. During my two years of involvement, I have had the opportunity to experience the roles of both mentee and mentor. I have watched the program evolve into a more secure and rooted entity in the college, and at the same time, I have evolved into a more confident person from my participation in it. Reflecting on my experience in the program, I can see the skills that I have learned from it have enabled me to persist and flourish in the academic environment.

The transition from high school to college held many new challenges for me, primarily because I was left responsible to find or create support systems to succeed. Having no experience like this before, I did not know exactly where to begin. My background at a small, single-sex, independent high school gave me a false sense of security concerning what college life would be like. Although I felt my academic preparation had been sufficient, I soon realized that this alone was not enough to succeed in my field of studies. The large size of the lecture classes made me feel small and insignificant. I was reluctant to approach my professors for fear of imposing on their time. Although I had been informed of several resources available for finding internships and academic help, I was not entirely confident about when and how to use them. Apart from the new academic stress upon me, I also had to contend with the financial and emotional stress associated with being the first in my single-parent family to move away and attend a four-year college. For me, as well as for other first-year students, this period was a very trying time. Just as I was discovering and developing my emerging identity as an individual, I found myself displaced in this foreign environment. This limited experience left me reeling and feeling lost.

Becoming a mentee allowed me to find my roots in this new arena. I heard about the mentoring program from a flyer in my mailbox. Enticed by the promise of ice cream and pop, I showed up at the organizational meeting, and soon afterwards was assigned to a mentor. I really enjoyed our relationship, and I feel that I benefited from it. My mentor shared with me her enthusiasm for the sciences and her confidence. She encouraged me in my endeavors and helped me to overcome obstacles that confronted me along the way. She never allowed me to proclaim defeat when the obstacles seemed insurmountable. We found that we shared not only academic interests but also similar family backgrounds to which we could relate. She helped to keep me motivated through the highs and lows of my first year. My commitment to the program provided a constant reminder of my larger goals and purpose in being at school. By the end of my first semester, I had become much more involved in academic-related groups, including compiling the newsletter for the American Chemical Society student affiliates; regularly attending the weekly brown-bag lunch presentations given by the chemistry department; and serving as the secretary of the Pre-Health Society. I also found my support network apart from academic life by becoming involved in other groups such as in my dorm, church, and the Latina organization on campus.

After my positive experience as a mentee in the program, I decided to apply for a position as a mentor in the following year. I was a little afraid that I would not be adequate, since I was still trying to find my own place in this environment and had my own challenges to face. I continued to struggle with the daunting class sizes and with shyness around certain professors. My mentor encouraged me to apply, reminding me that I did not have to be an ideal student to be a mentor, but rather I had to be willing to share my positive and negative experiences with my eventual mentee. I finally decided to apply for this reason and because I believed strongly in the purpose of the program.

Mentoring has been as rewarding as being mentored myself. The mentor-mentee relationship is flexible; its dynamics depend on the needs of the particular student. The mentor can serve just as someone to listen, or she can offer a more experienced perspective. One way in which the dynamics of this relationship are determined is by the nature of the mentor-mentee weekly meetings. These reunions can be centered around academic or nonacademic settings or events. Sometimes we end up using our meeting time as a break from the hustle of the academic week. Our gatherings have taken place at lectures, department picnics, coffeehouses, organized study breaks, and other settings. Other participants in the program have expressed that they feel the nonacademic meetings are just as important as the more focused meetings, and they help the mentor and mentee to develop a more trusting relationship. I feel close to my mentees because of experiences we share and our shared love of science.

The relationship between the mentor and the mentee has also proved to be a reciprocal learning experience. I feel that I learn as much from my mentees as they learn from me. Although the mentor is selected through a competitive application process as someone capable of guiding the mentee, she is also still a student herself. The mentor is not chosen for being the "perfect" student, but rather because she is someone who is willing to share successes as well as failures with the mentee. One of the fringe benefits to mentoring is learning about oneself in the process. An example of something I have learned throughout this process is to take my own advice on certain issues, such as the value of being assertive. Often it seems we know what we have to do to succeed, but we have trouble getting there due to a lack of confidence. When I advise my mentee to approach a problem in a particular way, I have to make sure that I follow through in the same manner with my own challenges. The commitment to this program reminds me weekly of my commitment to the sciences. The role of a mentor also provides me a certain amount of motivation for attending more of the departmental offerings or other academic events with my mentee, such as the presentation of the major, networking conferences, and visiting lecturers.

One important aspect of the program is the manner in which the mentors are paired with the mentees. The fact that mentors are matched with the mentees on the basis of common interest rather than ethnicity helps to build bridges toward cross-cultural mentoring. Common experiences shared between ethnic groups show that many students often encounter the same types of obstacles. Learning to find mentors from other cultural groups is a valuable lesson because this will often prove to be a necessity for minorities in a given field. It is more productive to focus on common interests than on differences between groups; we create a stronger voice for ourselves by working together for a singular goal.

Diversity within the group of mentors is thus complemented by the unity encountered through the common purpose. The group of mentors is a closely working unit brought together by their interest in the sciences and their desire to help other students. The mentors represent a wide variety of backgrounds, ethnicities, and class years, ranging from sophomores to seniors. More than just supporting our mentees, we learn to support one another. During the group meetings, we occasionally discuss personal concerns or problems. Additionally, we share our successes with the group. The fact that the meeting schedule is worked around the individual schedules of *all* of the mentors shows that the opinion of each of the mentors is valued. Although not a requisite for becoming a mentor, many are introduced to the program as mentees and bring additional insight to the program from their own experience. Mentors often work as a group on problems, utilizing the collective experience of the members to focus on a particularly difficult situation.

The most common difficulty encountered by the mentors is keeping in contact with the mentees. Science majors often have very busy schedules as they try to juggle labs, classes, and extracurricular activities. Mentors usually assume the responsibility of setting up the first several meetings of the semester. Oftentimes mentors have experienced difficulty in contacting the mentee—she fails to return phone calls or respond to other means of communication. The mentee sometimes expresses a decline in interest in the program when academic demands increase as the semester progresses. In response to this, mentors have developed creative ways to contact the mentee. One mentor solved this problem by leaving a photocopy of her schedule in the mentee's mailbox and asking the mentee to write in a time to meet and to then return the sheet through campus mail. I have found that keeping a consistent weekly meeting time agreed upon early in the semester has proved to be one of the most successful ways to maintain the commitment between the mentor and mentee.

Another disappointing situation is when the mentee seems to lose interest or show limited enthusiasm for the sciences. It is a tough situation for a mentor when the mentee does not respond to her attempt to help. In order to avoid this situation, the responsibilities of both the mentor and the mentee are outlined in detail at the first meeting. A mentor-mentee "contract" is drawn up to avoid any confusion about the seriousness of the commitment and to stress the importance of this relationship from the outset. However, a mentor must also pay close attention to what other factors could be contributing to a decline in interest by the mentee, such as trouble with class material or with a professor, or biased incidents in the classroom or dorm.

The support network for the mentoring program provided by the directors is an invaluable part of the program. With each new challenge or problem that develops, the directors find a way to adjust and prevent future occurrences. Thus, the program seems to evolve slightly each year in response to the apparent needs of the students. The one-on-one monthly meetings between a director of the program and the mentor serve to provide new ideas and an objective approach to the situations encountered during the semester. The advisors gently guide the mentors with suggestions and help when needed. They also serve as a resource when the mentor feels that there is a problem larger than she can handle alone, such as a racist incident. The directors bring the group of mentors together and keep them organized with the periodic mentor meetings and events. I have found this aspect of the program to be very helpful in keeping operations running smoothly. I also feel very comfortable in having an additional resource to help me so that I do not feel overwhelmed.

The concept of a mentoring program designed primarily to support minority women in the sciences may seem exclusive. Other students in the sciences may be resentful if there is no program designed to support their needs as well. However, the majority of the students and faculty in the sciences do reflect the dominant culture. It is no coincidence that certain groups are underrepresented; there are widely discussed reasons for this based on our society and culture. Many minority students, although not all of us, come from backgrounds where we have no precedent for going to college or studying science. Often, we have families who can't understand why we feel we have to go away to study. Additionally, once we get to college, often we have to carry the burden (willing or not) of acting as representatives of our racial or ethnic group, or gender. Peer mentoring gives us the opportunity to recognize the cultural influences that impede us from succeeding, and it teaches us the skills we need to overcome them.

Although the program is currently limited to supporting underrepresented students of color, the peer mentors often serve as a resource for a larger number of students within the college residences and other structures. Several of the mentors in our program are actively involved in leadership roles in their college houses. When I am asked why the program is limited to minorities, students usually understand when I explain that although I believe *all* women are underrepresented in the sciences, our group is designed to support those that have the *least* representation and thus are least likely to find mentors (and certainly role models). Ideally, it would be best to have a mentoring program for all women in the sciences, but until we can realize that goal, we need to focus our energy in the area where it is most needed. In the end, I believe that everyone benefits from a more culturally diverse scientific community.

By having a group specifically designed to support underrepresented students in the sciences, we learn to recognize the ways in which cultural bias affects our lives and, also, how to get beyond these obstacles. The program not only works to support the ethnic groups that are the most underrepresented in scientific fields, but it also gradually explores the reasons why these groups are underrepresented and attempts to ameliorate them. Often the obstacles preventing these groups from succeeding are so subtly ingrained within society that they are difficult to identify.

Through our mentoring program, I believe we are creating not only future scientists but future mentors as well. We are learning the value of networks and support structures that will ultimately help each of us on the path toward our goals. Although college is a unique experience, it is not at all isolated from the problems of the rest of the world. Learning strategies to deal effectively with obstacles at this stage will help us when we are presented with new challenges in the future.

Notes

1. National Science Foundation, *Task Force on Women, Minorities, and Handicapped in Science and Technology, Interim Report* (Washington, D.C.: National Science Foundation, 1988).

2. National Science Foundation, *Women, Minorities, and Persons with Disabilities in Science and Engineering* (Washington, D.C.: National Science Foundation, 1996).

3. Paula Rayman and Belle Brett, *Pathways for Women in the Sciences: The Wellesley Report*, part 1 (Wellesley, Mass.: Center for Research on Women, 1993).

4. National Science Foundation, *Women, Minorities, and Persons with Disabilities in Science and Engineering*, 1.

5. Betty M. Vetter, *Professional Women and Minorities: A Manpower Data Resource Service*, 9th ed. (Washington, D.C.: Committee on Professionals in Science and Technology, 1991), 127.

6. Franklin and Marshall College, *Baccalaureate Origins of Doctorate Recipients*, 7th ed. (Lancaster, Pa.: Franklin and Marshall College, 1993).

7. National Science Foundation, *Women, Minorities, and Persons with Disabilities in Science and Engineering*, 35.

8. Stephanie G. Adams and Howard G. Adams, *Techniques for Effective Undergraduate Mentoring: A Faculty/Student Guide* (National Consortium for Graduate Degrees for Minorities in Engineering and Science, GEM, Notre Dame, Indiana, 1993).

9. Peggy McIntosh, "White Privilege: Unpacking the Invisible Knapsack," *Peace and Freedom*, July/August, 1989.

10. "Mentoring Means Future Scientists: A Guide to Developing Mentoring Programs Based on the AWIS Mentoring Project," executive summary (Washington, D.C.: Association for Women in Science, 1986), 5.

Gender Bias in Biological Theory Formation

Colleen M. Belk

Treating women's biology as a deviation from the male norm marginalizes women and can lead to the formation and acceptance of gender-biased theories. These theories, in turn, can serve to limit the types of questions scientists ask and can perpetuate cultural norms that are not always beneficial to women's well-being.

In this essay I identify two basic biological concepts—the production of gametes by the process of meiosis and the notion of a biological clock—that display this type of gender bias and then reformulate these theories from a feminist perspective. In doing so, it will be made apparent that listening to feminist voices leads to different, but equally valid, interpretations of these processes and data. Reformulation of these ideas from a feminist perspective can thereby facilitate the asking of a greater diversity of questions, the hallmark of good science. Changing pedagogical strategies in an effort to avoid couching science in language, images, and examples that are overwhelmingly masculine can subtly tell women students that their biology is not simply a biology that deviates from the male norm but that their biology can also be the norm. This reworking of the language of science so that there are more female-friendly nuances may well allow women to feel more comfortable as scientists, and it could help women to question ideas about their bodies that are not based in biology but rather are based in gender-biased theories.

To illustrate this point, I describe in this essay the manner in which the topics of the production of gametes by the process of meiosis and the notion of a biological clock are generally taught in college level courses. I then demonstrate the fashion in which a feminist perspective can alter these commonly held notions to provide a more accurate approach to presenting these concepts in college classrooms and texts.

Meiosis

Meiosis is a process that occurs in both women and men in order to make gametes (egg cells in women and sperm cells in men). Men make their gametes in the testicles via this process, which initially duplicates all of the DNA in a parent cell, then splits what is now two times the normal amount of DNA into each of four daughter cells. This reduction and apportioning of DNA is affected through two separate meiotic divisions of the cell's nucleus. The DNA is housed in the nucleus on chromosomes. Humans have forty-six chromosomes. These chromosomes are found in pairs, with a given individual inheriting one member of each pair from her/his mother, that is, in the egg cell, and the other member of each pair from her/his father, that is, in the sperm cell. These twenty-three pairs of human chromosomes are called homologous pairs.

Prior to meiosis, all forty-six chromosomes are duplicated and the copy is attached to the original. The first meiotic division in men ends when the parent cell has had its twenty-three homologous pairs of chromosomes separated into two cells, both containing one member of each pair. At this point, each of the two daughter cells' DNA is composed of still duplicated chromosomes. During the second meiotic division in men, each still duplicated chromosome is pulled apart, leaving four daughter cells with half the amount of DNA as the original parent cell. Virtually every general biology text book on the market today describes the process of meiosis as the chromosomal division that results in the production of four daughter cells.

However, this is not at all the case in women. The cells inside the female ovaries undergo meioses that result in the production of one or, should fertilization occur, two daughter cells. The first meiotic division in women proceeds from an eccentric spindle, resulting in one large daughter cell and one very small daughter cell. The spindle apparatus is made of proteins that physically attach themselves to chromosomes in order to pull them apart. The larger of the two cells receives the majority of the original cell's nutrients, leaving the smaller cell too few nutrients to survive and incapable (normally) of finishing the second meiotic division. This smaller cell, called a polar body, is ultimately resorbed by the female body. The remaining larger cell may then be ovulated. Once released from the ovary into the oviduct, the egg cell can exit the body or be fertilized. In the event of fertilization (clearly the minority occurrence for most women) the egg cell undergoes the second meiotic division, yielding one egg cell and the second polar body. Therefore, in human females, the result of meiosis is one daughter cell or, rarely, two daughter cells.

One can see from these descriptions that the process of meiosis in men differs significantly from the process of meiosis in women. Why, then, is the male model of meiosis, with its production of four daughter cells, considered meiosis proper, and the female model of meiosis considered a variation of this norm? When young scientists, male and female, are taught that maleness is normal and femaleness is a deviation, does this not render them more accepting of biological theories that further marginalize women? Are scientists more willing to accept theories that marginalize women since they have been taught over and over again that women's biology is a collection of oddities? I believe this to be the case, and my next example, based on our cultural acceptance of the male model of meiosis as the norm, illustrates the dangers of this dogma in a broader, societal context.

Is the Biological Clock More Alarming for Women than for Men?

In our culture, the notion of the biological clock generally brings to mind scenes of young to middle-aged women desperately scrambling around in an effort to find a mate. This is thought to be due to women's shorter reproductive life span and the increased incidence of birth defects in children born to older women. The ticking of the biological clock can be misconstrued to imply that women who put off having children until their careers and finances are well established are jeopardizing the health of their unborn children, as well as jeopardizing their own ability to have children at all. Typically, this clock is presumed not to be ticking in men, who are therefore able to devote as much time and attention to their careers as they feel necessary. The idea that only women need to worry about having their children when young promotes the cultural norm of women having children before they establish careers and taking care of their husbands, while their husbands advance their own careers and earning potentials. While this arrangement may work well for some couples, we have all seen the disastrous effects this will have on the mother and children in the not so unlikely event of a divorce. This also promotes our culture's acceptance of older men discarding their wives of many years in exchange for younger, ostensibly more fertile mates. Ultimately, this biological clock shows no mercy for those women who chose to obtain some economic power of their own prior to starting a family. But is this notion true? Is there a biological clock that ticks only for women? The answer is a resounding no, as I will detail in what follows. Again, my analysis attempts to exhibit how a feminist perspective can yield equally valid interpretations and steer the types of questions being asked in an alternative yet equally productive direction.

Biological Observation

Older mothers are more likely to have children with Down's syndrome. Down's syndrome results from the inheritance of an extra chromosome 21. Instead of having pairs of chromosomes, persons with Down's syndrome have three chromosome 21s. The inheritance of extra chromosomes is most commonly the result of a process called nondisjunction, in which the homologous pairs of chromosomes fail to separate during meiosis. This results in one daughter cell with no chromosome 21 and one daughter cell with two chromosome 21s. If a sperm or egg cell with two chromosome 21s fuses with a normal gamete (containing one copy of chromosome 21) a zygote with three chromosome 21s results.

Biological Theory

As women age, there is an increased likelihood of them producing a non-disjunctive egg cell, that is, Down's syndrome children most often inherit their extra chromosome 21 from their mother (Gaulden, 1992).

Feminist Perspective/Unanswered Questions

Does the inheritance of two chromosome 21s from the mother result in greater viability than inheritance of two chromosome 21s from the father?

Answer

Dietzsch et al. (1995) have shown that fetuses who receive their extra chromosomes from the egg cell survive longer in utero than do fetuses that receive their extra chromosome from the sperm cell. So it is indeed possible that men undergo an increasing rate of nondisjunction with age, but that the fetuses that result from nondisjunction of sperm are less often detected due to early spontaneous abortions. Further support for this idea comes from Spriggs et al. (1996). This group of scientists looked at the rate of nondisjunction in the sperm of healthy men. They found that chromosome 21 in men underwent nondisjunction at a much higher rate than any other chromosome. However, this study did not attempt to take into account changing rates of nondisjunction with increasing male age.

Biological Theory (Microcirculation Hypothesis)

Decreased blood supply as ovaries age and with hormonal changes decreases oxygen usage. Decreased oxygen usage results in the buildup of metabolic products that alter the pH and inhibit spindle apparatus functions (Gaulden, 1992).

Feminist Perspective/Unanswered Questions

How does decreased blood flow affect the testes?
Do hormonal changes in aging men decrease oxygen availability?
Are external genitalia more susceptible to decreased oxygen supply via constriction?

Biological Theory

The "long pause" at prophase I of meiosis renders the homologues more susceptible to nondisjunction.

Men begin meiosis at puberty and continually make gametes thereafter. Women begin meiosis in utero, pause during the first meiotic division (at prophase I) until puberty, and begin the second meiotic division after ovulation and fertilization. Based on the male model, the pause at prophase I is considered to be a long pause.

Feminist Perspective/Unanswered Questions

Does a short pause at pairing leave chromosomes more susceptible to mutagens? It seems reasonable to question whether the close appositioning of homologous pairs that occurs at prophase I in women may have some protective effect in terms of shielding portions of these chromosomes from chemical mutagens. This, in fact seems to be the case. Recall that men have testicles containing sex cells that do not undergo meiosis and sperm production until puberty. This facet of male gametogenesis causes men a unique set of problems not seen in women. Essentially, men begin each meiosis anew, whereas women start from chromosomes already at prophase I. Thus, men have to start meiosis from gametic progenitor cells that have been exposed to around thirteen years of environmental mutagens, which can cause damage to the chromosomal DNA of these cells. Consequently, when meiosis occurs from these cells, the resulting sperm cells have an increased number of genetic point mutations. These are mutations that affect individual genes, by either changing the protein that the genes code for or stopping the gene from coding for any protein at all. Moreover, these mutations accumulate over a man's lifetime (Chandley 1991), leading to what can only be described as a paternal age effect. Women, having already moved past the step in meiosis that uses progenitor cells, are not subject to these cumulative effects. So, while mothers are more likely to pass on (to their live born children) errors in chromosome number, fathers are more likely to pass on mutations that affect genes directly by the creation of new mutations (Grimm et al. 1994). Important to note is that errors in chromosome number can be detected prenatally by a host of diagnostic tests, while most disorders associated with new mutations cannot. This has led contemporary researchers to advise men to have their children before the age of forty (Bordson and Leonardo 1991). It is interesting that when one really looks at the data, in terms of producing healthy babies, the biological clock ticks loudly for men as well as for women.

How Reformulating Biological Theories from a Feminist Perspective May Help

- Fewer female science students and scientists feeling marginalized.
- Increased numbers of women in science, yielding a reduction in gender-biased theories.
- Less acceptance of marginalization may lead to less reticence, on the part of all scientists, to ask questions that challenge prevailing biological theories, especially when those theories are not based in science.
- More respect for the voices and styles of female scientists.

- The biological processes women's bodies undergo are wonderfully normal and should be celebrated. Science can only benefit from viewing women's bodies, voices, and work as wonderfully normal.

References

Bordson, B. L., and V. S. Leonardo. 1991. "The Appropriate Upper Age Limit for Semen Donors: A Review of the Genetic Effects of Parental Age." *Fertility and Sterility* 56, no. 4: 397–401.

Chandley, A. C. 1991. "On the Paternal Origin of de novo Mutations in Man." *Journal of Medical Genetics* 28, no. 4: 217–23.

Dietzsch, E., M. Ramsey, A. L. Christianson, B. D. Henderson, and T. J. deRavel. 1995. "Maternal Origin of Extra Haploid Set of Chromosomes in Third Trimester Triploid Fetuses." *American Journal of Medical Genetics* 58, no. 4: 360–64.

Gaulden, M. E. 1992. "Maternal Age Effect: The Enigma of Down Syndrome and Other Trisomic Conditions." *Mutation Research* 296, nos. 1–2: 69–88.

Grimm, T., G. Meng, S. Leichti-Gallati, T. Bettecken, C. R. Muller, and B. Muller. 1994. "On the Origin of Deletions and Point Mutations in Duchenne Muscular Dystrophy: Most Deletions Arise in Oogenesis and Most Point Mutations Result from Events in Spermatogenesis." *Journal of Medical Genetics* 31, no. 3: 183–86.

Spriggs, E. L., A. W. Rademaker, and R. H. Martin. 1996. "Aneuploidy in Human Sperm: The Use of Multicolor FISH to Test Various Theories of Nondisjunction." *American Journal of Human Genetics* 58, no. 2: 356–62.

Defending Feminist Territory in the Science Wars

Maureen Linker

For some of us working in the sciences and the humanities there has been, as of late, an increasing awareness of the tension between the two fields. However, what many may not realize is that we are apparently in the midst of a war. At least this was the word used in *Newsweek* magazine's April 14, 1997, article entitled "The Science Wars." The alleged war is described as having, on the one side, science studies scholars who include in their ranks multicultural theorists, feminist academicians, and cultural studies theorists, and, on the other side, realists and empiricists, many of those working in the so-called hard sciences, who hold an unwavering belief in the primacy of the physical world and in science's ability to correctly characterize the properties of this objective physical system.

The work of science studies scholars, which has increased over the past twenty or so years, essentially calls for an examination and evaluation of the cognitive authority that physics, chemistry, and biology have enjoyed for most of the twentieth century. To this end, research has been done to uncover cases of explicit race, gender, and cultural bias in data collection, interpretation, and methodology in the sciences. Much of this research has been done under the rubric of "feminist philosophy of science and epistemology." In addition to questioning scientific method, feminist and other science studies scholars have raised questions regarding the lack of public forums for understanding and evaluating the moral and social dimensions in science research and spending. These issues have come to be combined with a postmodern skepticism regarding absolute and objective truths discovered empirically. As a result, the latter half of the twentieth century is being described by many in the humanities and social sciences as the end of an era. The era is seen, generally, as arising from the early hopes of white European and North American male philosophers who were committed to the ideals of the Enlightenment and early scientific method, then continuing on to the actual practice of the industrial revolution, and ending finally with the last gasps of positivist science. Needless to say, the postmodern analyses offered by science studies scholars have been met with real resistance by scientists, philosophers, and historians who are still committed to the ideals of empirical truth.

The actual published material devoted to the science wars spans the academic and more mainstream presses. For example, there was a recent *Scientific American* issue that included several articles on the topic of science versus antiscience. Among these articles was "Science versus Antiscience,"[1] in which the question of evidence was examined from both feminist and nonfeminist standpoints. Authors Paul Gross and Norman Levitt published the 1994 book *Higher Superstition: The Academic Left and Its Quarrels with Science*,[2] which defended a more traditional realist view of science and dismissed the significance of social factors and bias in scientific practice and feminist critiques specifically.

Perhaps one of the most notorious episodes in the literature of the science wars was physicist Alan Sokal's 1996 contribution to the journal *Social Text,* an interdisciplinary journal of cultural studies. Sokal, a professor at New York University, was becoming increasingly frustrated with what he saw as a lack of substantive arguments in feminist, multicultural, and postmodern analyses of science. To address this he wrote a faux piece on the history of physics and its relation to Freudian psychology that included patently false assertions concerning some of the results in quantum theory. Sokal then submitted the article under his own name and rank to *Social Text.* The article was accepted, and upon its publication Sokal came out publicly to say the article was a hoax and its publication evidence of the lack of standards in science studies scholarship. A flurry of articles, news radio programs, and op-ed pieces followed, with the majority opinion that feminist, multicultural, postmodern analyses of science are fuzzy-headed, illogical, or worse—intellectually dangerous.

Adding to this recent literature, the philosophical journal *The Monist* came out with an issue in 1994 devoted entirely to the question of feminist epistemology and philosophy of science. The issue is entitled "Feminist Epistemology: For and Against,"[3] and in it several authors, including

Harriet Baber, Barry Gross, Iddo Landau, and Alan Soble, voice their objections to the pursuit of epistemology and philosophy of science from a feminist perspective.

Many of the writers in this issue who take a position against feminist philosophy of science studies echo the objections raised in the sources mentioned earlier. For this reason I would like to look more carefully at the objections in *The Monist* and use them as a starting point. In my reading of this literature it seems that three different types of criticism emerge. I would like to divide up the criticisms, examine each type in turn, and then offer reasons why, ultimately, they should be rejected. In my view the critics of feminist philosophy of science offer no compelling reasons for discounting the enterprise of feminist science (and with it perhaps other social studies of science). Hence, my hope is to diffuse critics and defend feminist territory in the volatile climate of the science wars.

Three Types of Criticism

The Detriment Argument

The first type of criticism of feminist epistemology to be considered here is the detriment argument. The basic idea behind this criticism is that feminist epistemology is detrimental to and in fact at odds with the egalitarian interests of women and, likewise, all marginalized groups. Harriet Baber's article, "The Market for Feminist Epistemology,"[4] typifies this criticism.

Baber reasons that a way of doing philosophy and epistemology described as "feminist" paves the way for "pink ghettos"—small, undervalued areas circumscribed for women's work in philosophy (419). Aside from a distaste for ghettoization, Baber also offers an argument for why women qua women should not be understood to have a unique way of knowing or experiencing reality.

Baber argues that feminist theorists draw on work in sociology, psychology, political science, and the natural sciences hoping to build on a "woman's perspective," something along the lines of the "different voice" described by Carol Gilligan in her work.[5] Baber claims that if Gilligan is to serve as an example, feminist theorists will soon be out of a job because Gilligan's work is so questionable. Baber cites Carol Tarvis, who argues that Gilligan's ideas lack empirical support.[6] Tarvis's conclusion is based on the results of several follow-up studies done after Gilligan.[7] Baber explains that behaviors linked to gender have very little to do with one's sex and much more to do with what a person does for a living and her situation in life. The myth of a different voice is likened by Baber to the myth of mother-infant bonding, debunked by Diane Eyer.[8] These so-called scientific myths are supported, according to Baber, by popular beliefs about men and women as well as the institutional goals of the society. They are appealing in that they reaffirm folk wisdom regarding gender differences that "many people have traditionally found intuitive."[9]

Baber refers to an example in Tarvis's study of a law professor who presented Gilligan's material to her class and received "vociferous resistance" from both male and female students. As the professor describes it, "many of the women in class plan to be litigators and they don't consider themselves naturally soft or pliable or less capable of justice based forms of moral reasoning" (413). Hence Baber concludes that Gilligan's study and any subsequent study of a "female voice" or perspective is doomed to failure, as there is no consistent set of facts that captures all women's experiences. Moreover, any attempts that say there is something consistent or patterned in women's experience will be dangerously limiting for those women who do not share the perspective. (I will readdress this last concern of Baber's in my response to the third type of criticism of feminist epistemology.)

Baber's reliance on Tarvis to undermine Gilligan's view, and feminist epistemology along with it, fails to take some obvious considerations into account. For instance, the issue of whether gender differences are biologically determined, psychologically determined, or culturally enforced remains an open question. Yet Baber characterizes Gilligan as offering a view of difference that depends on "deeply entrenched biological and developmental differences which are difficult to alter" (404). Gilligan is explicit in *A Different Voice* about not attempting to settle the issue:

> The different voice I describe is characterized not by gender but theme. It is primarily through women's voices that I shape its development. But this association is not absolute.... No claims are made about the origins of the differences described or their distribution in a wider population, across cultures, or through time. Clearly, these differences arise in a social context where factors of social status and power combine with reproductive biology to shape the experience and thought of males and females. (2)

Having misconstrued the scope of Gilligan's analysis to be a rigid study of biological and psychological sex differences rather than an exploration into an alternative and misunderstood moral perspective, Baber goes on to say that a more accurate criterion of "psychological and behavioral differences which do exist are better explained ... by one's current situation in life. What one does and needs to do."[10] This criterion is being offered by Baber as a contender against a gender-based explanation. However, where one is situated in life is significantly determined by one's gender. In the SEEDS series, a study of global labor divisions organized by the Population Council, Martha Chen states:

> Gender is one of the most significant determiners in how a person will be effected by socioeconomic and demographic trends. More-over, there are continuing aspects of the traditional systems—dis-criminatory customs and norms regarding the sexual division of work, marriage, family and the inheritance of property which con-tribute to unequal gender distribution around the world.[11]

By shifting the focus to one's situation in life, Baber begs the question of difference, given that a crucial factor in the division of labor and social sta-tus is determined by gender. Regardless of whether there are essential bi-ological sex traits, men and women are socialized differently and occupy different roles within a society. One of the empirical studies Baber relies upon to dismiss Gilligan's work ends with the statement "conditions of em-ployment, not qualities of the individual determine what people value about their work ... when men and women hold the same prestigious jobs, their values and behaviors are similar."[12]

However, men and women are a long way from holding "the same prestigious jobs." Therefore, the differences noted by Gilligan can reason-ably be attributed to the previously mentioned economic and labor divi-sions along with obvious facts of different experiences of socialization. But the point is that neither Gilligan nor those subsequently interested in her work who identify themselves as feminist epistemologists attribute the dif-ferences noted in the study to be the result of what Baber calls "virtually ineradicable" qualities in men and women (407). The fact is that Gilligan "traced" the difference through the voices of women, and subsequently an overwhelming number of women and men saw the model as a springboard for articulating alternative, feminist-based research programs.

It would be truer to Gilligan's work, and the work of feminist epistemologists who have found the study compelling, to see it as a reevaluation
of a mode of thinking and acting that has historically been undervalued,
considered irrational, and stereotypically been attributed to women. The
theoretical communities that have acknowledged Gilligan as something of
an influence do not stand or fall with the question of the accuracy of her
empirical findings. Rather, the study is taken to be more useful by many
because it has provided a framework for investigating normative questions
of moral reasoning rather than facts of biological sex-trait differences.[13]
Gilligan's approach has given a sense to the kind of conflicts of interest
many feminists (and some nonfeminists) have experienced in their theoretical challenge to accepted models of knowledge and value.

As far as Baber's reference to the law class in which Gilligan's work was
seen as offensive to women, the fact could more likely be attributed to the
inadequate way in which the material was presented, as opposed to what
actually appears in the work. Gilligan suggests that girls and women in her
study interpreted moral questions from the perspective of a care-oriented
approach. She stresses several times that this perspective employs a logic
and mode of reasoning that assumes responsibility to others and the maintaining of connection rather than a logic of rights and individual autonomy. Nowhere does she imply that this perspective is "soft" or "pliable." In
fact, in the abortion study, Gilligan goes to great lengths to emphasize the
level of complexity and sophisticated deliberation employed by women
when taking into account the needs of all persons involved in the
dilemma.[14]

Baber's final point is that even if Gilligan has gotten hold of something,
and there are some patterned differences in male and female approaches
to certain kinds of problem solving, it should still be downplayed because
it is an idea that could be too easily abused and used to justify preventing
women from reaching equal status in society. Clearly, the fact that an idea
can be misused and misinterpreted is not reason enough to prevent the exploration and understanding of that idea. If Baber's point is just an en-
lightened warning, then feminist epistemologists can acknowledge it and
continue on with their work. However, Baber seems to have something
more in mind.

Feminist epistemology and philosophy represent the "pink ghettos" of
women's work that Baber finds abhorrent. Ironically, her reaction perpet-

uates the undervaluation of "female-identified" labor. She sees little worth
in countenancing an area of scholarship described as "feminist epistemology" and denies the opportunity it could provide for those philosophers
who seek to analyze institutionalized systems of knowledge, value, and
power. Moreover, she sees danger in accounts that rely on gender divisions
to explain how knowledge is defined and produced.

As an example, Baber cites Ellen Swallow Richards—the first woman
to attend MIT, a chemistry major, and the founder of "home economics"
in the 1880s—as an example of a builder of pink ghettos, similar to feminist epistemologists of today. Richards, as Baber describes her, was happy
to use science to formalize the domestic duties associated with women
rather than pursue the more equalizing route taken by feminists of the
time who sought entrance into male-dominated fields. Richards is por-
trayed by Baber as a naive conspirator, aiding sexists of the day to keep
women confined to less worthy roles in academic and social life.

Yet, Baber fails to mention the ways in which Richards was not such a
sexual segregationist. In 1878, soon after MIT began admitting women directly, a lab was set up to study sanitation. The lab was the first of its kind
in the United States. Richards, who had earned her degree in chemistry,
was hired as an instructor of sanitary chemistry and held the position until her death. Richards worked with MIT professors analyzing water samples, an experience that led to her interest in the composition of food and
groceries, safe drinking water, and low-cost diets for the poor. In 1889,
Richards started the "New England Kitchen," where she and several of her
female students from MIT prepared nutritious soups for the city's poor.[15]

Richards's work could be interpreted as radical in that she struggled
to have science be shaped and directed by women and what they knew,
rather than have women conform to a field that they did not have a hand
in organizing and that was in conflict with their social experience and sense
of responsibility. The discipline of home economics arose from a sphere
traditionally assigned to women, yet it challenged that sphere's assigned
boundaries and used its sources of strength.

The fact is that Richards and women like her, who sought to enlarge
the opportunities available to women and who took seriously so-called feminine work, experienced ghettoization not because they saw their work as
separate and less valuable but because others did. Critics like Baber, who
feel, as she says, that they must "actively distance themselves from this en-

terprise, remaining aloof from women's organizations in the profession and even denying that they are feminists,"[16] relegate feminist epistemology to the ghetto not because they have cogent reasons and valid philosophical differences but because they fear that, by condoning the study of feminist issues in philosophy, they will incur guilt by association and lose the ground they have struggled to earn. Hence, the detriment argument comes down not to an argument but to the fact that feminist epistemology is too closely identified with women and, as such, has the potential of becoming the "home economics" of philosophy. Rather than risk this possibility and have talented professional women go into such a segregated and undervalued area, proponents of this argument wish to do away with the field altogether.

The Unimaginability Argument

I call the second type of criticism the unimaginability argument. This criticism—typified in Barry Gross's article "What Could a Feminist Science Be?"[17]—makes the claim that science, and the epistemological reconstruction of scientific methodology, are gender-neutral enterprises involving such nonsocial concepts as "evidence," "justification," and "confirmation." Gross's central concern is illustrated in the example he gives of a murder. Jones is standing over Smith, who lies dead on the floor. Jones is holding a smoking gun. This is good, albeit not conclusive, confirming evidence that Jones killed Smith. Then, as Gross asks in frustrated astonishment, how would this fact be understood any differently in a world that incorporated a feminist view of science (442)?

Gross's inability to imagine something like "feminist science," and therefore a feminist epistemology that describes the methodology of this enterprise, is due mostly to what he describes as the "very large and ambitious nature of the project. It is so large a project that one is hard-pressed to believe that anyone even thinks it could be carried out in some stepwise fashion" (442). The excessive magnitude of the project, as Gross sees it, stems from the fact that feminist science entails an unimaginable "reinventing" of traditional science. While Gross grants that the tools of science may have been used in oppressive ways, the essential and time-tested methods and techniques of science seem themselves to be neutral with regard to social and political issues. So therefore, to reinvent science in the light of political concerns would do nothing imaginable to change the essential characteristics of scientific methodology.

Gross makes a comparison with a transportation system. If a racist, sexist society used a transportation system, and that society experienced a political revolution and restructuring such that it was no longer racist and sexist, that would not change the essential features of the transportation system; it would still be essentially a system whereby goods and people were carried by some mechanical means over distance in a reasonable time. As Gross says, a "feminist transportation system" is an absurd notion in the same way that "feminist science" is (439).

The first problem with the way the question is posed by Gross is his uneasy talk of "a" scientific methodology. Consider two quotations from his article:

1. Parenthetically, it hardly seems to make sense to talk of science or method as a global phenomena. There are different sciences and different branches and different subfields and specialties within them. (443)

2. One can no more have a science that eschews *all* the time-tested methods and techniques of the natural sciences as we know them— than one can have the transportation system just described. (436; emphasis mine)

Comparing these two quotes illuminates a tension that can be felt in Gross's wish to admit the variety and complexity of science while at the same time being committed to some kind of an essentialist characterization. However, the features that make up the essential methodology of science are left to the imagination. Gross gives a few examples of medical achievements throughout history to show the positive results of traditional science (a reminder to the "anti-authoritarian" feminists who, he thinks, seem to forget the "miracles of medicine" [436]), but he never offers the kind of clear picture of the essential elements of science that he does for the transportation system.

Now this could be chalked up to the fact that it is difficult to elucidate something like the essential features of the complex set of systems known as natural science. However, if this is true, Gross should show some restraint in making an argument on the basis of unimaginability. If there exists a complex system whose foundations are difficult to characterize, and a proposal is on the table for changing some basic tenets of this system, then the ramifications of the change could be vast and intricate enough that to simply imagine them would be difficult. It would seem more correct to understand Gross's question not as a matter of a priori analysis or unimaginability but rather as a matter for a posteriori investigation within a knotty problem in the philosophy of science.

Putting aside the issue of simple unimaginability, a more interesting concern raised by Gross is the question of "particulars." How would the particular aspects of science, elements like "evidence," "justification," and "confirmation" be altered by a feminist perspective in epistemology and science?

If we return to Gross's original example, how would a feminist perspective alter the judgment of evidence we now make as to the fact of Jones's being a likely suspect in the slaying of Smith? The simple answer to Gross's question is that it would not alter *that* judgment in any way. The question of evidence that Gross presents contains none of the controversial features that are in dispute for feminist epistemologists. It is not a point of contention for feminist epistemologists to argue that *every* human inference involves a bias toward the undervaluation of women and nonwhite males, the continuation of a discriminatory social structure, and the reverence for white Western male virtues. Contrary to straw-man stereotyping, feminist theorists do not categorically see biased inferences being drawn everywhere. Such a characterization provides critics with a reason not to take feminist arguments seriously. The thinking goes: If you see discrimination everywhere, then you are not seeing it anywhere specifically, and hence you have an exaggerated and useless analysis. As a result of this way of thinking, the actual particulars of feminist criticism are lost.

To be more accurate, feminists do see bias in many places, even in more places than some might imagine, but it should be from within the range of cases criticized that the debate is framed, not in examples like the one Gross gives, which is irrelevant to the discussion. The example is irrelevant because Gross seeks to establish a point about the role of evidence in science, but the case he gives could only be settled in a court of law. The methodology and practice of science and law differ; hence the burden is on Gross to explain why he connects them.

Separating out the error in Gross's conflation of the question of evidence, we can look at legal theory and science in turn. Feminists working in law have marked off some important cases that can help to shed light on the question. If we exchange Gross's murder case with one of these, the question of evidence is no longer so simple to answer. For example, historically in legal theory the notion of "social equality" has meant that equals should be treated equally. This has meant that if men and women are equals, they should be treated, according to law, in the same way. However, some feminist legal theorists have argued that this sense of "equality" has unfair implications for women, since it ignores the differences in the social realities facing the two genders.[18] In a 1986 case, *Rabidue v. Osceola Refining Company*,[19] extremely disparate views of the facts and findings by a team of circuit court judges concerning sexual harassment indicated to legal theorists that the majority and the dissent operated from different underlying assumptions about what reasonably counts as evidence of sexual harassment and sexual hostility. The majority assumed that men and women were equal and used a "reasonable person" standard to decide that women should not have judged the workplace to be "hostile."

The dissent, on the other hand, utilized a "reasonable woman's" standard, because they found the reasonable person's perspective "failed to account for the wide divergence between most women's views of appropriate sexual conduct and those of men." The dissent report went on to say: "Unless the outlook of 'reasonable woman' is adopted in cases of this nature, the defendants as well as the courts are permitted to sustain ingrained notions of reasonableness and evidence fashioned by the offenders."[20]

Now if we compare this case with Gross's case of Smith and Jones, we can see how in the Gross case a smoking gun is an instance of evidence that is given no new light by a feminist perspective. However, in cases of harassment, the question of evidence and its relationship to feminist theory raises significant issues.

To move from law to science, a feminist perspective on the question of evidence also applies in a range of relevant cases. In a paper by the Biology and Gender Study Group entitled "The Importance of Feminist Critique for Contemporary Cell Biology,"[21] the authors explain that questions of gender bias should be posed at the outset of any scientific research program so as to provide critical rigor and avoid possible errors. The focus of the group is on the ways in which cultural norms and gender inequalities have led to the formation of particular interpretations in biology that excluded or ignored available valid evidence.

One example the study cites involves a well-entrenched theory, considered to be a "textbook" explanation of fertilization, that purports the ovum to be a passive participant in the act of fertilization and the sperm as "the active agent that must move and penetrate the ovum. The egg passively awaits the sperm."[22]

However, in recent investigations by Gerald and Heide Schatten[23] using electron microscopy, they were able to show that when the sperm contacts the egg, it does not "burrow through." Rather the egg directs the growth of microvilli—small fingerlike projections of the cell surface—to clasp the sperm and slowly draw it into the cell. The phenomenon of microvilli extending to the sperm has been known since 1895, when E. B. Wilson published the first photographs of sea urchin fertilization. But as the Biology and Gender Study Group says, "this evidence has been largely ignored until recent studies, and its new role remains controversial in the field."[24] The Schattens consider rethinking of standard sex-role stereotyping as an influence in their investigation of microvilli. The members of the Biology and Gender Study Group credit this kind of rethinking to the increase in feminist critiques of cell and molecular biology. They refer to the work of biologists Ruth Hubbard and Marian Lowe and their research for the Committee for Responsible Genetics and the research of Eva Eicher and Linda Washburn of the Jackson Laboratory on genetics and sex determination.[25] The Group sums up their report with the comment: "A feminist critique of molecular and cell biology involves being open to different interpretations of one's data than is traditionally taught and having the ability to ask questions that would not have occurred within the traditional context."[26]

These examples show that the concept of evidence and its extension, as well as the related concepts and extensions of justification and confirmation, are not only able to be explored from the perspective of gender but may actually be more adequately understood by the normative controls this perspective provides when gathering evidence and analyzing data. Hence Gross's inability to see a relationship between gender and evidence is a result of his failure to consider relevant cases.

The Perspective Argument

The last criticism of feminist epistemology I will address concerns the question of a woman's perspective or standpoint and is raised by authors such as Alan Soble and Susan Haack.[27] The criticism maintains that there is something paradoxical in the view that the perspective of women is essential for science, since there does not seem to be something like "the perspective of women." A characterization of women's essential perspective can be challenged by any woman who argues that it fails to capture her experience. Moreover, if the view is reformulated to mean only a "feminist woman's perspective," then there is no reason to include nonfeminist women in science, unless the point is that all perspectives should be included in science. However, assuming this is the case, we will easily be led into a degenerate pluralism whereby a feminist perspective offers nothing unique to science. What is needed is some argument that will give us identity conditions for a person's "social location" and explain how these conditions contribute to something novel in the production of scientific knowledge. Hence, we need to get a handle on the notion of "perspective," otherwise the identification of perspectives will have no predictive force. So in essence the criticism comes down to a challenge to make clear what a "feminist perspective" is and how it could uniquely contribute to science and epistemology. I call this objection the perspective argument.

Both Soble and Haack are proponents of the perspective argument. Soble, in investigating the writing of Evelyn Fox Keller, finds that Keller's arguments regarding a "feminist style of thinking" are groundless. The result for Soble is a general skepticism regarding any account of the role of gender in scientific knowledge. Haack argues that most of the accounts feminists have put forward are significantly defective for two reasons. First, the accounts fail to take into consideration the work of mainstream philosophers of science, specifically Rudolph Carnap, Carl Hempel, Karl Popper, or Paul Feyerabend. Haack notes an occasional reference to Thomas Kuhn, but not enough to merit the omission of these other important theorists in the philosophy of science.[28] Second, feminist philosophy of science and epistemology attempt no serious analysis of the concepts of rationality, objectivity, or value-ladenness, which are crucial for their arguments. Haack, like Soble, concentrates on Keller, since in her view "Keller is the most sophisticated and thoughtful representative of the feminist critics of science" (16). Other representatives of feminist epistemology and philosophy of science, such as Hilary Rose, Donna Haraway, Helen Weinrich-Haste, and Brian Easlea,[29] are rejected for various reasons by Haack. Rose's work is rejected because it is "so clotted with Marxist jargon as to be unreadable," Haraway's because Haack had to struggle with "convoluted banalities of recent French philosophy," and Weinrich-Haste's because it was, in Haack's words, "titled in such a repulsively cute way that I was tempted to not read it at all." Finally, with Easlea's article, Haack says that it had such a "broad streak of wooly romanticism, I probably missed its substantial points out of sheer irritation" (16).

Haack's admitted frustrations and biases are not reassuring if we look to her work hoping for good philosophical reasoning. Her argument is a clear case of an ad hominem abusive attack; thus it offers no insight into the worth of the arguments put forward by the philosophers she criticizes. Haack's ultimate assessment of feminist epistemology and philosophy of science, based on her reading of Keller, is that if it is the case that girls and women are brought up in such a way that they employ methods of reasoning and objectivity in a way that is different from what is required by science, then girls should be brought up differently. What should not follow is that science and epistemology be required to account for this deficiency in the upbringing of women. However, this is not to say that Haack rejects looking at science from a feminist perspective. She states:

> Some no doubt, would regard the whole project of feminist science and epistemology as absurd. I think they would be wrong; for looking at science from this perspective one encounters, from a promisingly unfamiliar angle, a whole host of good, hard questions. However, in the work that I have been discussing, regrettably, the soggy and self-indulgent predominates over the detailed and discriminating. (18)

I want to note a conclusion of Haack's, namely, that if girls and women reason in a way that is different from what is required by science, then this difference need not be of interest to theorists of science. Given this view, I am puzzled as to why Haack thinks the questions a feminist perspective raises are "good" ones. In what way could the results of such an investigation of difference yield relevant information for philosophy of science and epistemology if, on Haack's view, science and epistemology are justified in their present construals of reason and objectivity?

I will leave this question to turn to the general problem raised by both Soble and Haack, the problem of trying to account for a "feminist perspective." Clearly there is difficulty in trying to characterize both the factors that contribute to a "feminist perspective" and a normative epistemic principle. Given this, is there still a chance for defining the project of feminist epistemology? In my view, the answer is yes. Following a proposal by Terri Elliot in her article "Making Strange What Had Appeared Familiar,"[30] feminist epistemology can be understood firstly as a reconstruction of a *pattern* of marginalizing experience. This is not to say that the experiences of persons who are socially marginalized are the same. However, it is also not to deny that an analyzable pattern emerges in the investigation of the experiences of members of social groups. The emerging pattern serves as the object of investigation in a feminist or social epistemology.

Elliot's account advocates a more moderate version of standpoint theory and provides an epistemically useful analysis of perspective. Her view resurrects Heidegger's notions of "readiness-to-hand" and "presence-to-hand" to shed light on the question of perspective (428). For some, engagement with the world involves circumstances and objects that are ready-to-hand, in that they are easy to use and present no noticeable obstacles. So for someone who is healthy and able to walk, a flight of stairs presents no noticeable challenge and therefore is ready-to-hand. However, for others, the same situation can result in a presence-to-hand, in that it presents noticeable obstacles and a *conspicuousness* regarding the particulars of the situation. So for someone who is bound to a wheelchair, the flight of stairs becomes present-to-hand and noticeably unusable.

Elliot's point in bringing up the distinction is to show how aspects of the social order are conspicuous for marginalized persons, in that they are unusable for them. Given that gender is the earliest and most pervasive determiner of social role and expected behavior, and gender inequalities exist, women are in a position to notice how certain aspects of institutional knowledge are merely "present-to-hand" for them and hence problematic. These experiences can arise in a range of circumstances—from the way in which labor is divided to how scientific methodology is understood.

The sexual connotations rife in metaphors used in science pedagogy, including examples of "hard" or "soft" science, "rigor" versus "softness," or the "seminal" quality of an idea, have been described extensively in the literature of feminism.[31] My purpose in bringing them up here is to provide one example of how our public picture of science can present women with a problematic situation. Encountering such descriptions of science may not present a woman with an entirely unusable situation, but it requires her having to work around an obstruction to derive the meaning of the metaphor. On the other hand, for a man, the same description can be an invitation to join in a collective enterprise, presenting no noticeable obstacles to his sense of self.

Now as Elliot makes clear, this does not mean that unusability will necessarily be the experience of all woman. Some may be able to be engaged, interpret circumstances as ready-to-hand, and not feel hindered by the predominance of male references. How can we understand this?

Elliot explains that a perspective on the unusability of certain aspects of social experience is something earned; it is not a birthright. The emergence of an individual perspective on unusability may then be joined by others to reflect a repeated pattern. Moreover, contrary to theorists like Nancy Hartsock or Sandra Harding, to describe a pattern of marginalizing experience is not to point to a perspective that is epistemically privileged. Rather, what we find is a perspective that is uniquely sensitive to circumstances that assume value-neutrality but contain elements of exclusivity and marginalization. This information is significant, as it can expose the apparent implementation of objective methods of reason and justification, which may be far less than reasonable or objective. But the perspective does not address directly the question of how to evaluate these procedures, assuming their inherent reasonableness or objectivity. As such, they are informative and potentially corrective but not always epistemically superior.

Yet the feminist perspective can have normative force on two fronts. The first comes from the demand put upon societal institutions to acknowledge the reality of systematically exclusive and unusable circumstances. The second involves the development of methodological principles that can be used to uncover the exclusive nature inherent in background assumptions and evidential criteria. Returning to the perspective argument, we can respond to the concerns it raises by recognizing that what should underlie an adequate feminist epistemology, or any socially motivated account of knowledge, is not a monolithic group perspective but rather a pattern of repeated exclusivity that has been overlooked or deliberately suppressed in more individualistic accounts of knowledge.

It is conceivable that someone could accept all of the reasons I have given for the legitimacy of looking at epistemology and philosophy of science from this wider perspective but not accept that this work is particularly "feminist." I would argue against this claim on the grounds that the link between knowledge and social and political factors develops out of the critiques of science, reductionism, and individualism made by feminists in the early literature of feminist philosophy of science. Moreover, in none of the more mainstream accounts of science and knowledge, including the work of philosophers such as Wittgenstein and Kuhn, is there a recognition of gender and power. This contribution to science studies is significantly feminist and should not suffer the "erasure" that such contributions often face.

Notes

1. Gary Stix, Sasha Nemecek, and Philip Yam, "Science versus Antiscience," *Scientific American,* January 1997, 96–101.
2. Paul Gross and Norman Levitt, *Higher Superstition: The Academic Left and Its Quarrels with Science* (Baltimore, Md.: Johns Hopkins University Press, 1994).
3. *The Monist* 77, no. 4 (October 1994).
4. Harriet Baber, "The Market for Feminist Epistemology," *The Monist* 77, no. 4 (1994): 403–23.
5. Carol Gilligan, *In a Different Voice: Psychological Theory and Women's Development* (Cambridge, Mass.: Harvard University Press, 1982).
6. Baber, "The Market for Feminist Epistemology," 406.
7. Carol Tarvis, *The Mismeasure of Woman* (New York: Touchstone, 1992).
8. Diane E. Eyer, *Mother-Infant Bonding: A Scientific Fiction* (New Haven, Conn.: Yale University Press, 1992).
9. Baber, "The Market for Feminist Epistemology," 413.
10. Baber, "The Market for Feminist Epistemology," 408.
11. Martha Chen, introduction to *Supporting Women's Work Around the World: SEEDS,* vol. 2, ed. Anne Leonard (New York: The Feminist Press, 1995), 5.
12. Baber, "The Market for Feminist Epistemology," 408.
13. See especially Eva Kittay and Diana Meyers, *Women and Morality* (Totowa, N.J.: Towman and Allenheld, 1986).
14. See Gilligan, *In a Different Voice,* 106–27.
15. Margaret Rossiter, *Women Scientists in America* (Baltimore, Md.: Johns Hopkins University Press, 1982), 68–70, 74.
16. Baber, "The Market for Feminist Epistemology," 421.
17. Barry Gross, "What Could a Feminist Science Be?" *The Monist* 77, no. 4 (1994): 434–44.
18. See Catherine MacKinnon, "Feminism, Marxism, Method and the State: An Agenda for Theory," in *Feminist Theory: A Critique of Ideology,* ed. Nannerl O.

Keohane, Michelle Z. Rosaldo, and Barbara C. Gelpi (Chicago, Ill.: University of Chicago Press, 1982).

19. *Rabidue v. Osceola Refining Company,* U.S. Court of Appeals for the 6th Circuit, Fair Employee Practice Case 631, November 13, 1986.

20. Ibid.

21. Biology and Gender Study Group, "The Importance of Feminist Critique for Contemporary Cell Biology," in *Feminism and Science,* ed. Nancy Tuana (Bloomington: Indiana University Press, 1989), 182–87.

22. W. C. Keeton, *Biological Science,* 3d ed. (New Haven, Conn.: Yale University Press, 1976), 394.

23. Gerald Schatten and Heide Schatten, "The Energetic Egg," *The Sciences* 23, no. 5 (1983): 28–34.

24. Biology and Gender Study Group, "The Importance of Feminist Critique," 177.

25. See Ruth Hubbard and Marian Lowe, *Genes and Gender II: Pitfalls in Research on Sex and Gender* (Staten Island, N.Y.: Gordian Press, 1979); and Eva M. Eicher and Linda Washburn, "Genetic Control of Primary Sex Determination in Mice," *Annual Review of Genetics* 20 (1986): 327–60.

26. Biology and Gender Study Group, "The Importance of Feminist Critique," 179.

27. Alan Soble, "Gender, Objectivity, Realism," *The Monist* 77, no. 4 (1994): 509–30; Susan Haack, "Science 'from a feminist perspective,' " *Philosophy* 67 (1992): 5–18; and "Knowledge and Propaganda: Reflections of an Old Feminist," *Partisan Review* 60 (1993): 556–64.

28. Haack, "Science 'from a feminist perspective,' " 16.

29. Articles by all these authors appear in *Perspectives on Gender and Science,* ed. Jan Harding (London: The Falmer Press, 1986).

30. Terri Elliot, "Making Strange What Had Appeared Familiar," *The Monist* 77, no. 4 (1994):424–33.

31. Sandra G. Harding, *x*(Ithaca, N.Y.: Cornell University Press, 1986).

Strong Objectivity and the Language of Science

Andrea Nye

That women should succeed in the sciences is an irreproachable goal. Science and technical applications of science provide good jobs, and women should have their share of those jobs. More important, these days science is where our world is made and where much of how we live is determined, whether in health, the environment, how we communicate with others, or how we live together. Certainly, women should be part of that determination.

At the same time, it can seem that feminist critiques of science run the danger of discouraging women from getting involved in science.[1] Some feminist epistemologists, critics argue, make it seem that objectivity and scientific method are a masculine plot. Postmodernists go even further, it is charged, and say that science consists of discardable sexist texts with dubious credentials, subject only to symbolic or cultural fashion and on an equal footing with literature or myth. The result is that science is "deconstructed" rather than fostered as an area of increased opportunity for women.

What I argue in this essay is that such a caricature of recent critical feminist theory, popular as it may be in conservative circles, does not capture the root impulse of feminist epistemology. Rather, what is in question in feminist debates about science is something more simple and more existential. Success is a good thing, but only when you know what it is at which you are succeeding. Without that understanding, success can lack meaning, or worse, can fail to achieve anything important or useful. In the simplest terms, I would claim that "knowing at what you are succeeding" is the idea behind the "strong objectivity" promoted in feminist philosophies of science. And I would say further that every young woman choosing or shaping a career in science should take that idea to heart.

One way of thinking about success in science and science-related fields is institutional. Are you in the right Ph.D. program? Are you working with, or taken under the wing of, the acknowledged leaders in a field? Are you associated with the most prestigious laboratories? Are you involved with the best-funded projects? Certainly, if you do not have some of this kind of institutional success, you have no success at all. Today very little science can be done at home in the kitchen sink. To get into the science game, to become a player, you must learn a discipline, learn accepted methods and procedures, learn to negotiate a culture still predominately male. Too many false steps, too many of the wrong kind of questions, too much allegiance with the wrong persons, can be fatal. Many women who have been through graduate school in any discipline have walked a tightrope, balancing between two abysses: on the one hand, self-destructive insubordination and on the other, an even more frightening loss of self.

The question is whether such experiences are appropriate or necessary in the sciences. In a "fuzzy" humanities discipline like philosophy, it might be argued, where there is no accepted method and procedure, authority, as a matter of course, must be magisterial. In contrast, it seems, the great thing about science is that it is not ruled by intellectual fashion but by truth, and truth does not play favorites, demand a return for patronage, or practice deceit for personal profit. In short, unlike the egocentric or seductive thesis advisor, truth, though temporarily defeated, is never corrupted. There are heroic stories of women who served scientific truth and triumphed, who in the end won the professorship, or membership in the Royal Society, or even a Noble prize. Marie Curie, Barbara McClintock, Rosalind Franklin, who was posthumously recognized for her photograph of the double helix, and many others could be and are cited as examples.

These are women who did groundbreaking work that contributed to some of the most striking modern technologies: atom splitting, genetic engineering, the cloning of complex organisms. Few would dispute that under the standard of truth these women often had to do so against bias. And only slightly more would contest the claim of recent feminist philosophers that this bias was not only against women in a male field but sometimes took the insidious form of favoring constricting and misleading masculine metaphors and ways of thought, such as hierarchical pacemaker cells or macho, dominant DNA molecules. Feminist historians have taught us about the social history of science, with all its unfair exclusion; feminist philosophers like Sandra Harding, Donna Haraway, and Evelyn Fox Keller have shown how evidence can be fudged and margins of error exploited to sustain a pet theory. They have shown how established patterns of thought can skew the way experiments are judged, how hypotheses are framed, and how problems and experiments are constructed, so that one can gloss over phenomena discovered by women, such as the transposition of genes or the cooperative behavior of cells.

Nevertheless, what might seem to put the lie to any simplistic post-modernist constructionism is that after any form of bias has been defeated, science "works." And what more reliable test of truth and success can there be than being able to participate in that working? Lay abstention from interference with the tremendous success of science is constantly ratified in current mainstream nonfeminist philosophy of science. Reference, many current leading philosophers tell us, is determined within science; real objects are not what we can touch and feel and talk about but the objects measured and counted up in laboratories. Take W. V. Quine, for example, perhaps the leading academic philosopher of our time. Scientific theories, Quine argues, are revisable nets cast over reality. There are no places where science's edges tie down tightly to reality, no raw or indubitable naive observations that are certainly true and theoretically innocent, no necessary truths except perhaps the truths of logic. Science decides which among alternative possible theoretical configurations is preferable, and we must think that what there is in the world are the objects of whatever theory is chosen by science. Or take another leading philosopher of science, Hillary Putnam. Rigid designation of a specific object, like a natural substance, *is* possible, he argues against Quine, but for the essential identifying features of a thing we have to trust to scientific experts; they will tell us what a thing is. When or if they change their minds, there will be a new truth about what that substance is for us to accept. As another leading philosopher, Jerry Fodor, put it, speaking of the mind: All "sensible" people must now accept the findings of cognitive science. Philosophers can help a little; they might look at psychology and help to point out what it is that science says is the mind. Psychologists in turn may more clearly structure their experiments according to the philosopher's clearer understanding of their object. But, said Fodor, if and when cognitive science decides it has been wrong, right-minded sensible philosophers will accept the verdict; what they are doing will have been wrong too.[2]

But here is where I think there is a place for the important message of recent feminist philosophies of knowledge. Science remakes the world, but as what? What is it that the mathematical formulas—which so few of us can follow—really map? What is it that geneticists are researching? What are the things they are telling us truths about? What is it that science is researching? Is it the release of energy for affordable electricity in rural homes? Or is it the explosive capabilities of matter? Is it parthenogenesis or human cloning? Surrogate mothering or the farming of women's bodies? The reprogramming of disruptive ways of thinking or the development of diverse human potentials? Assuring educational equality or tracking students by race and class? Ensuring sustainable agriculture or getting quick profits from a tract of land? Are fiber optics a delivery system for knowledge or only for entertaining and distracting information bytes? A major achievement of feminist and other critical epistemologies has been to point to questions like these, which the procedures and disciplines of ordinary scientific objectivity cannot answer, questions that truthful reporting of quantitative data and that theories accurately extrapolated from that data cannot decide. If we do not address these questions—whether we are women who work in science, nonscientists who consume science, or citizens who directly or indirectly influence research policy—we may know truths, but we do not know what the truths are about. We may succeed, but we do not know what it is at which we are succeeding.

For example, in 1905 a Frenchman named Alfred Binet set out to try to measure academic disadvantage in schools in order to see which students might need extra help. He devised an "IQ," or "intelligence quotient," test to identify those who would profit from remedial teaching. In the United States, however, his methods were adapted in a revised Stanford-Binet IQ Test, and this time what was measured as intelligence was not socially induced deficiency but an intelligence deficit that could be used to track students. "Truth" about this intelligence provided a beginning point for further studies, of correlations between race, gender, and intelligence, for examples. Such studies could be carried out according to proper empirical methods of data gathering and interpolation. Ambitious psychologists achieved "success" in documenting and proving correlations. Or they had success in pointing out how the numbers had been fudged or misrepresented. But here is where feminist epistemologists have drawn attention to a deeper question: What is this "intelligence" about which researchers prove truths? Are scientists studying differences that we want to maintain? Are they studying fixed human potentials? Or is the restricting and fixing of human potential what is in question?

In standard philosophical accounts of scientific logic, these questions cannot arise. The logician Alfred Tarski, for example, whose truth theory is the basis for virtually all mainstream current philosophical accounts of the logic of science, explicitly cites IQ as exemplary of properly rigorous scientific method. As long as you stay with the messiness of ordinary conceptions of intelligence, he argued, science cannot be rigorous or true. When you define intelligence as a set of specified answers to specified questions on an IQ test, however, then science can find out truths about intelligence, truths that, as Tarski puts it, are "truths-in-a-language," the only truths that it is possible to have.[3]

But here again is a question: Truth about IQ as determined in standardized testing is truth about what? About how to keep racial lines drawn? About how to police sets of gender-specific behavior, like the ability to do math? About how to retain classes of tracking in education? If there is resistance to asking these kinds of questions, it is understandable. Answers can cut deeply into vested interests in funding and policy. A deeper resistance may be philosophical. We philosophers have an old dream: an ideal language that will automatically deliver truth. The current version of the dream dates back to Descartes's seventeenth-century vision of a universal science expressed in clear and distinct mathematical terms. Questions such as those asked here about IQ tests threaten to awaken one from any such dream to a more complex and ambiguous reality, one in which educational policy is anything but clear.

And there are other more existential forms of resistance. Questions about the nature of intelligence go to the heart of our human identity. Are we genetically African, or were there several racial strains of early humans? Is humanness linked to brain capacity or to social behavior? Are our minds complex computers programmed for survival at all costs, or do we have souls or minds under conscious control?

Here is where the concept of strong objectivity, developed by Sandra Harding and other feminist philosophers, has been useful. The objectivity of standard empirical methods, these philosophers have argued, is weak objectivity when it leaves questions of value, social implications, and vested interests unasked. A stronger objectivity requires researchers to take their own interests, institutional affiliations, ruling metaphors, and experimental designs under critical review, along with the collection and interpolation of data. In assessing the science of IQ tests by this standard, more than the proper tabulation of test results is necessary. The design of the testing instruments, the definition of theoretical objects, the social class of the researchers, the use made of results, preformed assumptions about the nature of intelligence embedded in testing methods all must be critically examined.

In some surveys of current feminist epistemology, sides are drawn up in oppositional terms. On the one hand, feminist empiricists argue that truth results when accepted procedures of experimentation are observed, procedures that have passed the communal test of expert practice. In other words, they believe, with Quine and Putnam, that science provides its own internal standards. In opposition, nonobjectivist postmodernists debunk the idea of truth in science, or anywhere, and suggest that women should either shun science as a masculine endeavor or encourage forms of science in which interpretative creative theorizing is tolerated.

But these two extreme alternatives do not capture the heart of feminist epistemology as I understand it. Rather, what has emerged from recent feminist theorizing is something like this: Standard versions of objectivist truth, whether defined as the eighteenth-century Enlightenment ideal or as positivist verifiability, are in fact not objective enough. If you study intelligence in the way that Tarski suggests, in tabulating results about "the variables over which a theory ranges"—in this case, test scores—the actual "objects" being studied are not known. Perhaps, in one sense of truth, you discover truths, but since you do not know what those truths are about, their value is unclear. You might be able to "do something" with the "facts" you discover, but what that something is remains undetermined. This does not apply only in social sciences; it may also be true for "harder" sciences, like physics. What are quarks? Well, they are shorthand for certain laboratory effects. Yes, but what are those effects? Are they destructive and dangerous? Or are they liberating and productive? Why do we care about them? What are these objects being studied in nuclear physics?

The distinction commonly made between pure and applied science only obscures the issue. It is not that there is some hard fact of the matter that scientists, hopefully pure of politics or bias, are privy to and that politicians then use for worthy or nefarious purposes. It is rather that questions about the things that scientists study are all too often swept under the rug as questions not to be brought up in the midst of a well-funded program of research, or too "confusing" to be dealt with in science classrooms, or too destructive of accepted habits of thought. As the members of several of the science departments where I teach put it—they were refusing to participate in a core course on science, technology, and society—"we do science, we don't talk about science." In its simplest terms, the lesson of recent feminist epistemology is that science is not immune from the danger in doing something without thinking about what you are doing. What I understand Evelyn Fox Keller to say in her later work, as well as Sandra Harding, Lorraine Code, and others, is that we must ask questions about meaning and value. We must do so as strongly objective researchers, researchers capable of reflection on our own methods, on our own assumptions, capable of reflection on the objects of our interest. Do we want to research more objects of destruction, more ways to profiteer in human bodies, more ways to speed meaningless message bytes around the world for the entertainment of a privileged techno-elite?

These are not questions in which value can be separated from fact, but rather questions about the naming and identifying of facts or things. What do we care about? What should we care about or not care about? There is no way to identify objects except in the kind of evaluative talk that goes on at family tables, in classes, in Congress, at faculty meetings, in laboratories among researchers, in this book, or in political campaigns. And the discussion must go on in natural language. No matter how complex and sophisticated the latest mathematical idioms or computer programming models are, to be successful science must come back to where it begins, back to words, to words that name objects of interest among people, to words in which we express to each other what we care about, what we want to change, and what we would like to have happen.

Here is where the old philosophical dream of a logically perfect language of science has gotten in the way. Since the seventeenth century, science expressed in mathematical terms has been privileged as an idiom that might eventually represent the whole exact truth about the world with no intervening messiness of connotation, emotion, or ambiguity.[4] Unfortunately, numbers have no reference. One can count; one can arrange numbers in elegant and increasingly complex formulas, but unless one knows what it is that is being counted, the process is useless. Mathematical language might even be dangerous if it gives an illusion of perfect knowledge and mandates action with undetermined results. The fact is that given the nature of what it is to be human, the only way those results can be assessed is in the ordinary language of words made to stretch in meaning as they are used by different people of diverse perspectives. Is the widespread use of pesticides an environmentally dangerous cover-up for bad cultivation practices or an efficient way to increase production of food? Is nuclear power a safe and clean way to produce energy or an uncontrollable interference with natural forces? What is a "safe" food source or an "efficient" way to produce energy?

Using only the mathematical formulas that specify chemical compounds or atomic structures these questions cannot be answered, or even asked. If philosophers are to blame for isolating science from critical scrutiny with our positivism and scientific realism, feminist epistemologists have played a role in bringing science back into the mainstream of human life. They argue that policy, principles, values, and ideals are an integral part of the truth-seeking process. They argue that objects that science researches, if they are to be real objects, must be objects of interest that make life easier and healthier for people of all classes, cultures, races, and genders. It is not that there is a "politically correct" feminist categorical imperative to research the effects and cure for malnutrition instead of investigating the charm of quarks, or to engage in research that will minimize rather than document differences between races or genders. The point is a much deeper ontological insight about the truth-seeking process: to be successful in science is not just to "do science" but to know, for better or for worse, what it is that one is doing when one does science.

Notes

1. Some of the major texts include Lorraine Code's *Epistemic Responsibility* (Hanover, N.H.: University Press of New England, 1987) and *What Can She Know? Feminist Theory and the Construction of Knowledge* (Ithaca, N.Y.: Cornell University Press, 1991); Donna Haraway's *Primate Visions: Gender, Race, and Nature in the World of Modern Science* (New York: Routledge, 1989); Sandra Harding's *The Science Question in Feminism* (Ithaca, N.Y.: Cornell University Press, 1986) and *Whose Science? Whose Knowledge? Thinking from Women's Lives* (Ithaca,

N.Y.: Cornell University Press, 1991); Evelyn Fox Keller's *Reflections on Gender and Science* (New Haven, Conn.: Yale University Press, 1985) and *Secrets of Life/Secrets of Death: Essays on Language, Gender, and Science* (New York: Routledge, 1992); Helen Longino's *Science as Social Knowledge: Values and Objectivity in Scientific Inquiry* (Princeton, N.J.: Princeton University Press, 1990); and Lynn Nelson's *Who Knows: From Quine to a Feminist Empiricism* (Philadelphia: Temple University Press, 1990).

2. Representative works by W. V. Quine, Hillary Putnam, and Jerry Fodor include Quine's *Word and Object* (Cambridge, Mass.: Harvard University Press, 1990) (see also his recent simplified summary of his philosophy in *The Pursuit of Truth* [Cambridge, Mass.: Harvard University Press, 1998]); Putnam's *Reason, Truth, and History* (Cambridge: Cambridge University Press, 1982); and Fodor's *The Language of Thought* (Cambridge, Mass: Harvard University Press, 1990).

3. Alfred Tarski's classic paper, "The Semantic Conception of Truth and the Foundations of Semantics," was first published in *Philosophy and Phenomenological Research* 4 (1943–44): 341–75.

4. I discuss this point at some length in *Words of Power: A Feminist Reading of the History of Logic* (New York: Routledge, 1990), where I describe the genesis of contemporary mathematical logic in Gottlob Frege's ultimately unsuccessful attempt to fuse the meaning-carrying function of words with the quantitative precision of mathematics.

Feminist Theories of Knowledge

The Good, the Bad, and the Ugly

Jody Bart

In 1952 Simone de Beauvoir made the claim that "representation of the world, like the world itself, is the work of men; they describe it from their own point of view, which they confuse with absolute truth."[1] This has continued to be a major underlying assumption in much feminist theory since the 1970s and has resulted in the emergence of a type of feminist theory concerned with questions of knowledge, referred to as "feminist epistemology." It might be thought curious that this surge of interest among feminists in epistemology should occur at a time when there appears to be a growing philosophical movement away from epistemological questions in general, and foundationalism in particular.[2] But this becomes less curious when we remember that feminism, which refers to all those who seek to end women's subordination, is social-political philosophy. Feminism shares the view of Karl Marx, expressed on his monument stone in Hyde Park: "philosophers have only interpreted the world in various ways. The point however is to change it." Therefore, feminist theory is political theory, even when its object is not overtly political. For instance, feminist psychoanalytic theory is concerned with, among other things, the disparity between women's experience and the traditional psychoanalytic representation of human development. This latter view portrays women's psychology in a fundamentally negative light. Feminist theories are committed to uncovering the mechanisms involved in women's psychosocial development and psychological difficulties. Also, these theories attempt to show the unacceptability of traditional psychoanalytic theories that have served to perpetuate women's subordination. While women's psychology is the explicit object of inquiry, the implicit aims of such research are political—that is, to contribute to the struggle to end the oppression of women.

The same aims underlie feminist epistemological projects. The recognition that epistemological assumptions have political implications has had a dual effect on feminism. First, it stimulates an internal "theoretical self-consciousness concerning the intellectual presuppositions of feminist analyses."[3] For example, third-world women and women of color question the ability of any particular group of women, namely, Western, white, middle-class women, to "know" what is in the interest of all women.[4]

Second, it has led to the identification of androcentric biases in the sciences by challenging epistemological assumptions with negative social or political consequences for women. Men's claims to "know" women's natures, abilities, limitations, and so forth have been a fundamental element of feminist criticisms since feminism's genesis, primarily because it is precisely these claims that are used to justify the social and political subordination of women.[5] For instance, to the epistemological question "Who can be legitimate knowers?" the answer historically has been "not women." The denial that women can be fully rational agents has a long history. Aristotle, drawing on principles of biology he believed to show women were both physically and mentally inferior to men, argued that "The women have [a deliberative faculty] but it is without authority."[6] Therefore, "The man is by nature superior and the female inferior; the one rules and the other is ruled."[7] This attitude was continued with few revisions throughout the history of Western science, and it is both noteworthy and problematic that evidence confirming the aptness of this stereotype of women is often adduced from sources and by methods that appear to comply, at least at the time, with acceptable standards of objectivity. Londa Schiebinger illustrates:

> In the mid-nineteenth century, social Darwinists invoked evolutionary biology to argue that a woman was a man whose evolution—both physical and mental—had been arrested in a primitive stage. In this same period, doctors used their authority as scientists to discourage women's attempts to gain access to higher education. Women's intellectual development, it was argued, would proceed only at great cost to reproductive development. As the brain developed, so the logic went, the ovaries shrivel. In the twentieth century, scientists have

given modern dress to these prejudices. Arguments for women's different (and inferior) nature have been based on hormonal research, brain lateralization, and sociobiology.[8]

Feminist analyses have significantly illuminated the epistemological and political consequences of male bias in the sciences, in philosophy, and in many other fields. These consequences are not trivial and have had a serious impact on women's lives. Therefore, feminist criticisms, which uncover these biases, deserve serious attention. But feminists do not stop here. Feminist epistemologists seek to construct a distinctively feminist epistemology, that is, a feminist theory of knowledge. These theorists hope to modify or reconstruct the theoretical structures that shape epistemological and scientific investigations. Their aim is to yield a better picture of reality than the so-called androcentric picture that now prevails.

Clearly, this project raises significant questions. To begin with, what is a "feminist" epistemology? What makes a theory of knowledge different enough to count as an epistemological endeavor distinct from the rest of nonfeminist epistemology? After all, it is argued, epistemology, the study of knowledge, is gender neutral, isn't it? There are all kinds of theories of knowledge, ranging from skepticism, which doubts the possibility of knowledge, to theories that postulate that knowledge is possible to various degrees of certainty. Some theories argue for various justification strategies for cognitive claims, while others argue over the epistemic relationships of "knowing how" to "knowing that" to "knowing plus some direct object." Still, it is all epistemology.

Critics of feminist epistemology also assert that even where these projects seem to generate new facts, new knowledge, or more humbly, better theories, the evidence used in support of these claims is generally not substantially different from the kinds of evidence used to support conventional claims. For instance, Carol Gilligan's work challenges the basic premises of Lawrence Kohlberg's theory of moral development, in which women's moral experience has fallen into a shadowy realm of the not properly moral.[9] Gilligan asserts that the apparent failure of women to achieve autonomy and moral maturity as measured on Kohlberg's scale is more plausibly interpreted as evidence of inadequacy in the scale itself than as a demonstration of natural female inadequacy. Gilligan's claims, however, are assessed in terms of the scope of her investigation, the breadth of her research, the scale of her evidence, and the explanatory force of her theory. For critics of feminist epistemology, a specifically feminist theory of knowledge is superfluous because it appears that the results of feminist research are justified (or not justified, as the case may be) in noncontroversial, traditionally acceptable ways. Even if, these critics argue, gender does play a decisive role in shaping our perspectives, the question of what, if anything, makes one perspective better than another, remains. Wouldn't one theory be better than another because its evidence is more unbiased, more comprehensive, more inclusive (i.e., accounts for more of the phenomena in question)?

What distinguishes feminist epistemologies from nonfeminist epistemologies is precisely the emphasis feminist theory places on the role of gender in shaping our perspectives. When used as an analytical technique to evaluate epistemological claims, these theories have been immensely valuable. Many feminists have made significant contributions to the epistemological terrain as regards questions such as who can be knowers, or what sorts of experience can count as justification of knowledge claims. But the development of a distinctively feminist theory of knowledge premised on the supposed superiority of women's gender-conditioned experience is a shaky endeavor at best, a politically disastrous project at worst. It is shaky because there is no good reason to believe that women are any less prone to error, deception, or distortion than men or to believe that all women in all social-historical conditions share the same or similar experience of reality. The project of developing a specifically feminist theory of knowledge that rests on the assumed corrective power of women's perspectives smacks of a kind of essentialism from which women have been trying to extricate themselves for centuries. It implies, among other things, that women's experiences and perceptions are essentially one way and not another. This could have politically disastrous effects for women. Throughout history women have had to overcome beliefs that we are "essentially" nonrational, emotional, nurturing, and so forth. The identification of these supposedly essential characteristics have then been used to restrict women from most political, social, and economic spheres. Reclaiming or revaluing women's so-called essential characteristics still limits women's autonomy by asserting a determined or fixed women's nature.

In this essay, I identify the current feminist epistemological strategies that I feel are inadequate, particularly when used to support the general

feminist political aim of ending the oppression of women (thereby increasing women's autonomy). I focus on various feminists' claims and criticisms regarding objectivity and show some of the strengths and weaknesses of these positions. I then turn to several nonfeminist views on
objectivity to show some similarity these theories share with their feminist
counterparts, as well as some of their weaknesses. It is my position that,
while the stress on the role of gender is unique to feminist epistemological critiques, they emerge from and are contiguous with a long history of
prefeminist and nonfeminist criticisms. Recognizing this intellectual heritage and philosophical connectiveness will have the political advantage of
placing feminist epistemological theory squarely within a historical discourse, rather than marginalizing it as a subject of interest to women only.

If male-dominated conceptual frameworks yield a flawed or incomplete picture of reality, what are the alternatives? Sandra Harding surveys
three types of feminist epistemological strategies: feminist empiricism;
feminist standpoint theory; and feminist postmodernism.[10]

Feminist empiricism would retain the two basic philosophical assumptions of science. The first assumption, philosophical realism, asserts
the existence of the world as the object of knowledge independent of the
human knower. The second assumption is the empiricist conviction that
all knowledge derives from experience through the senses. Feminist empiricists assert that by the inclusion of women (which means literally including more women as scientists and researchers, as well as including
more women's experiences as objects of inquiry) in all phases of observation and theory formation, gender bias can be eradicated and objective
knowledge achieved. Harding notes:

> There are facts of the matter, these critics claim, but androcentric sci-
> ence can not locate them. By identifying and eliminating masculine
> bias through more rigorous adherence to scientific methods, we can
> get an objective, de-gendered (and in that sense, value-free) picture
> of nature and social life. Feminist inquiry represents not a substitu-
> tion of one gender loyalty for another—one subjectivism for an-
> other—but the transcendence of gender which thereby increases ob-
> jectivity.[11]

Feminist empiricism suffers from most standard criticisms of foundationalism and empiricism, beginning with the Humean problem of in-

duction. Antifoundationalists are quick to point out that observation generates correlations that cannot prove causation. No matter how strong the evidence we have for assessing probabilities may be, we can never attain uncontestable truth. If traditional empiricism underestimates the role of theory in shaping perception, feminist empiricism overestimates the power of women's perspectives to increase objectivity.

Feminist standpoint theories appropriate the Marxist belief in the epistemological superiority of the perspective of the oppressed class, in this case, women. These theories reject the notion of an unmediated truth, arguing that knowledge is always mediated by a myriad of factors related to an individual's particular position in the sociohistorical landscape, at a specific point in history. Mary Hawkesworth explains:

> Although they repudiate the possibility of an unmediated truth, feminist standpoint epistemologies do not reject the notion of truth altogether. On the contrary, they argue that while certain social positions (the oppressor's) produce distorted ideological views of reality, other social positions (the oppressed's) can pierce ideological obfuscations and obtain a correct and comprehensive understanding of the world.[12]

Although feminist standpoint theories assert that concepts of knowledge are historically and sociologically variable, other features of their arguments contradict this claim. Claiming the existence of a distinctive women's perspective that has privileged insight into the nature of reality is tantamount to asserting the existence of a uniform and universal women's experience that generates this univocal vision. But this position ignores the social, historical, and cultural differences among women. This view fails to explain why some women see the truth and some do not. Faced with competing feminist knowledge claims and political agendas, a universal women's standpoint theory can have little adjudicating force. There is no homogeneous women's experience and hence no singular women's standpoint.

The third category of alternative epistemologies vying for feminist allegiance is feminist postmodernism. These theories challenge the notion that there is such a thing as objective reality to be structured. Given the situatedness of each finite knower, and the various conditions that shape individual identities, postmodern feminists are skeptical about the idea of any unitary women's consciousness or unitary women's experience. These views reject all universal or universalizing claims about existence, nature, and the powers of reason. Postmodernists encourage instead "a commitment to plurality and the play of difference," unhampered by any predetermined gender identity or "authoritarian impulses of the will to truth."[13] The attraction of feminist postmodernism is that it seems to hold out the promise of an increased freedom for women. But it also tends to foster a politically paralyzing relativist stance. To mobilize a social movement you must offer a positive alternative, a vision of the better society toward which you ask people to struggle. An ideology that claims only subjective veracity can have little persuasive force for social change.

Brief as this summary of these alternative feminist epistemologies is, it exhibits the difficulties each theory has in addressing all feminist concerns. Both feminist empiricism and feminist standpoint theory, which sustain claims concerning a privileged perspective of the world, are challenged by insights generated by the long struggle of women of color within the feminist movement—that there is no uniform "women's reality" to be known, no coherent perspective to be privileged. Feminist postmodernism's plea for tolerance of multiple perspectives is in conflict with feminists' desire to develop a successor science that can refute androcentric biases in the sciences and support feminists' positive political aims. I will now turn to some feminist epistemological critiques.

Many aspects of feminist epistemological critiques are now well-known. Much of this work has been extremely valuable, yet some trends in feminist theory have been less positive. For instance, responding to abusive intellectual practices that have oppressed women throughout history, feminist analyses have, understandably, often subtly shifted from the identification of misinformation about women to the conspiracy theory of a design by men to disseminate disinformation about women. It is not necessary to engage in discussion on the merits of this position to recognize that this shift in emphasis from misinformation to disinformation has had unfortunate effects on feminist approaches to epistemology. Concentrating on the source of knowledge—men—rather than on the validity of specific claims advanced by men has shifted the analysis away from issues of justification toward psychological and functional analyses. The result has been a slide from epistemology per se to sociology of knowledge that, in turn, has allowed several highly controversial epistemological assumptions regarding the nature of knowledge, the process of knowing, assessment criteria, and standards of evidence to be incorporated unreflectively into feminist arguments.

One of the more controversial of these positions suggests that the whole notion of objectivity expresses a fundamentally male approach to knowledge and the world. Ruth Blier expresses this idea:

> Science is the male intellect: the active, knowing subject; its relationship to nature—the passive object of knowledge—is one of manipulation, control and domination; it is the relationship of man to woman, of culture to nature.[14]

Yet another feminist critique refers to "the ostensibly non-involved stance" as the male epistemological stance that "does not comprehend its own perspectivity."[15] The assertion is that what has traditionally been accepted as unbiased and objective is, in fact, intricately embedded in a particular worldview. This perspective, it is argued, is "specifically male and tends to exclude or devalue the experiences and the points of view of women."[16] These types of critiques deny the objectivity of traditional standards of objectivity and advocate the inclusion of women's experience in scientific research and theory formation to correct our perceptions.

Some feminist treatments of knowledge approach the problem of objectivity by suggesting that part of the difficulty emerges from the dualistic categories into which we have tried to place all knowledge. This approach includes the curious claim that reason is gendered:

> The claim here is that science rests on and is defined by the assumptions of a polarity between man and woman that structures our views of and investigations into what constitutes men's and women's natures.[17]

Rationality, a tough, rigorous, impersonal, competitive, unemotional, objectifying stance, is said to be "inextricably intertwined with issues of men's gender identities," such as obsession with separation and individuation.[18] Evidence from many areas, most notably biology, anthropology, and sociology, is often used to reinforce the stereotype of "male" as active, rational, superior, and of "female" as passive, emotional, inferior. Paradoxically, these stereotypes are adduced from animal behaviors onto which are falsely projected human sex roles. This research is then used as evidence for the claim that these roles are biologically determined. The contention is that the assumption that active behavior on the part of an organism exemplifies the male principle, and passive behavior the female, leads biologists to "see" in certain theory-determined ways. While in very recent history these types of claims have come under criticism, the stereotypes persist.[19] It is argued that these assumptions underlie all our views about what constitutes knowledge. Across the board, our culture accepts and perpetuates these dualisms in art, literature, science, philosophy, and all social institutions. Our customs and social structures reflect our belief that these dualisms really exist in the world, particularly in the natures of men and women. An alternative view argues the converse, that these dualisms do not exist in nature but are our way of describing, ordering, and analyzing our perceptions and experiences. In the words of Ruth Blier, "We tend to mistake our cognitive techniques to comprehend the universe for the universe itself."[20]

Lorraine Code, puzzling over the knowledge/experience dichotomy, asserts it to be of a piece with several other dichotomies standardly taken to mark crucial philosophical distinctions, all of which have epistemological implications: namely, the mind/body, reason/emotion, theory/practice, and public/private dichotomies, among others.[21] Feminists are now considering the male/female dichotomy as similar to these and are thinking that, along with the other dichotomies, the distinction between male and female is evaluative and not merely descriptive. In each dualistic relationship, the left-hand term is the more highly valued and the right-hand term is often outright denigrated. Feminist critiques claim that to treat such dualisms as representing contradictory and mutually exclusive spheres is to perpetuate false dichotomies, not because these ways of classifying do not order our perceptions, for clearly they do, but because they leave out or undervalue women's experiences. For many feminists, these false dualisms actually represent continua whose extremes are not separable but continuously interact with one another.

Feminist analyses that concentrate on men as the source of knowledge and the social purposes served by androcentric rationality as the central epistemological issues are premised on many highly problematic assumptions about the nature of reason and the process of knowing. Rather than acknowledging that reason, rationality, objectivity, and knowledge are themselves essentially contested concepts that have been the subject of centuries of philosophical debate, there is a tendency to conflate all reasoning with one particular conception of rationality.

Objectivity is often attacked, even by nonfeminist realists, for its inherent limitations: every observer, by the very act of observing from a single vantage point, must be to some extent subjective. Scientific method employs many safeguards that limit subjectivity, but inevitably the constraints of perspective remain. Israel Scheffler argues that these very restrictions can direct us toward a greater objectivity:

> Our categorizations and expectations guide by orienting us selectively toward the future; they set us, in particular, to perceive in certain ways and not others. Yet they do not blind us to the unforeseen. They allow us to recognize what fails to match anticipation, affording us the opportunity to improve our orientation in response to disharmony. The genius of science is to capitalize upon such disharmony for the sake of a systematic learning from experience.[22]

This view, not surprisingly, assumes a unified ontological ground: "reality itself ... independent of human wish and will, progressively constrains our scientific beliefs."[23] Scheffler sees observation as the prime methodology of scientific evaluation, providing, in spite of its innately subjective nature, an objective counterpoint to the predisposing factors of assumption and conviction.

In the late nineteenth century, Charles Peirce advanced a definition of truth that parallels Scheffler's defense of observation. Peirce held that human opinion is not only subject to inaccuracy and error, but that acknowledgment of the error factor is "an essential ingredient of truth."[24]

> The confessed fallibility of our beliefs works as a permanent stimulus to further inquiry.... This idea of confessed inaccuracy [is] not only a condition of the truth of assertions, but an essential characteristic of scientific method.[25]

While no single scientific statement can be known with certainty to be true, the principle of fallibilism leads always toward an idea of finished scientific knowledge. Although this ideal is, in practice, unattainable, fallibilism is said to guide us unerringly in its direction. Objective truth, for Peirce, is what the rational processes of human intellect would arrive at if all the facts were known.

Karl Popper regards objectivity in a different light. While not renouncing realism altogether, he considers that we are more severely limited in what we can know of reality. He writes:

> My use of the terms "objective" and "subjective" is not unlike Kant's. He uses the word "objective" to indicate that scientific knowledge should be justifiable, independently of anybody's whim: a justification is "objective" if in principle it can be tested and understood by anybody.... Now I hold that scientific theories are never fully justifiable or verifiable, but that they are nevertheless testable. I shall therefore say that the objectivity of scientific statements lies in the fact that they can be intersubjectively tested.[26]

While sounding very much like fallibilism, Popper's vision stops short of the Peircean ideal of ultimate truth. Perhaps Popper is more skeptical of the potential accomplishments of human rationality. Certainly he considers that our discoveries about reality are more sharply constrained by the limits of subjectivity. Since there is no escape from the limits of point of view, intersubjectivity is the best we can do.

In case it should be thought that only some feminist theorists suggest the deployment of a knowledge that is intuitive, emotional, engaged, and personal, let me point out the philosophy of Michael Polanyi. He dispenses with objectivity by redefining it beyond recognition. He associates objectivity with passion and intuition, not with detached observation. Polanyi would discard the tenets of scientific methodology for the purportedly superior approach that he calls "personal knowledge." Passionate commitment, a sense of cosmic responsibility, and utter confidence in one's personal authority constitute the salient ingredients of this exotic prescription. The scientist becomes a shaman, assigning greater weight to personal conviction than to sensory evidence.

> It is the act of commitment in its full structure that saves personal knowledge from being merely subjective. Intellectual commitment is a responsible decision, in submission to the compelling claims of what in good conscience I conceive to be true. It is an act of hope.[27]

It is certainly that. If conscience is the principal criterion to which intellectual commitment must submit, then this hope could more properly be called beatific faith. Rationality, for Polanyi, is not a human faculty to bring to bear upon observed fact but is a characteristic of nature itself. Objectivity is a property rather mysteriously engendered by passion and faith, and truth is linked to a vision "far beyond our comprehension" (65). While he posits a unified reality, a "universe which can speak for itself" (5), his notions of how to read that reality are as unilluminating as personal accounts of mystical experience.

Hillary Putnam would preserve truth through a pragmatist hybrid he calls "internal realism," which claims that "realism is not incompatible with conceptual relativity."[28] Our conceptual schema give intelligibility to our questions and answers. Truth and falsity are preserved, but only within conceptual frameworks. This view rejects the spectator view of "truth as correspondence to a pre-structured Reality" (43).

Truth, on this conception, stands in peril of dismemberment by the claims of relativism. If my truth about a given situation differs from yours, and there is no possibility of an arbitrating standard, doesn't the very notion of truth lose its meaning? No, argues Putnam, because the "facts" remain. "There are 'external facts,'" claims Putnam, "and we can say what they are. What we cannot say—because it makes no sense—is what the facts are independent of all conceptual choices" (33). By citing "externality," Putnam hopes to obviate the charge that he appears to claim that facts do and do not have independent status, but he gives an equivocal defense:

> We can and should insist that some facts are there to be discovered and not legislated by us. But this is something to be said when one has adopted a way of speaking, a language, a "conceptual scheme." To talk of "facts" without specifying a language is to talk of nothing. (36)

Inquiries are conducted by applying the rules of the particular game (the conceptual framework) to the facts at hand, but the shape and existence of the facts themselves depend on the rules. Putnam goes a step beyond Kant, who says that we can't know about the noumenal world. For Putnam the very notion of a noumenal world is unintelligible: "Internal realism says that we don't know what we are talking about when we talk about 'things in themselves'" (36). Putnam declares that there are no intrinsic properties, so how can there be "external facts"?

For Putnam, there can be no objective standards of truth or ontological status. People arguing from different positions have no recourse to external, arbitrating criteria. Putnam's view does not require—indeed, does not admit—a "best version":

> One does not have to believe in a unique best moral version, or a unique best causal version, or a unique best mathematical version; what we have are better and worse versions, and that is objectivity. (77)

This is a peculiar sort of objectivity, and it is difficult to see what relation it could have to the word's denotation as it is commonly understood. Because his "internal realism" admits of "better and worse versions," Putnam believes that it is saved from the paralyzing skepticism that nullifies the possibility of rational discourse across perspectives or conceptual frameworks. But, on his own account, there can be no standard by which to measure "better" and "worse."

What, indeed, has become of truth? If the assumptions of Putnam are correct, there is no objectively ascertainable truth. Traditional objectivists like Scheffler fail to solve the problem of conflicting points of view. Popper is well on his way down the slippery slope of relativism, and Polanyi is evidently off in a world of his own. If there is an objective reality to be investigated, I am unpersuaded that a feminist epistemology will be any more successful in its attempt to offer an exclusive premium on truth. It does seem that some sort of synthesis is in order, incorporating not only the perspectives of women but of other disempowered groups as well. We would still, however, require some sort of objective—or consensual—standard by which to guide such a synthesis.

Given the very long and eclectic history of epistemic debate, and the apparent movement in philosophy away from foundationalism, feminist efforts would be more productively engaged in developing a critical feminist epistemology rather than a uniquely feminist theory of knowledge. Recognizing the complexity of all knowledge claims, feminism as a set of social-political philosophies need only adopt a minimalist standard of rationality that requires belief be apportioned to evidence and that no assertion be immune from critical assessment. With this standard, feminist analyses can achieve their various social and political aims: they can refute unfounded claims about women's "nature"; they can identify androcentric bias in concepts, methods, and theories; and they can point out the practical implications of these biases that obstruct women's full participation in social, political, and economic life.

Feminists need not claim a universal, ahistorical validity for their analyses or claim that women have an exclusive window on truth. Many feminists recognize this and encourage a plurality of perspectives. Feminist claims derive their justificatory force from their capacity to illuminate existing social relations, to show the weaknesses in alternative explanations, and to debunk opposing views. Feminist analyses confront the world by providing concrete reasons in specific contexts for the superiority of their views. These claims to superiority are not derived from some privileged standpoint of the feminist knower but from the strength of rational argument and the ability to demonstrate point by point the deficiency of alternative positions.

Notes

1. Simone de Beauvoir, *The Second Sex,* trans. H. M. Parshley (New York: Vintage, 1972), 161.
2. Jacques Derrida, *Dissemination* (Chicago: University of Chicago Press, 1981). Discussions concerning excessive preoccupation with epistemology abound. Another good essay is Paul Kress, "Against Epistemology," *Journal of Politics* 41, no. 2 (1979): 526–42. Even more arguments may be found against foundationalism, such as Richard Rorty, *Philosophy and the Mirror of Nature* (Princeton, N.J.: Princeton University Press, 1979). By this, I do not mean to suggest that foundationalism is in any way "dead" as a philosophical topic. Nor do I suggest that there are no foundationalists. Philosophical trends can be pointed out, and there is a growing body of literature that is nonfoundational or antifoundational in contemporary philosophy.
3. Mary E. Hawkesworth, "Knowers, Knowing, Known: Feminist Theory and Claims of Truth," *Signs* 14, no. 3 (1989): 533–56. See also Nancy Hartsock, "The Feminist Standpoint: Developing a Ground for a Specifically Feminist Historical Materialism," in *Discovering Reality: Feminist Perspectives on Epistemology, Metaphysics, Methodology, and Philosophy of Science,* ed. Sandra Harding and Merrill Hintikka (Dordrecht, Netherlands: D. Reidel, 1983).
4. Angela Davis, *Women, Race, and Class* (New York: Random House, 1981).
5. Mary Wollstonecraft, *Vindication of the Rights of Women,* ed. Charles Hagdman (New York: Norton, 1967). This is but one example of an early critique; many others could be cited, notably John Stuart Mills, *The Subjection of Women* (Cambridge, Mass.: MIT Press, 1970). The critique continues today. Andrea Nye, *Feminist Theory and the Philosophies of Man* (New York: Routledge, 1989) is a well-discussed overview of such critiques. Allison Jaggar, *Feminist Politics and Human Nature* (Totowa, N.J.: Rowman and Littlefield, 1983), chapter 11, is an attempt

to show the importance of epistemology to feminist political aims. Carol Gilligan, *In a Difference Voice: Psychological Theory and Women's Development* (Cambridge, Mass.: Harvard University Press, 1982), raises many questions regarding the ways in which gender-biased assumptions influence scientific methodology and theory formation. It also has become a classic example of the very practical consequences of these assumptions for women, in this case, regarding the psychological development of female human beings.

6. Aristotle *Politics,* 1.13.1260.a113.

7. Ibid., 1.15.1254.b13–14.

8. Londa Schiebinger, "History and Philosophy," in *Sex and Scientific Inquiry,* ed. Sandra Harding and Jean F. O'Barr (Chicago: University of Chicago Press, 1987), 26–27.

9. Carol Gilligan, *In a Different Voice: Psychological Theory and Women's Development* (Cambridge, Mass.: Harvard University Press, 1982).

10. Sandra Harding, *Whose Science? Whose Knowledge?* (Ithaca, N.Y.: Cornell University Press, 1991), chapter 4. This is the most recent articulation of the alternatives and stems from her earlier work, *The Science Question in Feminism* (Ithaca, N.Y.: Cornell University Press, 1986).

11. Harding, *Whose Science?* 289.

12. Hawkesworth, "Knowers, Knowing, Known," 536. I might add that this essay attempts to sketch an alternative feminist epistemological direction, different from those surveyed here. See also Hartsock, "The Feminist Standpoint."

13. Jane Flax, "Post-modernism and Gender Relations in Feminist Theory," *Signs* 12, no. 4 (1987): 621–43. Harding (see note 10) has a thorough discussion of feminist postmodernism, or you can go to the wellspring, the French feminist, in an anthology such as *French Feminist Thought: A Reader,* ed. Toril Moi.

14. Ruth Blier, *Science and Gender* (New York: Pergamon, 1984), 196.

15. Catharine MacKinnon, "Feminism, Marxism, Method, and the State," *Signs* 13, no. 5 (1982): 538.

16. Marsha Hanen, "Feminism, Objectivity, and Legal Truth," in *Feminist Perspectives: Philosophical Essays on Method and Morals,* ed. Lorraine Code, Sheila Mullett, and Christine Overall (Toronto: University of Toronto Press, 1988), 30. This work gives an excellent overview of the types of epistemological issues that Canadian feminist philosophers are concerned with. This anthology particularly emphasizes questions about the relationship of knowledge theory with moral theory.

17. Ibid., 29. A full discussion of the epistemological/political consequences of the tenacity of stereotypes in determining women's place in an epistemic community may be found in Lorraine Code, "Credibility: A Double Standard," in *Feminist Perspectives: Philosophical Essays on Method and Morals,* ed. Lorraine Code, Sheila Mullett, and Christine Overall (Toronto: University of Toronto Press, 1988).

18. Susan Bordo, "The Cartesian Masculinization of Thought," *Signs* 11, no. 3 (1986): 439–56.

19. Lord Zuckerman, "Apes Are Not Us," *New York Review of Books* (May 1991). And many other critiques of imposing any anthropormorphism on nonhuman species abound. But the impact of these ways of thinking is very much with us. Lorraine Code's most recent work, *What Can She Know: Feminist Theory and the Construction of Knowledge* (Ithaca, N.Y.: Cornell University Press, 1991), is one of the most coherent discussions concerning the lingering effects of stereotypes of women, regarding their epistemic inferiority, on mainstream Anglo-American epistemology.

20. Blier, *Science and Gender,* 197.

21. Code, "Credibility," 75–76.

22. Israel Scheffler, *Science and Subjectivity* (Indianapolis: Bobbs-Merrill, 1967), 44.

23. Ibid., 11.

24. H. S. Thayer, "Pragmatism," in *A Critical History of Western Philosophy,* ed. D. J. O'Connor (London: Free Press of Glencoe, 1964), 445.

25. Ibid., 445–46.

26. Karl Popper, *The Logic of Scientific Discovery* (New York: Basic Books, 1959), 44.

27. Michael Polanyi, *Personal Knowledge* (Chicago: University of Chicago Press, 1958), 64–65.

28. Hilary Putnam, *The Many Faces of Realism* (LaSalle, Ill.: Open Court, 1987), 17.

Gender and Physical Science

A Hard Look at a Hard Science

Amy Bug

> The reader should be reassured again that I do not intend to throw out the baby of science along with the bath water of false views about science. My concern is to identify more carefully where the baby ends and the bath water begins.
>
> Sandra Harding, philosopher of science

> Re: identifying where the baby ends and the bath water begins, it is easy: Define an order parameter that is one within baby space and 1 in the water space. The baby ends at zero regardless of the sharpness of the front.... So, although according to the bible water (-1) was good to Moses $(+1)$, leading him to the king's court and heart, I would still run a Landau-Ginzburg equation just to verify....
>
> Rafi Blumenfeld, physicist

This essay explores some aspects of the interplay between gender issues and physical science. At the start, we acknowledge the paradoxical status of physics (Keller 1985, chapter 4) as both gender free (an impersonal enumeration of mathematical truths to which our universe adheres) and highly gendered—of the male variety. If physics were not free from the influences of gender, race, and class, how could men and women all over the world reproduce the same experiments with the same results (to ten or eleven decimal places in some cases)? If it were not highly gendered, then would it not be equitably integrated, and would images of physics and of physicists not conflate with images of male activities and male people in most of our minds?[1]

Organizing one's thoughts on issues of women in physical science is a tough task. Immediately, the question arises: Which issue is paramount? There are many questions that compete for attention, among them:

Did/do men outnumber women (the participation, persistence issue)?
Is/was there an exclusion of women from institutions of learning and power?
Is there a gendered quality to the science itself?
Need we assess/reform physical science education?
What are the images of science and scientists that are ingrained within our society?

Though these questions are quite distinct, they resist being answered in isolation, and their answers are intertwined in interesting ways. Further, they have a continuity across time and place. They could have been asked about science and society 200 years ago, 500 years ago, as well as now, and the answers in different eras would inform one another. "We feel a lack of intellectual respect from classmates. We often feel patronized in homework sessions" is a paraphrase of a comment made by a physics major at our small college. "I did not dare lay bare my impulse and intention to any of the wise by asking for advice, lest I be forbidden to write because of my clownishness" is a quote from the tenth-century scientific scholar and cleric Hrosvitha (Wertheim 1995, 43). One gets a strong sense that these two quotes, separated by a thousand years, might have emerged from similar sources—from women struggling in a male-identified scholarly sphere.

The current wave of feminist scholarship has produced enormously interesting work on the aforementioned questions. The plan of this essay is to touch on a few of them. Perhaps this essay will serve best as an introduction for people who are experienced in science but new to the field of women's studies (like me). Women's studies has much to say about who does science, how it is done, and how the character of the science and the scientist are coupled.

Participation

A woman physics major looks around her physics classroom and, at most coeducational institutions, finds herself in the clear minority. In the early

1990s she could expect to find that women comprised about 25 percent of her introductory physics class, about 15 percent of physics majors, and about 3 percent of physics professors (about 1 percent more at a liberal arts college, about 1 percent less at a university). If she attended a large university, the most probable number of women who would eventually graduate with a Ph.D. in physics would be between 1 and 5, the next most probable, zero; these numbers reflect the fact that women in physics are clustered at some institutions and completely absent from many others (American Institute of Physics 1990). In the American Physical Society (the largest professional organization of physicists) in 1990, women comprised 14 percent of members under age 30 and only 3 percent of members over age 40 (American Physical Society 1993). This is a hopeful sign that women are in the process of better populating the field. But a less hopeful sign is the disproportionate way that women leave the discipline at all levels—the so-called leaky pipeline. Also, apparent progress in women's participation, like the proportion of women earning physics Ph.D.'s, which rose from 5 percent in 1975 to 10 percent in 1990, is negated if one looks only at U.S. women (Fehrs and Czuijko 1992). Their participation, as a percentage of all physics Ph.D. recipients in the United States, was virtually unchanged during that time. The increasingly international character of graduate student populations had produced the rise in women's participation. What explanation for these lopsided numbers can one give the young woman in college today? What reassurance can one offer that a life in physical science is well within her reach?

As historians and philosophers of science know well, the history of women in physical science (and participation in public scholarship in general) has not been monolithic. Women's participation has ebbed and flowed. One period of flow began during the Renaissance, when humanism allowed some of the ancient, gender-based prejudices to be questioned on several grounds (Jordan 1990; Scheibinger 1989). There were defenses of women from such thinkers as the Jesuit priest François Poullain de la Barré, from whom comes the quote "The mind has no sex" (quoted in Scheibinger 1989), and the use of Cartesian ideas as inspiration and to demonstrate sex differences were limited only to sex organs. Even Leibniz, though largely silent on the issue, asserted that women had leisure at home and so should study (Scheibinger 1989, 39), and defenses based on women's innate superiority of nature were offered as well. This was also a period when, according to Scheibinger, there were "lexicons listing female worthies in the arts and sciences." But in the eighteenth century, as the prestige of science began to grow, there were attempts to deny that women had ever contributed to development of the sciences, or of the arts. Scheibinger (1993) discusses the movement among eighteenth-century individuals to prove the intellectual inferiority of women to men, and non-Europeans to Europeans. This was a time, argues Martin Bernal, when there was an attempt to de-emphasize African and Asian roots to science and to focus solely on the Greco-Roman contributions (Bernal 1993). For example, one can read in some histories of science, as well as some current elementary physics textbooks, that Galileo was the first to invent and/or turn the telescope heavenward with the full intent to study celestial objects, despite the fact that Galileo himself acknowledged that ancient North Africans had optical devices that were essentially telescopes, and that they used them for celestial observation (Van Sertima 1983, 13). Moreover, the Western scientific revolution had firm roots in Arabic-Muslim and Asian science and mathematics (Hess 1995, chapter 3).

There was a very dark period for remembering/crediting women and non-Europeans in Europe and the United States from about 1920 through 1970. This facilitated the public perception today that, as Sharon McGrayne, author of *Nobel Prize Women in Science,* puts it, "there's been only one woman scientist, Marie Curie. And people don't know much about her, so they think she's boring. If they know about other women scientists, they assume they don't do world class work" (Hess 1994, 9). Happily, today there is a comparatively rich supply of biographical material available on the "forgotten" women of science, as well as on living women scientists.[2]

Opportunity or Exclusion?

It seems important to put the scarcity of women's faces and names in science textbooks in historical perspective, and to consider the historical participation of women in scientific and educational institutions. (While the history I mention is a Western one, there is an important message in the fact that African and Eastern educational history is so divergent; for example, that colonial forces denied the African system of universities, which flourished during medieval times, an opportunity to continue [Pappademos

1983].) There was a curtailment of women's educational opportunities in medieval Europe that coincided with their expulsion from positions of authority in the church. By the ninth century, there were new church schools, only open to boys; girls had no access to organized education (Wertheim 1995, chapter 2). David Noble traces this parallel exclusion of women from the church and from the practice of science as it culminated in the scientific revolution (Noble 1992). The scientific revolution was a time of conventional piety when science and church had not yet parted ways, but both presented a united front against the participation of women. Wertheim takes the "physicist as priest" metaphor to heart; the maleness of the two archetypes allowed them to reinforce one another historically and, Wertheim argues, today as well (Wertheim 1995, introduction and chapter 10). Women were excluded from the medieval universities and from the modern ones that cropped up during the Renaissance. Isolated exceptions were Italy and Germany. But no woman who attended ever set a precedent for the admission of women. For example, the illustrious Laura Bassi, a physicist, attended and then became a professor at the University of Bologna in the eighteenth century. Her chair at the university was established in such a way that it would dissolve when she left it, to avoid setting a precedent of having a woman in that place (Scheibinger 1989, 16, 17). Consider how differently we might view the historical impact of women physicists were there a Bassi Chair in physics at Bologna, the occupation of which conferred honor on the occupant. (And occupation of which by an illustrious physicist would reflect honor back on the chair, as does the Lucasian Chair in physics at Cambridge, once occupied by Newton and currently by Stephen Hawking.) The university educational situation in Europe did not even begin to amend itself until the turn of the last century. For example, Lise Meitner, an Austrian physicist, was lucky that Vienna opened its doors in 1901, and she was able to take classes there, and then with Max Planck at the University of Berlin. Still, there was a chemical institute nearby where she did her experiments and where they had classes. She was not allowed upstairs and had to hide under the auditorium seats to listen to lectures (Wertheim 1995, 193–97). Agnes Pockels, keeping house for her father in Germany in the latter part of the nineteenth century, had not even this meager opportunity. Her scientific knowledge was based largely on books to which her brother, a university-educated

physicist, provided access. Her dozen or so papers on the physical properties of liquid surfaces were based on research performed entirely in her
kitchen (Tanford 1989, chapter 11).

M. Sadker and D. Sadker provide an excellent summary of the history
of women's education in the United States (Sadker and Sadker 1994, chapter 2). No public schools were open to women until the early nineteenth
century. Oberlin was the first U.S. college to admit women, men, and racial
minorities of both sexes. But the "ladies' course" was second rate. (Additionally, the women had to do the men's laundry and serve them meals.)
Coeducation in universities began in the mid-nineteenth century when the
number of men attending dropped after the Civil War. But a subsequent
backlash against coeducation caused some formerly coed universities to
instead establish women-only, affiliated colleges. In the late nineteenth century, "real" women's colleges (as opposed to institutions that were, essentially, finishing schools) began to open their doors; Vassar was the first. In
the middle of the twentieth century, most major universities and colleges
finally went coed. Even then, as conversations with women who matricu-
lated at that time reveal, women were regularly channeled into traditionally feminine vocations (Sadker and Sadker 1994, 33–35).

A similar cycle of advancement and retrenchment was experienced by
women scientific professionals, according to Margaret Rossiter (Rossiter
1995a; 1995b), whose monumental works delineate the educational and
working conditions for women scientists in America. During the middle
of the twentieth century, women scientists were scarce in colleges, industry, and government, and the fit was often less than perfect. For example,
because of anti-nepotism rules, physicists Maria Mayer and Libby Marshall
were appointed as "volunteer professors" at the University of Chicago, a
situation that was "awkward ... but humane," according to Rossiter
(Rossiter 1995a, 138). A quest for institutional prestige eroded the progress
women had made in securing faculty positions, even at women's colleges
(Sadker and Sadker 1994, chapter 2; Rossiter 1995a, chapter 10). On the
other hand, for some physicists with the highest levels of research aspiration and talent, work at small colleges was not the best fit. Emmy Noether,
a mathematical physicist (who had never secured a paid position during
her many years at Göttingen University), spent the end of her career at
Bryn Mawr College (Wertheim 1995, 190–93). But we should no more
imagine this brilliant researcher being completely fulfilled in an under-

graduate teaching environment than we could imagine Einstein being so. Lise Meitner, despite her growing desire to emigrate from Berlin in the early 1930s, refused to consider a position at Swarthmore College, because of its insufficient laboratory space, and/or lack of assistants for her work, and/or inability to allow her to work with large amounts of radioactive materials (Sime 1996, 149).

The Woman behind the Curtain

The theme of invisibility is one that pervades the study of women in science. In an apocryphal story, the woman scholar gives her scientific lectures from behind a curtain, so that listeners (male) will not be distracted by her beauty. (Sometimes the story is told with Laura Bassi as the subject, sometimes it is another historical woman worthy.) This veiled woman is a potent metaphor for the fact that women's contributions, and the names of the women who made them, are often obscured. The Sadkers describe an exercise wherein people are given 5 minutes to write down 20 famous women—no sports figures or entertainers allowed (Sadker and Sadker 1994, chapter 1). How hard my class found the exercise when one of my students suggested we try it![3] When we restricted the exercise to names of scientists, it became virtually impossible. Why? Clearly our early education bears some responsibility; the impressions that our early social studies teachers and books have made last a lifetime. (Students tell me that high-school texts now put marginalized people in blue boxes. In my day, they didn't even have the boxes.) But this begs the question of why, in the first place, women worthies should be marginal characters, and whether their lesser historical and demographic weight is compounded by the fact that their achievements are underestimated or underreported.

The model of women inventors is an interesting one to consider. The Sadkers report that they saw middle-school teachers write lists of inventors on the board, all male (Sadker and Sadker 1994, chapter 1). There was no mention of how hard it was for women to get patents in their own name until very recently; of new scholarship that shows that the routinely cited discovery, the cotton gin, formerly credited to a man, was invented by a woman. There was no suggestion that some enormously important devices have been invented by women in the twentieth century (like the computer compiler, invented by Grace Hopper, or the tunable dye laser, in-

vented by Mary Spaeth). Sadly, despite the fact that women inventors are
now on about 8 percent of patent applications,[4] despite the fact that at the
time the Sadkers did their research there were numerous books in print, at
various grade levels, describing the achievements of women inventors,[5]
the enduring stereotype is that women invent nothing, as described in this
excerpt of a letter that H. J. Mozans reproduces:

> I was out driving once with an old farmer in Vermont, writes Mrs.
> Ada C. Bowles, and he told me, "You women may talk about your
> rights, but why don't you invent something?" I answered, "Your
> horse's feed bag and the shade over his head were both of them in-
> vented by women." The old fellow was so taken aback that he was
> barely able to gasp, "Do tell!" (Mozans 1913, 346)

According to Steven Shapin, a great deal of the hands-on scientific
work during the English scientific revolution was done by technicians who
were "triply invisible" to historians, to other scientists, and as relevant actors with control over the laboratory where results are produced (Shapin
1994, chapter 8). A minority of scientists, Robert Boyle among them, mentioned their technicians by name in print. Shapin compares these technicians to the Victorian domestic servants, who were "not there." Class intersected with educational opportunity, which determined whether one
was an assistant with "mere skill" or a collaborator with "genuine knowledge." While women did not occupy these jobs in England, one can see
this sort of role being played in the series of women astronomers from the
sixteenth century onward (Wertheim 1995, chapter 3), people like Maria
Winkelmann, the eighteenth-century astronomer for the Berlin Academy.
Most of these women worked in Germany, all worked in family observatories "under" husbands, fathers, brothers (like the sixteenth-century Dan-
ish astronomer Sophe Brahe), or even sons whom they had trained. All can
be viewed as examples of people working from a tradition identified by
Scheibinger as a craft, or artisan, tradition (Scheibinger 1989, chapter 3).
The work was hands-on and not viewed as very cerebral—charting astronomical objects, preparing calendars. There is an interesting carryover to
the history of U.S. astronomers from the late nineteenth century onward.
Certain subspecialties were considered acceptable for women, those that
involved "large scale processing of data" (Mack 1990). These gave women
a path to professional employment as astronomers. Many women's col-

leges supported programs (e.g., Maria Mitchell's program at Vassar in the nineteenth century) that produced graduates who supplied major observatories. Pamela Mack notes that from 1890 to 1920 women authored 4 percent of astronomy papers in the three major journals. Of these, about 48 percent came from women at women's colleges. However, many of the women who made technical contributions to papers in that era do not appear as authors; the papers are written in supervisors' names (Mack 1990, 75). Again, here are contributions of "invisible" women.

Joan Hoffman, one of my students at Swarthmore College, drew a parallel (antiparallel?) between the way a gentleman scientist heading a lab in the seventeenth or eighteenth century might merely enable research, yet receive full credit, and the way women like Robert Boyle's sisters enabled his research, yet received no credit. (Boyle's older sister actually had his chemistry laboratory commissioned and built for him in her manse, and both of his two sisters provided constant intellectual, social, and emotional support [Shapin 1994, chapter 8].) Ruth Bleier makes the observation that in modern times as well, eminent scientists have "a veritable army of unpaid or underpaid women behind them" (Bleier 1986, 4). Clearly, though, the observation that women often receive inadequate credit for their roles as enablers generalizes far beyond science to women's roles in the workplace and in the world economy.[6] The discussion comes full circle if we observe, with Namenwirth, that today "[s]cientific research ... becomes an arena of competition for prominence and authority, not unlike the arenas of business and politics," and that in this arena there is a "[f]usion of the scientist's image with a masculine authority stereotype" (Namenwirth 1986, 23). An excellent summary of work by Merton, Traweek, and others on the competitive culture of science appears in appears in the Wellesley "Pathways" Report (Rayman and Brett 1993).

It is important to acknowledge that science was not what we would consider a job in the modern sense—and indeed the word "science" was not even coined—until the nineteenth century, when the word was used by William Whewell (Whewell 1834). Understandably, the gentleman "scientists" of sixteenth- through eighteenth-century Europe had a common background of class, money, and leisure in which to conduct their work, and scientists who rose from humble beginnings were rare.[7] From the early years of the scientific revolution, some women participated. But their participation was at the fringes of scientific society, and only noble women like Queen Christina of Sweden or Margaret Cavendish, Duchess of Newcastle, could do so. Acceptable roles consisted of sponsoring learned men in one's court or home and engaging learned men as tutors. Acceptable, too, was a father's arrangement of tutoring in science or mathematics for his daughters. But a woman's trajectory always stopped short of an institutional affiliation. The British Royal Society was established in the late 1600s, and the French Academy around the same time. They both admitted their first woman about 300 years later. Margaret Cavendish was permitted into the Royal Society only for a visit, and only once (Scheibinger 1989, 25, 26). Although there were individual members who very much supported her admittance, the French Academy failed to vote to admit Marie Curie, even after she had won her (first) Nobel prize (McGrayne 1993, 29–30; Scheibinger 1989, 10). This limited trajectory for qualified women reminds one of Rossiter's term "the American Inconsistency," which refers to the fact that until only recently, American society educated, but did not employ, scientific women.

Scientific books were sometimes published by women worthies, but the identity these books always seemed to forge for their authors was that of commentator, expositor, facilitator, not the originator of any of the ideas they espoused. Emilie du Chatelet produced the first (and still the only) French version of Newton's *Principia*. Jane Marcet's extremely popular series of books, *Conversations on Chemistry*, was credited with influencing the young Michael Faraday to take up chemistry, particularly electrochemistry and the study of "voltaic current" (Miller 1990; Bordeau 1982, 110).

Harriet Zuckerman's book *Scientific Elite* is an interesting study of the sociology around that ultimate route to visibility in science, the winning of a Nobel prize. Bearing in mind that the elites in "nearly all departments of social life come in disproportionate numbers from the middle and upper occupational strata" (Zuckerman 1996, 63), she finds it to be manifestly true for the U.S. scientist laureates, as measured by occupational rank of one's father, which in turn correlates with other measures of socioeconomic status. "While inequalities in the socioeconomic origins of American scientists at large have been significantly reduced during the past half century, this has not been the case for the ultraelite in science. Even in a system as meritocratic as American science, in which identified talent tends to be rewarded on the basis of performance rather than origin, ... the ultraelite continue to come largely from the middle and upper middle strata"

(Zuckerman 1996, 67). Clearly, women are likely to occupy Zuckerman's "41st chair" (a reference to the French Academy, which has only 40 chairs). Jocelyn Bell, the discoverer (while a student) of pulsars, did not win along with her adviser. Lise Meitner never won, though she was nominated in nine different years, almost always jointly with her coworker Otto Hahn.[8] Yet, Zuckerman reports, when Hahn won with Fritz Strassman, he reports it was "given to me for work I had done alone or with my colleague Fritz Strassman," and washed his hands of Meitner's reported "unhappiness" at being left out (Zuckerman 1996, xxiii; Sime 1996, chapter 14 and page 342).

In summary, we encourage our students to think of science as a field in which excellent ideas are unambiguously so. We like to think of it as a meritocracy, not subject to the fickleness of history, because one's scientific work speaks for itself. But if one is excluded from the only scientific society in one's country, its journal won't accept one's paper, people of one's sex are not even permitted in the university faculty club, one has no way, either speaking or writing, to communicate one's thoughts to peers— all of these being the status quo for women until the latter part of this century—one's work can't speak for itself; it is silenced.[9] In the words of Margaret Cavendish: "Being a woman (I) cannot . . . Publicly . . . Preach, Teach, Declare or Explain (my works) by Words of Mouth, as most of the Famous Philosophers have done, who there by made their Philosophical Opinions more Famous, than I fear mine will ever be" (qtd. in Scheibinger 1989, 37).

Feminist Physics?

The issue of whether there is a gendered quality to physics itself is extremely complicated. One might begin with the hypothesis that all human activities are deeply impressed with culturally determined gender norms (Harding 1991).[10] The error we physicists might be making, if we claim that our subject is free of gender content, is to overlook how much our humanity shapes our professional activities at all levels (Easlea 1986).[11] (Often, as with racism, the majority group has the luxury of overlooking such things, whereas the minority group does not.) As Elizabeth Fee notes, "the scientist, the creator of knowledge, cannot step outside his or her social persona" (Fee 1986, 53). One might continue by observing with Schuerich that "Good work depends on exclusion of bias; value free science. Feminists' claim is opposite. But feminist revisions can correct previously un-

detected bias. The conventional scientific method makes no claim that discovery is context free, only that justification is" (Schuerich 1992, 3). The scientist and feminist Ruth Bleier goes further yet, suggesting that "the scientific method is generally viewed as the protector against rampant
subjectivity and the guarantor of the objectivity and validity of scientific
knowledge. Yet each step in the scientific method is profoundly affected by
the values, opinions, biases, beliefs and interests of the scientist" (Bleier
1986, 3). Clearly, ideas like these open the door to a fascinating debate,
which is currently unfolding in the literature thanks to the attention of
philosophers of science, Sandra Harding, Evelyn Fox Keller, Helen
Longino, and Karen Barad among them (Harding 1991; Keller and Longino
1996; Barad 1996).

Henry Bauer, in his book *Scientific Literacy and the Myth of the Scientific
Method,* points out how new is the interest of historians of science in the
"externalist" view, that the "context of discovery"—not just the "context
of justification"—is quite worthy of study, and quite fundamental to the
definition of science. The context of discovery was traditionally excluded
from consideration because it was a nonrational part of human experience
(Bauer 1992, chapter 6). Hence, it was defined to be irrelevant to science,
which was in turn defined as the rational side of the enterprise—a circu-
lar definition. Thomas Kuhn, of course, started the "externalist" revolution when he argued that the actual practice of science does not adhere to
the "scientific method" (Kuhn 1970). An important distinction made by
Bauer is between frontier science and textbook science. He argues that it
is impossible to have feminist textbook science, in the sense of a feminist
Newton's law or periodic table. Textbook science is rectified by time, dis-
tilled into pure law, and represents a logical and coherent body of knowledge with a broad base of people who have confidence it its veracity. The
creation of frontier science is a human activity, and the body knowledge
on the frontier is incoherent and unreliable. Feminist and other critiques
have a real foothold there (Bauer 1992, chapter 6).

As one example of a cultural context for frontier science, Stevenson
and Byerly point out that British home life had for centuries encouraged
the sort of "enjoyable tinkering" (on the part of the men) that led to prominent scientific discoveries (Stevenson and Byerly 1995, 71, 72). Indeed, there
was some snobbery about this; they quote physicist P. Blackett as distinguishing this from the French tradition of idling around in cafés when in-

stead people should be home in their sheds. Blackett was a photographer who toiled in *his* shed; he looked through tens of thousands of alpha particle tracks that he photographed to find the first nuclear reaction, a collision with an alpha particle and a nitrogen molecule. (In response to Blackett, though, we might point out that his French contemporaries Marie and Pierre Curie toiled for years in *their* shed to purify radioactive ores.) The shed versus café debate was the heir to an earlier debate between the salon-based, feminine science of France and the institute-based, masculine science of England. We might symbolize the steps that French science, and ultimately world science, took toward adopting the English scientific culture, by contrasting the early-eighteenth-century collaboration of Voltaire with the physicist Emilie du Chatelet (she helped him with his math) with the later-eighteenth-century attitude of Rousseau, and also of Voltaire by midcentury, whom Scheibinger quotes as pronouncing that "all the arts have been invented by man, not woman" (Scheibinger 1989, chapters 4 and 8, and page 102).

To define physical science in a certain way, following the lead of European "gentleman" scientists from the seventeenth century onward, has brought the field of physics profound successes. Electromagnetism, thermodynamics, relativity, and quantum physics have all produced quantitative predictions about the universe that hold with marvelous success—"unreasonable" success, according to Eugene Paul Wigner—that "we neither understand nor deserve." What is the secret to this success? Bruce Gregory asserts that "Physics is primarily procedural. Its procedure is to uncover the value of a theory by determining its consequences and then seeing if these predictions are confirmed by measurements" (Gregory 1988, 187). Though this is indeed a recipe for success, it is not a recipe unique to physics. Yet, among scientists, there exists what Stephen J. Gould has referred to as "physics envy," and a notorious snobbishness of physics toward sciences with less of a claim to universal truth.[12] The subversive (for a physicist) thought arises that we owe our success not to having such great answers, but to confining ourselves narrowly to such great questions. Wertheim makes this point, noting that the *calculatores* of the fourteenth century were the first scholars to get a handle on velocity and acceleration, the fundamentals of a science of motion. But they also tried to quantify human stuff, such as sin and charity (Wertheim 1995, 53–54). Perhaps physics took a big leap forward around the time that Galileo dropped two masses from a tower in Italy, not because the methods changed but because physicists began asking only the questions for which their methods had good answers.[13]

Der Noether? Die Einstein

The following excerpt from a 1937 coffee-table book on chemistry speaks for itself, as its gendered language and subject matter stake out the field as a male domain: "Although nature, the great chemist, has provided man with the prototypes and methods by which he has attempted, with considerable success, to conquer his environment, her motives and objectives have seldom been man's. The beautiful silks with which man bedecks himself and his womankind, ... were created for far different purposes than those to which man has put them" (Morrison 1937, 13). Responsibility in language is one of the principles of feminist science espoused by Bleier, and others, in the volume *Feminist Approaches to Science* (Bleier 1986, 16). The choice of words in the teaching or practice of science will readily reveal gender inequities and can have the unfortunate consequence of maintaining them. One cannot only excise the flagrant examples of sexist language, as in the quote above. Inside the physics (and any other) classroom, even the gender of pronouns matters. Various studies have shown that in hearing or reading "he," as well as "man" or "mankind," readers and listeners presume they are hearing about a male (Henley 1989, 59–78; Kramer, Thorne, and Henley 1978; Schneider and Hacker 1973). There is a recent trend in elementary physics texts of depicting people in a way that is representative in terms of gender and race, which is well-founded in this regard. However, the unwavering custom in these same texts of giving names of famous scientists and biographical snippets works to undo this progress. (Anthony Standen criticizes this attempt in chemistry texts: "'Culture' and 'human interest' are dragged in by the scruff of the neck in the form of little potted biographies of famous chemists of the past ... without giving anything extra that would make the biographical facts interesting and worth knowing by tying them in with the rest of history" [Standen 1950, 80].) In elementary texts, we can see women as subject to the laws of physics as they throw Frisbees, ride bicycles, wire circuits, and fire lasers, but we are simultaneously reminded, thanks to these historical interludes, that not a single woman has "authored" a law of physics. And sadly, "each time a girl opens a book and reads a womanless history, she learns she is worth less" (Sadker and Sadker 1994, 13). Indeed, the importance of being first at articulating a physical principle or effect, which may or may not, depending on the vagaries of history, result in having one's name attached to it, is something that proponents of a feminist science would question. It is at odds with accepted principles of feminist science, which emphasize cooperativeness and collaborativeness (Bleier 1986, 16). Merton describes the "fierce competition among scientists throughout history to be recognized as 'the Discoverer'" (Merton 1962).[14] No less a scientist than Einstein commented on how inappropriate was this drive to be first in discovery, how reminiscent it was of the attempt to win a game, or at sports (Stevenson and Byerly 1995, 44).

The tension between a woman's scientific prowess and the societal norms for her gender may be revealed in the language with which her achievement is discussed. "Sich männlich erweisen" (has proven herself manly) was how a university rector commended Dorothea Erxleben, who was one of the first women to earn a German medical degree. "A Woman who has translated and illuminated Newton [is] in short a very great man" was Voltaire's comment on Emilie du Chatelet. "The best man at Harvard" was Edwin Hubble's pronouncement on astrophysicist Cecelia Payne Gaposchkin. "Monstrosity," said August Strindberg of the great mathematical physicist Sonya Kovalevsky. One could go on and on like this, but as Sandra Harding observes, "it is important to see that the focus should not be on whether individuals in the history of science were sexist. Most of them were; in this they were like most men (and many women) of their day. Instead, the point is that the sexual meanings of nature and inquiry ... express the anxieties of whole societies or, at least, of the groups whose interests science was intended to advance. Cultural meanings, not individual ones, should be the issue here" (Harding 1991, 44). This should indeed be the focus when we look at androcentric language in physical science. What factors in the culture at large, and in the culture of the science, allow us all to accept the unspoken premise of a joke that begins "Why do physicists have mistresses?"[15] What factors are at work to make the term *woman physicist* an oxymoron?

One interesting set of gendered metaphors within Western scientific culture are baby metaphors. They provide a revealing view of scientific activity through some scientists' eyes, particularly those of some nuclear physicists. Though it is only one subdiscipline of physics, thanks to various political factors the field of nuclear physics has intersected strongly with weapons research. It expanded enormously in the middle of the twentieth century and has thus set a certain pattern for the modern culture of physics as a whole. One might also take a broader view and observe that weapons research and physical science have long had a kinship. In the thirteenth century, Roger Bacon trumpeted the eventual development of optical weapons to his pope (Wertheim 1995, 51). Newton depicted hunters firing at game on the frontispiece of his book introducing calculus (reprinted in Scheibinger 1989, fig. 22.), and so on. The ready identification of physics with the military is, for example, one documented reason that many schoolchildren feel science is a subject meant for boys (Kelly 1981).

Brian Easlea discusses Earnest Rutherford, the "father of atomic physics," at length. In Rutherford's lab "the nucleus was born" (according to C. G. Darwin, his student) (Easlea 1983, 62). That so-and-so is the father of such and such field is a common cliché, yet it deserves a little thought. If so-and-so is the father, then who is the mother? Or is it understood, rather, that this is a special type of paternity, and no maternal element is required? If so, one needs to consider the notion of uterus envy, emphasized by Easlea, Frechet, and others.[16] On the other hand, if one considers, with Francis Bacon, that the scientist has established "a chaste and lawful marriage between Mind and Nature" (quoted in Keller 1985, 36), might Nature be thought of as the mother? This would bring us to the Nature-as-a-woman image with all of its complicated dimensions,[17] including her domination by a tyrannical, male science. As the poet e. e. cummings asks in a poem addressed to the earth, "how often ... has the naughty thumb of science prodded thy beauty?"

But whoever the mother of such and such a field is, if indeed there is a mother at all, she is of as little consequence as the mothers forced to remain behind curtains in Bacon's utopian community, Solomon's House. Keller notes, "In this inversion of the traditional metaphor, this veritable back firing, nature's veil is rent, maternal procreativity is effectively co-opted, but the secret of life has become the secret of death" (Keller 1992, 45).

The scientific humanist Jacob Brownowski starts his meditation *Science and Human Values* by discussing a visit in 1945 to Nagasaki, soon after it was destroyed by the atomic bomb. The popular song "Is You Is or Is You Ain't Ma Baby?" was playing on the car radio, and he asks whether the awful technology of nuclear weaponry, and the science itself, should be acknowledged as mankind's baby? (With Henley et al., perhaps we should understand the author to mean the male half of humankind.) Brownowski sees science as a precious aspect of our society and he feels that this baby should be acknowledged: "Science has nothing to be ashamed of even in the ruins of Nagasaki" (Brownowski 1956, 73). The community of defense professionals also take great pride (or hubris?) in this baby, as is revealed in studies by Carol Cohn. She has written a series of papers about her interactions with these intellectuals, almost exclusively male, who consult for the government, working at universities and think tanks on issues of nuclear armaments. While these professionals are not, in general, physical scientists, the physicist Freeman Dyson, who has consulted extensively with the military, has confirmed that there is a similarity between the "world of warriors" and of physicists. In both worlds there is a premium on staying cool, using language that emphasizes technical accuracy and objectivity (Dyson quoted in Easlea 1986, 146). They are both worlds where a certain type of cartoonish masculinity is valued. (I say cartoonish, for it is a special type of masculinity traditionally associated with scientists, one that, in many ways, stands in opposition to stereotypical masculinity in our society [see the works cited in note 1].) "Rutherford will think it very effeminate of us to use a null method when we might" is how one of Rutherford's students dismissed a detection technique he eschewed as, apparently, not macho enough (Easlea 1983, 61).

The atomic bomb project was, in Cohn's words, "rife with images of male birth" (Cohn 1987, 687). For example, Ernest Lawrence wrote to the University of Chicago physicists, "Congratulations to the new parents. Can hardly wait to see the new arrival" (quoted in Keller 1992, 44). At Lawrence Livermore National Laboratory, the H-bomb was "Teller's baby," though others said Stan Ulam was the father and Edward Teller was rather its mother (Cohn 1996, 177). The comment originated with Hans Bethe: "Edward was the mother, because he carried the baby for quite a while" (quoted in Easlea 1983, 131). Cohn notes that in this context, maternity is being belittled by being equated with nurturance, as opposed to being considered an agency of creation. (This also belittles nurturance.) Those at Livermore who wanted to disparage Teller's contribution would ascribe to him the maternal role (Easlea 1983, 131). The motherhood imagery was also used in the context of a new satellite system: "We'll do the motherhood role telemetry, tracking, and control the maintenance" (Cohn 1987, 687). The invitation to "pat the missile" that Cohn received on a nuclear submarine evokes for her several images—patting something small and cute, like a baby, is one of them.

Not only were atomic bombs not-of-woman-born, the ones that worked correctly were male (Jungk 1956, 197). "It's a boy," announces a telegram from Teller upon the successful test of the H-bomb (quoted in Easlea 1983, 130). Keller explains that a bomb with "thrust" is a boy baby; a girl baby is understood to be a dud (Jungk 1956, cited in Keller 1992, 197). The bombs dropped on Hiroshima and Nagasaki were dubbed "Fat Man" and "Little Boy," respectively. Curiously, when one sees photographs of nuclear generators—for example, the last image of Barnaby's *Man and the Atom* (Barnaby 1971, 207)—there is an unmistakable emphasis on the phallic character of the device.

Cohn, Easlea, Keller, and others make the point that this world of nuclear professionals is a strange and surrogate world. It is one where life and death are permuted, where bombs are babies, where creative people father destructive monsters, as J. Robert Oppenheimer quotes from the Bhagavad-Gita: "I am become Death, the shatterer of worlds" (Keller 1992, 45; Jungk 1956, 197). Given this bizarre culture, and given the assumption that it reflects scientific culture, should it surprise us that physical science will be perceived as very one-sided, very "masculine"? The epigraphs that began this essay play into this stereotype. Blumenfeld's comment was a lighthearted response to the Harding quote. He shows us how natural it is for a physicist, a true heir of Galileo, to gravitate toward the methods that have served physics traditionally very well. And how strangely these methods juxtapose with a reality that includes sin and charity, parents and children—as if Pharaoh's daughter needed a detailed calculation of statistical mechanics before plucking Moses from the river! To practicing scientists, women and men, a crucial question can be whether one can strike a balance between one's own generativities of babies and of science. Easlea relates that Frederic Joliot loved his new cloud chamber, and he would talk of the creating of a cloud trail by an elementary particle: "Is it not the most beautiful phenomenon in the world?" Whereupon, if Irene Joliot-Curie was in the lab (pregnant at the time), she would reply, "Yes, my dear, it would be the most beautiful phenomenon in the world, if there were not that of childbirth" (quoted in Easlea 1983, 66). These attitudes did not stop either parent from having children and creating artificial radioactivity, winning a Nobel prize, being among the first to identify the positron, and so on.

One of the strengths of women's studies is that, applied to a discipline, it can reveal it in a new light. Thinking about the interplay of gender and science brings fresh insights about science itself. "The culture of no culture" is what the anthropologist Sharon Traweek has called the view of physics that is traditionally held by physicists and their students (Traweek 1988, 132), one of perfect objectivity: mechanistic, no genders, inhuman. But how can this be? I have used the word repeatedly and somewhat matter-of-factly in this essay. This term might be defined as the "patterns of expectations, beliefs, values, ideas and material objects that define the taken for granted way of life for a society or group" (Anderson 1983, 382). According to this definition, how could the community of physical scientists not have a culture, and a rich one at that? We often lose potential physics students, the so-called "second tier" of Tobias's study (Tobias 1990), mostly women and people of color who rebel at what they either perceive to be Traweek's nonculture, or a culture to be avoided—like the culture of defense professionals, perhaps. But a modern understanding of the history and practice of physics, one that acknowledges formerly "invisible" participants and celebrates the collaborative aspects of research, portrays a very different side of the culture. Happily, the culture of physics can be heterogeneous without sacrificing any of the empirical soundness of physical theory thanks to (Wigner's blessed) appropriateness of a mathematical analysis of the world. Research in physical science has throughout history been a cooperative, as well as creative, endeavor.[18] Understanding old physics, and articulating new physics, does not require a Y chromosome. It does require chromosomes. It is something requiring intellect, passion, and personhood.

Notes

1. A few representative works on perceived qualities of scientists are D. C. Fort and H. L. Varney, "How Students See Scientists," *Science and Children* (May 1989), 8; M. C. LaFollette, *Making Science Our Own* (Chicago: University of Chicago Press, 1990); and R. D. Hanes, *From Faust to Strangelove: Representations of the Scientist in Western Literature* (Baltimore, Md.: Johns Hopkins University Press, 1994).
2. A few recent compendia on past and present women scientists are: B. F. Shearer, ed., *Notable Women in the Physical Sciences: A Biographical Dictionary* (Westport, Conn.: Greenwood, 1996); B. F. Shearer, ed., *Notable Women in the Life Sciences: A Biographical Dictionary* (Westport, Conn.: Greenwood, 1996);

H. M. Pycior et al., eds., *Creative Couples in the Sciences* (New Brunswick, N.J.: Rutgers University Press, 1996); M. Alic, *Hypatia's Heritage* (Boston: Beacon, 1986); P. G. Amir-Am and D. Outram, eds., *Uneasy Careers and Intimate Lives* (New Brunswick, N.J.: Rutgers University Press, 1987); M. B. Ogilvie, *Women in Science: Antiquity through the Nineteenth Century* (Cambridge, Mass.: MIT Press, 1990). Some books on contemporary women scientists are S. Ambrose et al., eds., *Journeys of Women in the Sciences* (Philadelphia: Temple University Press, 1997); M. Morse, *Women Changing Science: Voices from a Field in Transition* (New York: Insight Books, 1995). Some recent biographies of notable physicists are R. L. Sime, *Lise Meitner: A Life in Physics* (Berkeley: University of California Press, 1996); S. Quinn, *Marie Curie: A Life* (New York: Simon and Schuster, 1995); J. W. Brewer, ed., *Emmy Noether: A Tribute to Her Life and Work* (Ann Arbor: Books on Demand, 1981).

3. Indeed, it might have been better to see no names at all than to see a student produce a list like this: (1) Pochohontas (the Disney movie of that name had recently been released), (2) Lizzie Borden . . .

4. While the U.S. Department of Patents does not record the sex of patent applicants, they attempt to infer these data. A full report "Buttons to Biotech—U.S. Patenting by Women, 1977 to 1988," (U.S. Patent and Trademark Office Technology Assessment and Forecast Program, January 1989) chronicles the period mentioned in the title. Supplementary, updated figures show that the percentage of patents that include at least one woman inventor have grown each year from 1988 onward. The figure of 8 percent corresponds to the year 1993.

5. For example, J. M. Gage, *Woman as Inventor* (issued under the auspices of the New York State Woman Suffrage Association) (Fayetteville, N.Y.: F. A. Darling Printer, 1870), was followed in 1888 by a compendium of women inventors issued by the U.S. Patent Office. Among more recent books are P. C. Ives, *Creativity and Inventions: The Genius of Afro-Americans and Women in the United States and their Patents* (Arlington, Va.: Research Unlimited, 1987); E. A. Vare, *Mothers of Invention: From the Bra to the Bomb: Forgotten Women* (New York: Morrow, 1988); A. L. MacDonald, *Feminine Ingenuity: Women and Invention in America* (New York: Ballantine Books, 1992); A. Stanley, *Mothers and Daughters of Invention: Notes for a Revised History* (Metuchen, N.J.: Scarecrow Press, 1993). There are many more books on this topic available today.

6. See, for example, R. Steinberg and L. Haignere, "Separate but Equivalent: Equal Pay for Work of Comparable Worth" in *Beyond Methodology*, ed. M. M. Fonow and J. A. Cook (Bloomington: Indiana University Press, 1991); E. Boserup, *Woman's Role in Economic Development* (New York: St. Martin's Press, 1970).

7. Scheibinger notes that though the Royal Society was founded so as to be open to men of all backgrounds "both learned and vulgar . . . the vast majority of the members . . . came from the ranks of gentlemen virtuosi, or wellborn connoisseurs of the new science" (Scheibinger 1989, 25).

8. Sime's biography of Meitner provides many details about the Nobel prize, and the attitudes of Hahn and other scientists close to the issue (many of whom understood Meitner's partnership in the discovery and felt her lack of acknowledgment unjust). Meitner's comment was that Hahn "simply suppressed the past.... I am a part of that suppressed past" (Sime 1996, x).

9. "Let the data speak for themselves ... scientists demand. The problem with this argument is, of course, that data never do speak for themselves"—Evelyn Fox Keller (Keller 1985, 130–31).

10. See, for example, Anderson (1983), chapter 2, for a discussion of the interplay between culturally determined gender and everyday life. For arguments that scientific endeavors are not immune, see M. Namenwirth 1986, as well as Harding 1991.

11. See, for example, Stevenson and Byerly (1995) for an introduction to how scientists' activities are shaped by culture and society.

12. For example, chapter 3 of A. Standen, *Science Is a Sacred Cow* is entitled "Science at Its Best—Physics" and begins: "The various sciences can all be arranged in order, going from fairly good through mediocre to downright bad. Allowing the scientists to put their best foot forward, we may as well begin with the best of the sciences, which is physics" (Standen 1950, 59).

13. Interesting, in this regard, is Galileo's determination to distinguish quantities that are "really present in physical objects from those that are merely subjective qualities of human sensation" (Stevenson and Byerly 1995, 27), and to make the former the focus of his studies.

14. See also the case studies involving priority disputes among famous scientists in Stevenson and Byerly (1995) chapter 5.

15. Answer: So that they can tell their wives they are with their mistresses, and their mistresses that they are with their wives, and spend the night at the lab.

16. "Male science, male alchemy is partially rooted in male uterus envy, in the desire to create something miraculous out of male inventiveness."—Phyllis Chesler, *About Men* (quoted in Frechet 1991, 216, 217).

17. See, for example, C. Merchant, *The Death of Nature* (San Francisco: Harper and Row, 1980), chapter 7.

18. One book that emphasizes these and other feminine-identified aspects of scientific culture is L. J. Shepherd, *Lifting the Veil: The Feminine Face of Science* (Boston: Shamhala Press, 1993).

References

American Institute of Physics. 1990. Figures presented at the Conference on Recruitment and Retention of Women in Physics. Sponsored by the American Association of Physics Teachers, 12–13 October.

American Physical Society. 1993. *CSWP Gazette* 12, no. 3.

Anderson, M. L. 1983. *Thinking about Women.* Boston: Allyn and Bacon.

Barad, K. 1996. "Meeting the Universe Halfway: Realism and Social Constructivism without Contradiction." In *Feminism, Science, and the Philosophy of Science,* ed. Lynn Hankinson Nelson and Jack Nelson. Dordrecht, Netherlands: Kluwer.

Barnaby, F. 1971. *Man and the Atom: The Uses of Nuclear Energy.* New York: Funk and Wagnalls.

Bauer, H. 1992. *Scientific Literacy and the Myth of the Scientific Method.* Urbana: University of Illinois Press.

Bernal, M. 1993. "Black Athena: Hostilities to Egypt in the Eighteenth Century." In *The Racial Economy of Science,* ed. Sandra Harding. Bloomington: Indiana University Press.

Bleier, R., ed. 1986. *Feminist Approaches to Science.* New York: Pergamon.

Bordeau, S. P. 1982. *Volts to Hertz: The Rise of Electricity.* Minneapolis, Minn.: Burgess Publishing.

Brownowski, J. 1956. *Science and Human Values.* New York: Harper and Row.

Cohn, C. 1987. "Sex and Death in the Reational World of Defense Intellectuals." *Signs: Journal of Women in Culture and Society* 12, no. 4: 687–718.

———. 1996. "How We Learned to Pat the Bomb." In *Feminism, Science, and the Philosophy of Science,* ed. Lynn Hankinson Nelson and Jack Nelson. Dordrecht, Netherlands: Kluwer.

Easlea, B. 1983. *Fathering the Unthinkable.* London: Pluto Press.

———. 1986. "The Masculine Image of Science with Special Reference to Physics: How Much Does Gender Really Matter?" In *Perspectives on Gender and Science,* ed. J. Harding. New York: Falmer Press.

Fee, E. 1986. "Critiques of Modern Science: The relationship of Feminism to Other Radical Epistemologies." In *Perspectives on Gender and Science,* ed. R. Bleier. New York: Pergamon.

Fehrs, M., and R. Czuijko. 1992. "Women in Physics: Reversing the Exclusion." *Physics Today* (August): 33–40.

Frechet, D. 1991. "Toward a Post-Phallic Science." In *(En)Gendering Knowledge,* ed. J. E. Hartman and E. Messer-Davidow. Knoxville: University of Tennessee Press.

Gregory, B. 1988. *Inventing Reality: Physics as Language.* New York: John Wiley and Sons.

Harding, S. 1991. *Whose Science? Whose Knowledge? Thinking from Women's Lives.* Ithaca, N.Y.: Cornell University Press.

Henley, N. 1989. "Molehill or Mountain? What We Know and Don't Know about Sex Bias in Language." In *Gender and Thought: Psychological Perspectives,* ed. M. Crawford and M. Gentry. New York: Springer-Verlag.

Hess, D. J. 1995. *Science and Technology in a Multicultural World.* New York: Columbia University Press.

Hess, E. 1994. "An Interview with Elizabeth Hess." *Swarthmore College Bulletin* (February): 17–19.

Jordan, C. 1990. *Renaissance Feminism: Literary Texts and Political Models.* Ithaca, N.Y.: Cornell University Press.

Jungk, R. 1956. *Brighter than a Thousand Suns,* trans. James Cleugh. New York: Harcourt Brace.

Keller, E. F. 1985. *Reflections on Gender and Science.* New Haven, Conn.: Yale University Press.

———. 1992. *Secrets of Life, Secrets of Death.* New York: Routledge, Chapman and Hall.

Keller, E. F., and H. E. Longino. 1996. *Feminism and Science.* New York: Oxford University Press.

Kelly, A., ed. 1981. *The Missing Half.* Manchester, England: Manchester University Press.

Kramer, C., B. Thorne, and N. Henley. 1978. "Perspectives on Language and Communication." *Signs: Journal of Women in Culture and Society* 3, no. 3: 638–51.

Kuhn, T. S. 1970. *The Structure of Scientific Revolutions.* Chicago: University of Chicago Press.

Mack, P. E. 1990. "Straying from Their Orbits." In *Women of Science: Righting the Record,* ed. G. Kass-Simon and P. Farnes. Bloomington: Indiana University Press.

McGrayne, S. B. 1993. *Nobel Prize Women in Science.* Secaucus, N.J.: Carol Publishing Group.

Merton, R. K. 1962. "Priorities in Scientific Discovery." In *The Sociology of Science,* ed. B. Barber and W. Hirsch. New York: Collier Macmillan.

Miller, J. A. 1990. "Women in Chemistry." In *Women of Science: Righting the Record,* ed. G. Kass-Simon and P. Farnes. Bloomington: Indiana University Press.

Morrison, A. Cressy. 1937. *Man in a Chemical World.* New York: C. Scribner's Sons.

Mozans, H. J. 1913. *Women in Science: With an Introductory Chapter on Woman's Long Struggle for Things of the Mind.* New York: D. Appleton.

Namenwirth, M. 1986. "Science Seen through a Feminist Prism." In *Feminist Approaches to Science,* ed. R. Bleier. New York: Pergamon.

Noble, D. 1992. *A World without Women.* New York: Alfred A. Knopf.

Pappademos, J. 1983. "An Outline of Africa's Role in the History of Physics." In *Blacks in Science,* ed. I. Van Sertima. New Brunswick, N.J.: Transaction Books.

Rayman, P., and B. Brett, eds. 1993. *Pathways for Women in the Sciences.* Wellesley College Report, part 1. Wellesley, Mass.: Wellesley College.

Rossiter, M. W. 1995a. *Women Scientists in America: Before Affirmative Action, 1940–1972.* Baltimore, Md.: Johns Hopkins University Press.

———. 1995b. *Women Scientists in America: Struggles and Strategies to 1940.* Baltimore. Md.: Johns Hopkins University Press.

Sadker, M., and D. Sadker. 1994. *Failing at Fairness.* New York: Charles Scribner's Sons.

Scheibinger, L. 1989. *The Mind Has No Sex.* Cambridge, Mass.: Harvard University Press.

———. 1993. *Nature's Body.* Boston: Beacon.

Schneider, J., and S. Hacker. 1973. "Sex Role Imagery and the Use of Generic 'Man' in Introductory Texts." *American Sociologist* 8: 95–102.

Schuerich, J. 1992. *Methodological Implications of Feminist and Poststructuralist Views of Science.* The National Center for Science Teaching and Learning Monograph Series, no. 4.

Shapin, S. 1994. *A Social History of Truth.* Chicago: University of Chicago Press.

Sime, R. L. 1996. *Lise Meitner: A Life in Physics.* Berkeley: University of California Press.

Standen, A. 1950. *Science Is a Sacred Cow.* New York: E. P. Dutton.

Stevenson, L., and H. Byerly. 1995. *The Many Faces of Science.* San Francisco: Westview Press.

Tanford, C. 1989. *Ben Franklin Stilled the Waves.* Durham, N.C.: Duke University Press.

Tobias, S. 1990. *They're Not Dumb, They're Different: Stalking the Second Tier.* Tucson: Research Corp.

Traweek, S. 1988. *Beamtimes and Lifetimes: The World of High Energy Physicists.* Cambridge, Mass.: Harvard University Press.

Van Sertima, I., ed. 1983. *Blacks in Science.* New Brunswick, N.J.: Transaction Books.

Wertheim, M. 1995. *Pythagoras' Trousers: God, Physics, and the Gender Wars.* New York: Random House.

Whewell, W. 1834. "On the Connexion of the Physical Sciences, by Mrs. Somerville." *Quarterly Review* 51.

Zuckerman, H. 1996. *Scientific Elite: Nobel Laureates in the United States.* New Brunswick, N.J.: Transaction Publishers.

Inventing the Future

Women in Science, Technology,
Engineering, and Mathematics
at Purdue University Calumet

Barbara Mania-Farnell
and Colette Morrow

In 1994 the Women's Studies Program at Purdue University Calumet (PUC) in Hammond, Indiana, began developing a project aimed at encouraging women to pursue education and careers in science, technology, engineering, and mathematics (STEM). Project STEM has emerged as a leading initiative and garnered growing support among faculty, administrators, and community partners in northwest Indiana.

Project STEM evolved in response to specific campus and regional needs. Nevertheless, strategies that have contributed to its success are generic and can be employed in other contexts to develop similar programs. Similarly, obstacles that have impeded Project STEM's progress likely exist at other universities.

Four strategies that clearly contributed to the success of Project STEM have emerged in its first three years: (1) setting goals and communicating them clearly cultivates support among upper-level administrators; (2) aggressively pursuing on- and off-campus faculty development opportunities fosters interdisciplinary understanding of gender issues in STEM; (3) using the expertise of many players professionalizes the project and raises their sensitivity to gender issues; and (4) utilizing existing resources and administrative mechanisms increases opportunities for project growth.

Purdue University Calumet:
"Pride of Purdue ... Convenience of Calumet"

PUC is a regional commuter campus that is part of the Purdue University system. An early presence in northwest Indiana in the 1920s, later becoming an extension of Purdue West Lafayette during World War II, PUC is now a comprehensive institution of higher education. With an enrollment greater than nine thousand, PUC offers more than eighty associate, bachelor's, and master's degree programs in sixteen academic departments.

The Purdue system was founded in the land-grant tradition that created educational opportunities for midwesterners. Still dedicated to that tradition, PUC has a threefold mission:

> to provide its students with a liberal education which will prepare them for life or for the professions; to provide career-oriented curricula; and to provide programs that meet the professional, cultural and general education needs of a large urban-industrialized community.

Clearly this mission privileges vocational, that is, professional, education and ties degree programs and curricula to the needs of the surrounding region, whose economy, though changing, traditionally has been based on the steel industry and affiliated businesses. Hence, the STEM fields traditionally have been the university's central concern, and they attract students whose pursuit of postsecondary education is often motivated by a desire for better employment and upward economic mobility.

Currently, 56.1 percent of PUC's students are female, many having major professional and family responsibilities outside their academic studies. Many of these women are lifelong learners pursuing university education after being out of school for significant periods of time.[1] PUC's female students are a strong presence in the humanities, a group recognized as highly motivated, high-achieving students.

Women in STEM: The National Profile

At PUC, concerns about women's enrollment in STEM originally were based on informal, random observations and a commonsense suspicion that the situation described by national statistics existed at our campus as well. In contrast to their visibility in the humanities, social sciences, nursing, and education, few women appeared to be majoring in STEM areas. On the whole, it seemed that women usually took STEM courses at the introductory level when required for a non-STEM major.

Nationally, of course, women are underrepresented or underserved in the STEM fields at all junctures of the educational pipeline. According to the National Science Foundation (NSF), "The drop-off in the study of science among women is extremely steep from high school through Ph.D.s" (quoted in Alper 1993, 409). Of 730,000 high-school sophomores in 1977, for example, only 9,700 had earned doctoral degrees in science or engineering by 1992 (Alper 1993). Likewise, the U.S. National Center for Education Statistics reports that in comparison to men, the number of women completing postsecondary education in STEM decreases the more advanced the degree is (Alper 1993).

Starting from Scratch:
Setting and Communicating Goals

While national data suggest the need to encourage women to pursue education in STEM, there was no organized plan for such an initiative at PUC. Nevertheless, the perception that female enrollment in STEM at PUC reflected national patterns made women's education in science a cause of concern. Recruiting female students to STEM fields was identified as a program priority when the directorship of the Women's Studies Program was created in 1993–1994. The incoming director was charged with addressing this issue. Hence, Project STEM did not emerge from the Women's Studies Program itself.

The top-down nature of the STEM initiative has been a mixed blessing. On one hand, the project was born with substantial backing from at least one high-level administrator. On the other hand, the superimposition of Project STEM on the program initially deprived it of grassroots support from women's studies faculty, who, as is common elsewhere, were drawn primarily from the humanities. On the whole, they expressed little interest in expanding the scope of the program to the STEM areas. Consequently, Project STEM operated largely as a "director's initiative" for nearly two years, meaning that the director assumed administrative responsibility for it while collaborating with an ad hoc subcommittee of the Women's

Studies Advisory Committee that consisted of female faculty in STEM areas. Together, the director and the members of the subcommittee developed and implemented the project.

The subcommittee members, along with the director of the Women's Studies Program, were first-year faculty in October 1994 when they attended a Project Kaleidoscope (PKAL) regional colloquium, "Women in Science and Mathematics," in Berea, Kentucky.

PKAL, a national organization funded by both public and private institutions, works to strengthen undergraduate science and mathematics programs. At the PKAL conference, gender issues in science were theorized and model programs were described for participants. One of the requirements of the conference was that each university's team develop a preliminary plan for better supporting women in STEM at its campus and subsequently present that plan to upper-level administrators.

The PUC team identified nine goals, which have served as a blueprint for Project STEM and changed as campus needs became clearer and according to availability of resources. The key points of these goals included building an inclusive, inviting learning community for women; gathering quantitative and qualitative data describing PUC women's experiences in STEM; and broadening the scope of the Women's Studies Program, which was traditionally focused on the humanities, to include gender issues in STEM.

When the faculty team returned to PUC, they presented their report on the PKAL conference, including the goals that had been developed, to upper-level administrators. This strategy of articulating clear goals and communicating them to administrators has proven extraordinarily successful at PUC. Setting goals early in the process focused Project STEM. Presenting these goals to administrators cultivated support for the initiative. Such support has been evidenced by a willingness to fund STEM activities and establish networks on campus and in the regional community, leading to partnerships that make possible the realization of some STEM goals.

Faculty Development: Essential for Success

Although developing goals provided a focus for Project STEM from the beginning, none of the faculty involved had been trained in both STEM and women's studies. This made the process of identifying specific strategies for achieving project goals a slow one. Initially, it was unclear what steps could and should be taken in order to "build a STEM community," for example. Furthermore, all collaborators approached the project from diverse personal and disciplinary perspectives—biological sciences, engineering, and women's studies. While such diversity ultimately proved beneficial, it was at first disadvantageous because each faculty member had different priorities and often simply did not understand the others' views because they had been formed in the context of another field.

This became less problematic as faculty worked together over time. Participation in faculty development opportunities also played a key role in establishing a common ground and vocabulary among the faculty collaborators. In fact, faculty development played, and continues to play, such a large role in the formation of Project STEM that it must be identified as an essential component of success. Especially helpful were workshops and conferences that focused on changes in science education to make the field more inviting for all students; these included the Chautauqua Short Courses, an annual series of intensive forums where scholars working at the frontiers of science meet with undergraduate science teachers. Equally beneficial were conferences on women in science, such as the Midwest Region Women's Studies Association conference, "A Woman's Place: A Conference on Women in Engineering, Science, and the Humanities," held at Rose-Hulman Institute in 1996; and Sweet Briar College's 1997 conference, "Women Succeeding in the Sciences."

Data Collection: Confirming Suspicions and Raising Consciousness

While faculty development is an ongoing activity, gathering data describing women's experiences of STEM was the first task undertaken by the STEM committee. From the beginning, a commitment was made to collect both quantitative and qualitative data. This process not only confirmed the intuitive knowledge that PUC's enrollment of women in STEM reflected national statistics but also revealed one of our most successful strategies: availing ourselves of the expertise of various members of the campus community.

Initially, enrollment figures were analyzed in order to get a clearer picture of the distribution of gender among STEM majors. In all categories except computer information systems and biological sciences, women were found to be underrepresented in STEM at PUC. During the three semesters audited, women comprised 29 percent of the total enrollment in chemistry and physics, 35 percent in mathematics, computer science, and statistics, 11 percent in construction technology, 16 percent in engineering, 6 percent in electrical engineering, 41 percent in information systems and computer programming, and 28 percent in manufacturing engineering technologies and supervision. In order to determine whether women in STEM also were underserved or experienced differential treatment, a series of focus groups with students and alumnae were held. Because no one on the STEM committee was a specialist in communications or assessment, campus experts in these areas helped on the project. Faculty from the Department of Communications and Creative Arts and the director of Assessment and Testing contributed to the development of the questions posed to the focus groups. Faculty from the Department of Communications and Creative Arts facilitated the student focus groups and helped with data analysis.

Two sessions with students were held in March 1996. Based on these sessions, the committee made eight recommendations:

1. Support/Study Groups—Many of the women felt that support groups in their STEM majors would help them build confidence and get them through some of the more difficult aspects of their programs.
2. Mentoring Programs—Focus group participants thought that some form of mentoring would be helpful.
3. Women in Science Club—Forming a chapter of the Association for Women in Science was recommended.
4. On-campus Seminars by Women from Industry and Academics—Several of the focus group participants indicated an interest in seeing more speakers who could discuss issues that women face in the workplace.
5. Faculty Development—Most participants were generally satisfied with the climate in their departments. However, some had experienced gender bias from instructors. Some faculty probably used teaching methods with an embedded gender bias. Faculty development sessions could sensitize faculty to gender issues in STEM curricula and pedagogies.
6. Math Workshops—Several students indicated that some women, especially undecided majors, did not consider STEM fields because of

math anxiety. Students suggested that math workshops would build women's confidence.

7. Course(s) on Women in Science—Participants indicated that elective course(s) would encourage women to major in STEM and counter some of the stereotypes associated with women in STEM.

8. Outreach—Programs for youth and adults living in the region were considered good vehicles for increasing enrollment.

In addition to providing more accurate information about women's experiences of STEM, the focus groups had further-reaching consequences. The information gathered from enrollment figures and the focus groups generated greater support for Project STEM among upper-level administrators. In fact, the chancellor designated Project STEM a model academic program in the budget proposal he submitted to the state of Indiana in April 1996.

Furthermore, students' testimony of their experiences in STEM had a powerful effect on one of the facilitators, a senior faculty member and a longtime participant in the Women's Studies Program. Hearing students' experiences sensitized her to the need for the STEM initiative. She responded by lending support to the project and advocating it with other senior faculty from the Women's Studies Program. Such advocacy garnered support for Project STEM, creating a proprietary sense among faculty of the Women's Studies Program and members of the Women's Studies Advisory Committee.

Student focus groups were followed by two sessions with alumnae in June 1996. Once again, the STEM committee relied on the expertise of others, such as the director of Student Support Services and the training and career development specialist in Personnel Services, to facilitate the sessions.

In these sessions, emphasis was on factors to which participants ascribed responsibility for their success in STEM fields. At first, alumnae attributed their achievements solely to their own initiative and perseverance. As one participant said, "It was that determination of 'I will show you' that was my support." When they were probed, however, most alumnae were able to identify sources of support in their communities. The most often cited were family members, especially fathers working in STEM fields, with whom the women had positive relationships. Female support networks established informally at the university and on the job were also mentioned. Finally, some participants reported that they had been mentored by someone at the university or in industry, though not as the result of joining a formal mentoring program.

Women successfully working or who had worked in STEM fields credited PUC's emphasis on practical training, that is, curricula developed with local industries in mind. They also mentioned that courses taught by professionals working in the field were especially useful.

Like currently enrolled students, female alumnae experienced isolated incidents of gender bias at PUC from instructors or student peers. In most cases, they felt that simply being successful in their course work overcame negative stereotypes about women.

Mentoring: Conventional Wisdom Is Challenged at a Commuter Campus

Both conventional wisdom and the focus groups indicated that developing a formal mentoring program would encourage more women to enroll in STEM majors and, by providing support, increase retention rates. Furthermore, community partners have been eager to serve as mentors, especially the local chapter of the Association of American University Women, which for the most part draws its membership from PUC alumnae and other women with social and/or familial connections to the university.

At the beginning of the 1996–1997 academic year, the STEM committee was charged with developing a mentoring program. The committee used a two-pronged approach to this charge. It undertook a feasibility study while hosting various social and networking events to identify students who would join a formal mentoring program. For the most part, these events were poorly attended, and only a few students indicated that they could participate in a mentoring relationship. Furthermore, the director of Student Support Services, who is responsible for several other mentoring programs at PUC, advised the STEM committee that none of these have been particularly successful. The obvious difficulty in mentoring, she reported, is that PUC students have little time for extracurricular activities. As commuter students, they spend little time on campus beyond that required for courses, and they often have major family and work responsibilities. Hence, a traditional system of one-on-one mentoring is not well suited to PUC students, though clearly they would benefit from it.

In lieu of traditional mentoring, the STEM committee has found it expedient to utilize mechanisms already in place that would enable students to interact with successful role models. For many years the Women's Studies Program has sponsored brown bag forums as well as events celebrating Women's History Month in March. Furthermore, the university regularly offers faculty development sessions facilitated by outside scholars, who sometimes will meet with undergraduate students as well as faculty. The STEM committee has used all these forums to bring professionals and academics to campus.

In September 1995 a brown-bag forum on women in construction technology was presented by recent alumna Barbara Biernat, whose award-winning essay on this subject was published in *Constructor* magazine. In March 1996 the Women's Studies Program collaborated with the Department of Chemistry and Physics to sponsor a faculty development session, "A Molecular Model of Learning," conducted by Florida State University professor of chemistry Penny Gilmer. In November 1996 Fermi National Laboratory physicist Vivian O'Dell presented a brown-bag forum, "From Fission to Fusion to Feminism."

In February 1997 Sheila Tobias, author of several books in science and mathematics education, facilitated a faculty development workshop entitled "Peer Perspectives on Teaching" and met with women's studies faculty. Most recently, Joan Cadden, author of *The Meaning of Sex Differences in the Middle Ages: Medicine, Sciences, and Culture* and a professor of history at the University of California at Davis, gave several presentations on the history of women in science. She also facilitated a faculty development session for the Women's Studies Program in April 1997. In March 1998, Women's History Month explored the theme of women in science.

Although such programming has been helpful in educating faculty and administrators on issues relating to gender and science, only a handful of students attend these sessions. Again, the STEM committee interprets relatively low attendance as a consequence of the many demands on students' time and energy.

In the fall of 1997 the committee began work on developing a Leadership Institute for professional women working in STEM in northwest Indiana. In the course of a year and a half this effort became so extensive and attracted so much interest among STEM faculty that a separate subcommittee was convened in order to organize it. Three functions were offered through the Leadership Institute in 1999–2000. An open-house reception introduced the institute to the community in November 1999. In February 2000 a workshop for women working in technical fields introduced young professionals to strategies designed to assist them in assuming leadership roles in their companies. Finally, a banquet in April 2000 brought together current and aspiring leaders in local industry and business for the purpose of supporting networking among them. It is hoped that once professional women begin engaging with each other through the auspices of PUC, the Leadership Institute will become a forum for students to interact with them, creating an informal, de facto mentoring program.

Community Partnerships:
The Workplace Gender Equity Project

Although traditional mentoring has been less than wholly successful, the STEM committee's original goal of partnering with other educational institutions in the regional community has been fulfilled in unexpected ways. In August 1996 the vocational director at Hammond's Area Career Center contacted the director of the Women's Studies Program, requesting assistance in developing a far-reaching gender equities project. Key faculty from Project STEM subsequently collaborated with faculty and staff at Hammond's Area Career Center to write the grant proposal and administer the program. The total grant amounted to $46,000 for regionwide activities, including $7,000 for the university to host the Workplace Gender Equity Project (WGEP) for regional high-school students.

The goal of WGEP, a one-day workshop, was to encourage high-school students to pursue education and careers in fields traditionally dominated by one gender; hence, it served men as well as women. A team consisting of representatives from PUC and Hammond's Area Career Center as well as eight high-school students was responsible for planning the workshop, which was attended by more than eighty students. Approximately twenty professional role models from the community, representing nontraditional fields in terms of gender, made presentations to small groups of students. They provided information on the type and length of training required for their profession, employment opportunities, financial aid and scholarship opportunities, and professional organizations and shared personal experiences of being a gender minority in the field.

Students' evaluations of WGEP and anecdotal evidence from both students and professional role models indicate that it was successful. This project, with an additional provision for more participation by high-school counselors, was funded again in 1997–1998 and had even more student participants.

Looking toward the Future: Curriculum Development

Having made substantial progress in meeting its goals of establishing mentoring and outreach programs, the STEM committee will focus in the future on curriculum development. A first effort was made in that direction by faculty in the Department of Mathematics, who proposed a course entitled "Math for Everyone." This course was designed to support the development of thinking and problem-solving strategies through the exploration, analysis, and discussion of approaches to nonroutine, problematic situations grounded in everyday experiences. Clearly attempting to address the needs of students with math anxiety, the course would create a nonthreatening atmosphere in which students would be guided to the "mathematicization" of everyday activities. Course requirements included basic readings of bibliographical notes on women in math and science as well as culturally based mathematics activities.

Unfortunately, this first attempt was stalled by administrative concerns. The course was found insufficiently mathematical to grant it a math designator; hence, no funds were available for staffing purposes. Also, it was feared that a women's studies designator would discourage men from taking the course, thus inadvertently eliminating a potential audience and limiting enrollment. Moreover, the course did not feed into any PUC majors; as written it could only be used as an elective, raising concerns that enrollment would be low.

Clearly such hurdles must be overcome in order to offer an interdisciplinary curriculum in women's studies and STEM. Pursuing grants that would provide salaries for staffing "Math for Everyone" and similar courses that the Women's Studies Program cannot crosslist with another academic unit is one of the strategies that faculty in women's studies and mathematics are currently exploring. Recently, faculty in women's studies, the Department of Chemistry and Physics, and Information Systems and Computer Programming (ISCP) collaborated to develop a freestanding women's studies course, scheduled for fall 2000, on gender and science, technology, engineering, and mathematics. This course has four primary objectives. Students will examine women's contributions to science, technology, engineering, and mathematics. They also will explore the status of women and girls in these academic areas and associated fields of employment. Furthermore, a significant portion of the course will be dedicated to heightening students' awareness of educational and employment opportunities in science, technology, engineering, and mathematics. Finally, the course will introduce students to the role that gender plays in the production of scientific and technical knowledge and methodologies. The class will be taught collaboratively with a lead facilitator, and instructional staff will be "donated" to the Women's Studies Program by the Department of Chemistry and Physics and ISCP. Finally, the viability of a new initiative is currently being explored by an ISCP faculty member who joined PUC in fall 1998. This initiative would involve PUC and the University of Chicago in a collaborative research project on women's health care. At PUC, faculty in women's studies, nursing, and ISCP would contribute to the project's formulation and implementation, and the project would lead to the creation of a women's health center on campus. In addition to these possibilities, the STEM committee will be looking to other programs for creative solutions to the particular challenges that developing an interdisciplinary curriculum poses.

Conclusion: The Consequences of Gender Equity in STEM

After five years, STEM committee members are more than ever convinced of the necessity of this work. If nothing else, the economy in northwest Indiana dictates a certain urgency to the project of encouraging women to seek education and careers in STEM. In the region served by PUC, most job opportunities, especially those promising upward mobility, are in STEM areas.

If women as a class are implicitly or explicitly discouraged from pursuing these opportunities, they will remain economically marginalized. If individual women are discouraged from pursuing these opportunities, they will be prevented from fulfilling their abilities in STEM. This is a loss, not only to women, but to men as well, for everyone benefits from living in an equitable society.

Note

1. Of the total number of undergraduates, slightly over 50 percent are age 24 or older.

Work Cited

Alper, Joe. 1993. "The Pipeline Is Leaking Women All the Way Along." *Science* 260: 409–11.

Contributors

Madeline Adamczeski has been employed as a chemistry instructor in the Department of Math and Science at San José City College in San José, California, since January 1999. She thoroughly enjoys teaching introductory level chemistry courses for majors and nonmajors and is actively participating in the Chemistry Workshop Project <http://www.sci.ccny.cuny.edu/~chemwksp> and implementing the workshop model in her courses.

Jody Bart is an assistant professor of Philosophy and Women and Gender Studies and the director of Women and Gender Studies at Sweet Briar College. She earned her Ph.D. from Florida State University, concentrating in political philosophy and feminist theory. Dr. Bart's areas of research include the political philosophy of Emma Goldman and philosophical anarchism. She has written a book manuscript, currently under review, "If I Can't Dance Then It's Not My Revolution: The Political Philosophy of Emma Goldman," and she has authored numerous papers on Goldman and several other areas of feminist theory.

Colleen M. Belk is an instructor in the Biology Department at the University of Minnesota-Duluth. She has been teaching genetics, molecular biology, general biology, and biology of women for eight years.

Amy Bug is an associate professor in the Department of Physics and Astronomy at Swarthmore College in Swarthmore, Pennsylvania. She received her Ph.D. in physics from M.I.T. and did postdoctoral research at Exxon Research and Engineering Co. and Columbia University. In the year 2000, she will be spending her sabbatical leave at Lawrence Livermore National Laboratories in Livermore, California. Her research specialty is computational chemical physics.

Casey Clark has recently retired from Smith College in Northampton, Massachusetts, where she was the director of the Peer Mentoring Program and the coordinator of Science Inreach and Outreach Programs.

Julie Gess-Newsome is an associate professor of science education and interim chair of the Department of Educational Studies at the University of Utah in Salt

Lake City, Utah. She is also the president elect of the Association for the Education of Teachers in Science.

Ileana Howard graduated from Smith College in Northampton, Massachusetts, in May 1999.

Michelle Smoot Hyde received a Ph.D. in educational studies from the University of Utah in 1997 and an M.B.A. from Brigham Young University in 1984. She is currently a faculty member at Brigham Young University in Provo, Utah, in the Marriot School of Management, with a double emphasis in teaching and marketing. She is also a professional consultant.

Sarah E. Lazare is the coordinator of Tutorial Services at Smith College in Northampton, Massachusetts, and has also served as the assistant director of the Mentoring Program at Smith.

Nermana Ligata was an organic chemistry workshop leader in 1996 and 1997 for Madeline Adamczeski's courses at American University in Washington, D.C. In 1997 and 1998 she volunteered as a laboratory assistant conducting biochemical research in the Laboratory of Cellular and Metabolic Regulation and helped identify the protein serotonin transporter at the National Institutes of Health. In 1998 she graduated with a B.S. degree from American University.

Maureen Linker received her Ph.D. in philosophy from the Graduate Center at City University of New York and is an assistant professor of philosophy at the University of Michigan-Dearborn. Her research concerns conceptions of "reasonableness" in science and the law. She has published in the journals *Criminal Law Quarterly* and *Philosophy and Social Criticism*. She is currently working on gendered conceptions of reasonableness in theories of artificial intelligence.

Laura Malloy received her Ph.D. in physiology from the University of Virginia. She is currently dean of Academic Affairs and professor of biology at Hartwick College in Oneonta, New York. She has also held the Jane Watson Irwin Chair in Women's Studies at Hamilton College and maintains scholarly interests in feminist science studies, cardiovascular physiology, and science pedagogy.

Barbara Mania-Farnell received her M.A. in social sciences from the University of Chicago and her Ph.D. in neurobiology from Northwestern University in Evanston, Illinois. She is currently an associate professor in the Department of Biological Sciences at Purdue University Calumet.

Valerie N. Morphew is an assistant professor of education at West Virginia Wesleyan College in Buckhannon, West Virginia. Her professional interests include science education, instructional technology, and clinical experiences.

Colette Morrow is an assistant professor of English and the director of Women's Studies at Purdue University Calumet (PUC). She earned a Ph.D. from Texas

Christian University in Fort Worth, Texas, in 1994. She is currently engaged in several projects designed to recruit and retain female students in science, technology, engineering, and mathematics. These projects include the Leadership Institute at PUC and the development of women's studies courses that examine the roles that gender plays in the construction of scientific knowledge and methods.

Margaret A. M. Murray is an associate professor of mathematics at Virginia Polytechnic Institute and State University. She is the author of *Women Becoming Mathematicians: Creating a Professional Identity in Post-World War II America,* forthcoming in 2000 from MIT Press.

Andrea Nye is a professor of philosophy at the University of Wisconsin-Whitewater. Her recent books include *The Princess and the Philosopher: The Letters of Elisabeth of the Palatine to René Descartes* and *Philosophy of Language: The Big Questions,* an edited reader in philosophy of language that includes analytic, feminist, and multicultural perspectives.

Ruth O'Keefe is associate professor and chair of the Art History/Liberal Arts/ Sciences Department at Kendall College of Art and Design in Grand Rapids, Michigan. In the year 2001, while on sabbatical, she will be writing a math text for art and design students. She is also adjunct professor at Aquinas College in Grand Rapids.

Elizabeth Stassinos is an assistant professor of anthropology at Anna Maria College in Paxton, Massachusetts. She is currently interested in the intersection of anthropology and fiction.

Doreen A. Weinberger is an associate professor of physics at Smith College in Northampton, Massachusetts.

Index